DATE DUE

ABORTION
AND
PUBLIC POLICY

ABORTION
AND
PUBLIC POLICY

An Interdisciplinary Investigation within the Catholic Tradition

Edited by
R. Randall Rainey, S.J.
and Gerard Magill

CREIGHTON UNIVERSITY PRESS
Omaha, Nebraska
Association of Jesuit University Presses

©1996 by Creighton University Press

duced or transmitted in any form or
:chanical, including photocopying,
ɔrage and retrieval system, without
permission in writing from the Publisher, except in the case of brief
quotations embodied in critical articles and reviews.

Library of Congress Catalog Card Number: 95-083919
ISBN: 1-881871-17-7 cloth
1-881871-18-5 paper

EDITORIAL
Creighton University Press
2500 California Plaza
Omaha, Nebraska 68178

MARKETING & DISTRIBUTION
Fordham University Press
University Box L
Bronx, New York 10458

Printed in the United States of America

CONTENTS

PREFACE

Any observer of the social scene in America will acknowledge that abortion is a hotly contested issue. Although the 1973 decision of the United States Supreme Court in *Roe* v. *Wade* constitutionalized the right of abortion and legalized the act of abortion throughout pregnancy, the public controversy concerning abortion has intensified rather than diminished during the last two decades. Contrary to the *New York Times* editorial on January 24, 1973, the Supreme Court's decision did not provide "a sound foundation for final and reasonable resolution of a debate that has divide America too long." The dispute concerning the morality of legalized abortion has continued unabated not only in legislative chambers and university lecture halls, but also in our workplaces and in the streets of our cities. Unfortunately, this protracted debate or principled argument, call it what you will, too often has not been carried on at the level of productive interchange. Slogans, sound bytes, and placards have been the media for social exchange aimed at forming public policy. Discerning the public good in such an environment is exceedingly difficult.

Saint Louis University committed its institutional resources to facilitate that discernment of the public good. The conference on *Abortion and Public Policy: An Interdisciplinary Investigation within the Catholic Tradition* (March 11-13, 1993) was convened to that end and to provide a rigorous exposition of the complex issues surrounding abortion through the medium of interdisciplinary academic discourse within the Catholic tradition.

As members of a Jesuit university, the Conference Planning Committee desired to explore the rational basis of the moral teaching of the magisterium of the Church on this subject. And as citizens in a democratic society, the Committee also was aware of the need to present to a pluralistic society a more comprehensive explanation of that teaching. In seeking a nuanced and research-oriented interchange on the topic, the Committee hoped the act of abortion would be examined in a manner that would be as free as possible from the ideology that too often has displaced reasoned discourse in the formation of public policy regarding abortion. Accordingly, the Committee designed the program to gather leading scholars who not only would provide new insight into this social problem but who also would explore the parameters and substance of a sound public policy for the future.

An additional purpose was to serve Catholic decision-makers who have been entrusted with political and judicial office or who find themselves involved in drafting or implementing abortion public policy. With that end in mind, the Committee solicited a series of original papers that would help them—and anyone seriously interested in the topic—deepen their understanding of the scientific, philosophical, theological, legal, and political dimensions of the public policy of abortion. The Committee took great care in selecting those who would be invited to participate in the conference and those who would deliver original papers. We hope the reader will share the Committee's pleasure in the result of our efforts.

To underscore the fact that a lively Catholic faith can be reconciled with responsible democratic governance even within the abortion polemic, the Committee invited the Honorable Robert P. Casey, then Governor of the Commonwealth of Pennsylvania, to give the keynote address of the conference. The remarks of Governor Casey, delivered to the conference participants assembled in a restored courtroom in the original courthouse in which the Dred Scott decision was first rendered in Missouri, thoroughly demonstrate his commitment both to the rule of law and to thinking with the Church in the modern world. Governor Casey challenges all of us to face the tragedy of abortion with intellectual integrity, moral courage, and political will. Because the scientific data concerning the beginning of human life is a relevant but largely misunderstood issue in the debate, we sought scientific evidence for this aspect of human generation. The paper of Professor William S. Sly, M.D. of the Health Sciences Center at Saint Louis University entitled, "When Does Human Life Begin? Does Science Provide the Answer?" explores those questions in light of current genetic and embryological knowledge.

Professor Russell Hittinger, Ph.D., of The Catholic University of America, who received his doctorate from Saint Louis University, delivered a paper entitled, "Resolving Conflicting Normative Claims in

Public Policy." Having distinguished four types of normative conflict (any one or combination of which may characterize moral decision making in a pluralist democratic polity), Professor Hittinger focuses upon "conflicts over the ends and powers of government" regarding public morality and the act of abortion. He then offers a critique of the effect which the right of abortion has had upon our social contract regarding the use of deadly force in the United States. Professor James J. Walter, Ph.D., of Loyola University of Chicago, delivered a paper entitled, "Theological Parameters: Catholic Doctrine on Abortion in a Pluralist Society." Professor Walter's contribution is an elaboration of the foundations of the Magisterium's position on abortion. His exposition of four theological parameters—anthropological, ethical, value, and legal—within which the Church's position is fashioned and applied should prove especially useful to politicians who, as Professor Walter makes clear, need to identify "points of convergence and divergence... between the Catholic tradition and society's pluralist position on abortion."

The then President of the Catholic Theological Society of America, Professor Lisa Sowle Cahill, Ph.D., of Boston College, presented a paper entitled, "Catholic Commitment and Public Responsibility." Having first explored the conflict between fetal and maternal needs in Catholic teaching on abortion, her paper proposes that public policy concerning abortion should draw upon a more comprehensive social justice analysis of both the context and act of abortion. Accordingly, she examines both the individual and social nature of conscience, and concludes by presenting several political and legal solutions which Catholic politicians might consider in the formation of abortion public policy.

Turning our attention to the legal dimensions of this problem, Professor Basile J. Uddo, J.D., LL.M., of the School of Law at Loyola University of New Orleans, delivered a paper entitled, "The Public Law of Abortion: A Constitutional and Statutory Review of the Present and Future Legal Landscape." Written primarily for non-lawyers, Professor Uddo closely examines the decision of the United States Supreme Court in *Planned Parenthood of Southeastern Pennsylvania* v. *Robert P. Casey.* He argues that the Court substantially muddled the constitutional waters by introducing a new "undue burden" standard for testing the constitutional validity of state abortion laws and regulations. Following a review of the essential elements of the Pennsylvania statute, Professor Uddo explains the boundaries of permissible state regulation of abortion in light of the

Casey decision, and concludes by offering his assessment of the public policy challenges which face Catholic decision-makers.

The final two papers in this collection offer expositions of the nature of those challenges. Professor Hadley Arkes, Ph.D., of Amherst College, in his paper, "De Officiis: Catholic and the Strains of Office," makes the argument that politicians schooled in the Catholic natural law tradition of moral reasoning and in the limits of civil law should be well-suited to lead in the development of a just public policy concerning abortion "because they should be equipped with an even clearer sense of the distinctions that mark the boundary between private belief and public law." More significantly, Professor Arkes claims that a reappropriation by Catholic politicians of Catholic moral teaching, based as it is upon rational first principles, would do much to lead their colleagues and the electorate to rediscover a "moral tradition they may be surprised to find rather plausible and compelling after all." Professor J. Bryan Hehir, Th.D., of Harvard University, delivered a paper styled as "The Church and Abortion in the 1990s: The Role of Institutional Leadership." Father Hehir examines how the Church ought to exercise its institutional role in the abortion controversy and whether, in light of that evaluation, the Church should alter either its current strategy or some of its tactics. Having presented a critical retrospective of the institutional role of the Church in the last twenty years, Father Hehir offers a new abortion strategy for the final decade of this century.

In addition to the foregoing brief review of the contributors' articles, the reader may be interested in the following aspects of the conference. To foster a robust debate and definite conclusions, we invited a select audience of approximately 100 people, mostly from the academic community across the country. In a further effort to stimulate frank discussion and unfettered debate, the conference adopted the non-attribution rules of the American Assembly at Arden House of Columbia University. Accordingly, the statements of individuals could be quoted in the press but no statement could be attributed to any individual. Although the Committee did not seek formal media coverage, the conference did enjoy the participation of several prominent columnists and editors. To preserve a substantial record of the conference, the Committee elected to publish this selection of conference papers.

Primary financial support came from Saint Louis University through the leadership of its President, Reverend Lawrence Biondi, S.J. The conference was also made possible by a generous grant from the Webb Foundation of St. Louis, Missouri. Indeed, Virginia and Richard Fister of the Webb Foundation initially suggested the need for an academic exploration of this topic to Rev. Kevin O'Rourke, O.P., who in turn pursued a series of conversations which produced this national conference. Additional financial support was received from the Donahue Family Foundation of Pittsburgh, Pennsylvania.

Rev. Kevin O'Rourke, O.P., J.C.D., Director of the Center for Health Care Ethics, chaired the conference planning committee and did so generously and with good humor. We especially want to acknowledge with gratitude the efforts of the Conference Chairman, Professor George Dorian Wendel, Ph.D., who has served Saint Louis University with distinction for over forty-four years. His long experience in the Departments of Political Science and Public Policy Studies and as Director of the Center for Urban Programs was very helpful in the planning and execution of the conference. We also want to thank Reverend A. James Blumeyer, S.J., the Rector of the Jesuit Community at Saint Louis University and Assistant to the President for Mission and Ministry, who served as the Executive Secretary of the Conference Planning Committee.

We are indebted to Dr. Alice B. Hayes, Ph.D., the then Provost of the University and now the president of the University of San Diego, who took time out of her very busy schedule to serve on the Committee. She was not only helpful as an academic colleague—she is a biologist—but she also played an extremely important role in securing the significant financial support of the University for this project. We are also grateful for the service of John B. Attanasio, J.D., Dipl. in Law (Oxon.), LL.M., the Dean of the School of Law, and to Reverend Theodore Vitali, C.P., Ph.D., the Chairman of the Department of Philosophy. Their knowledge, experience, and insights were of great help in designing the program. Both of the co-editors served on the Conference Planning Committee: R. Randall Rainey, S.J., J.D., LL.M., was then a member of the Law faculty at Saint Louis University and is now a Senior Fellow at the Woodstock Theological Center at Georgetown University and the Director of its program area called Public Discourse and the Common Good; Gerard Magill, Ph.D., is the Director of the interdisciplinary Ph.D. program in Health Care Ethics at Saint Louis University's Health Sciences Center. Finally, we extend gratitude to Ann Coble and Marianne

Sheahan, Graduate Assistants whose cooperation contributed to the production of this volume.

While the results of the conference gathered in this volume may not change the way people in the United States think about the issue of abortion, this book will at least demonstrate that it is possible to examine highly controverted issues of moral complexity from the scholarly perspectives of interdisciplinary academic discourse within the Catholic tradition. On behalf of Saint Louis University, the Webb Foundation, the Donahue Family Foundation, the members of the Conference Planning Committee, and above all on behalf of the scholars who have contributed herein the fruit of their intellectual labors, we dedicate this collection to the Catholic community and to the Citizens of the United States who seek a just public policy solution to the tragedy of the estimated 35 million abortions in America since 1973.

ABORTION
AND
PUBLIC POLICY

Introduction:
Abortion, the Catholic Church, and Public Policy

R. Randall Rainey, S.J., Gerard Magill, and Kevin O'Rourke, O.P.

THE TEACHING OF THE CHURCH ON ABORTION

Although the political and social controversy regarding the act of abortion in the United States began in the late 1960s and has raged since the Supreme Court's 1973 decision in *Roe* v. *Wade*,[1] the opposition of the Catholic Church to every act of direct abortion is rooted in a two-thousand year moral tradition. Since the first century, the Church has taught that abortion at any stage of pregnancy is a moral evil.[2] In the Didache, for example, the Church enjoined the Christian community not to commit this species of homicide: "You shall not kill by abortion the fruit of the womb and you shall not murder the infant already born."[3] This teaching was confirmed by the Fathers of the Church,[4] and has remained unchanged throughout twenty centuries.

Following the natural law tradition of Aquinas,[5] Pope John Paul II in his Encyclical *The Gospel of Life* denounces abortion as a grave moral evil and sin against human nature, and insists that natural law must be a primary correlative of positive law and public policy.

> *I declare that direct abortion, that is, abortion willed as an end or as a means, always constitutes a grave moral disorder*, since it is the deliberate killing of an innocent human being. This doctrine is based upon the natural law and upon the written Word of God, is transmitted by the Church's Tradition and taught by the ordinary and universal Magisterium. . . .

1

> [A]n objective moral law[,] . . . [such] as the "natural law" written [by God] in the human heart, . . . [must be acknowledged as] the obligatory point of reference for civil law itself. . . . [C]ivil [and criminal] law must ensure that all members of society enjoy respect for certain fundamental rights which innately belong to the person, rights which every positive law must recognize and guarantee. First and fundamental among these is the inviolable right to life of every innocent human being.[6]

This recent papal teaching underscores the two central topics that are interwoven in the abortion controversy: the normative wrongfulness of the act of abortion and the obligation of society to proscribe abortion by law and public policy. The heart of the Catholic tradition on both matters is rooted in a full recognition of the transcendental nature of humanity which grounds the fundamental dignity and equality of all of us. The unborn, because of their humanity, possess this dignity and equality at all stages of development from syngamy.[7] On that account, abortion is wrong not only because it is a moral evil committed by those individuals responsible for the death of an innocent human being. It is also wrong because it constitutes a serious violation of basic human rights committed by any government which tolerates, permits, or fails to proscribe by public law the premeditated death of the unborn.

The affirmation of the transcendental nature of humanity—which must be respected by public authority—grounds the Christian commitment to an objective moral order and to the correlative demands of social justice. Consistent with that teaching, Vatican II made clear the theological and rational basis of its opposition to abortion.

> For God, the Lord of Life, has conferred on men [and women] the surpassing ministry of safeguarding life—a ministry which must be fulfilled in a manner that is worthy of [humankind]. Therefore from the moment of its conception life must be guarded against with the greatest care, while abortion and infanticide are unspeakable crimes.[8]

In the wake of the trend in western democracies to liberalize abortion laws, the Congregation for the Doctrine of the Faith explained church teaching on this matter in the 1974 Vatican *Declaration on Procured Abortion*.

> The first right of the human person is his [or her] life. [There are] other goods and some are more precious, but this one is fundamental—the condition of all the others.... In reality, respect for human life is called for from the time that the process of generation begins. From the time that the ovum is fertilized, a life is begun which is neither that of the father nor of the mother; it is rather the life of a new human being with [its] own growth. It would be made human if it were not human already.[9]

In the encyclical *The Gospel of Life*, Pope John Paul II strongly reiterates this recognition of the personal rights of the unborn:

> [T]he Church has always taught and continues to teach that the result of human procreation, from the first moment of its existence, must be guaranteed that unconditional respect which is morally due to the human being in his or her totality and unity as body and spirit: "*The human being is to be respected and treated as a person from the moment of conception*; and therefore from that same moment his [or her] rights as a person must be recognized, among which in the first place is the inviolable right of every innocent human being to life."[10]

This recognition is a moral imperative for individuals and for civil society as well. Consequently, Pope John Paul II explains that to counter "the culture of death"[11] in our societies, we have an "inescapable responsibility of *choosing to be unconditionally pro-life*"[12] and that in the face of laws permitting abortion "there is a *grave and clear obligation to oppose them by conscientious objection*."[13]

All of these instances of modern Church teaching underscore the depth and strength of this moral tradition. The Church throughout the centuries consistently has taught that abortion, defined as the delivery of a human fetus before viability or the killing of a fetus in the womb after viability, is a moral evil.[14] Because every human life is freely given and sustained by God, and because of the fundamental equality of all human beings, the Church teaches that human life should never be destroyed in

3

the absence of the gravest moral imperative. In the context of abortion, it holds no such imperative or ethical justification exists.[15] By reason of intention and direct action, every abortion unjustly deprives an innocent human being of the gift of life.[16] Accordingly, the Church denounces such action as an egregious sin against the love of God and neighbor.

The teaching of the Church concerning this matter is rooted in a theological anthropology which emphasizes the dignity of every human being. Scripture reveals to us that we are made in the image and likeness of God and that the universe of being is derived from God. Every human being, regardless of age, race, sex, physical condition, or bodily dependency, is a manifestation of God's creative love, intellect, and will. In this sense, each individual receives his or her life and personhood from God. All of us, including the unborn, thus share a fundamental moral equality, which together with human dignity constitute the profound moral significance of being human. These characteristics of the human being are not negotiable. Moral and legal recognition of this universal human dignity and equality therefore may not be conditioned upon live birth or viability or the absence of physical defect or upon any other human criterion.

While there has been philosophical uncertainty and scientific dispute throughout the ages concerning when human individuality and personhood were established prior to quickening,[17] the Church has never been in moral doubt concerning the evil of abortion.[18] However, even in the absence of philosophical certitude,[19] the rational basis for the Church's moral analysis is quite convincing, especially today when there are *no credible grounds for scientific dispute* about the beginning of human life. We know, for example, that life in the womb is human because it is the offspring of human beings. A human zygote is not any other species other than *homo sapiens*. We also know that it is life not only because it grows and develops, but also because it comes into being and possesses a unity of being in accord with a genetically unique identity and existence that emerge through the dynamic union of a single human male gamete and a single human female egg.[20] That unity of being exists until the death of that individual. Therefore, notwithstanding its nutritional and gestational dependence upon its mother, this new life has its own being which develops from the first division of one cell to increasingly complex stages of cell differentiation to bodily development (e.g., from syngamy to zygote to morula to blastocyst to embryo). Most importantly, this

4

early stage of human life, which lasts for approximately six days from fertilization to implantation in the mother's uterus,[21] is ordinarily that of a unique individual human being.

However, in the phenomenon of twinning we know that *more than one* unique human individual comes into being. Consequently, the Church cannot say that a *single* unique individual person exists at the moment of fertilization because the human zygote might twin. Nonetheless, the Church properly concludes and teaches that it is probable that *at least one* unique individual with a human soul comes into existence.[22] Following this insight into human reproduction, the Church recognizes within this spacial-temporal biological event that a new human life exists bearing an intelligible unity of being. It is genetically and physically differentiated from its father and mother and from every other person who does or could exist in the world. If left undisturbed in his or her mother's womb, barring any impediment to natural development, this unique human being will continue to grow toward live birth and subsequent human development from infancy to natural death.[23] Therefore, although the processes of fertilization and implantation are the objects of ongoing scientific and philosophical study, there is no doubt that what exists at syngamy is a member of the human species with a unique genotype.

The Church's teaching concerning abortion thus embodies an accurate understanding of human reproduction, a rigorous moral assessment of the nature of the act of abortion, and a faithful recognition of the dignity and equality of humanity that is revealed both in scripture and tradition.

Because of the social nature of humankind, however, the Church cannot rest only in teaching its own members but believes that it must function in active cooperation with civil society. Just as the Church's theological anthropology shapes its teaching on abortion, the Church's understanding of its involvement in society entails an ecclesiology—the self-understanding of the Church—that does not retreat from the world but tries to transform it[24] by enhancing the dignity of the human person in community.[25] This ecclesial involvement *in* the world—not *apart from* nor *over* it—undergirds the Catholic tradition of social justice. On this basis the Church encourages its members to participate in and to influence society by adding their voices to the public debate.[26]

Notwithstanding the clarity of its position and the depth of its moral commitment to defend human life in the womb, the Church's participation in public life in the United States means being involved not only with democratic pluralism but also with religious pluralism in which society is shaped by multiple communities of faith. Democratic pluralism requires the Church to express its moral teaching in the language of the public forum, that is, through reasoned analysis.[27] Religious pluralism requires the Church to draw upon the traditions and insights of all religious communities in its collegial effort to discover the moral wisdom necessary to assess and resolve the major issues facing society, shaping what John Courtney Murray called the "public consensus."[28] But precisely because its teaching is derived from reason within the context of religious belief, the Church is appropriately engaged in the development of public policy concerning abortion.[29] As a religious institution freely constituted under positive and divine law, the Church and its members (as citizens of different nations) are committed to participating in the development of public policy and law on social concerns like abortion, especially with regard to its ethical and political dimensions,[30] by presenting a coherent and consistent ethic of life.[31]

As the Church has made clear, the dignity and equality, and hence the moral value, of each human life are at the foundation of Catholic social teaching. This moral and religious insight invites, if not demands, a correlative political insight that is essential for the creation and preservation of a just society. The Church accordingly teaches that "the inalienable right to life of every innocent human individual is a *constitutive element of a civil society and its legislation.*"[32] This *fundamental right to life* is not the gift of civil society or its individual members. Accordingly, the dignity and equality of every human being, including the unborn, *must* be recognized by civil society and protected by just laws.[33] As an essential element in a just society, protecting and honoring the right to life of every individual from syngamy therefore has universal significance in Church teaching. Defending the right to life is *the* foundational moral duty which should guide the conduct of every political society which aspires to social justice and which labors to establish and maintain the conditions necessary for human flourishing in civil society.[34] Furthermore, this is not simply a Catholic position. It is most certainly *not* a matter of privacy[35] but a matter of utmost public concern.[36]

One of the objectives of the Church's participation in the public life of the nation is to ensure that the rights of individuals are understood as conditioned by the social nature of the human person and by the common good. In accord with this essential element in Catholic social justice teaching,[37] defending unborn life is an imperative of social justice. No one has *the right to choose to kill* an innocent person. To claim such *a moral or legal right* utterly misconstrues the nature and limits of human freedom. That is why the Church, not only in the United States but throughout the world, is so actively engaged in demanding civil rights and the full protection of the legal order for fetal life from conception. The failure to achieve this aspect of social justice threatens the very foundation of civil society.

The Church, based on its commitment to social justice and public discourse, has squarely faced the complexity of the circumstances that give rise to arguments supportive of legalized abortion and carefully has examined the hard cases that purportedly justify taking the life of a pre-born human being.[38] Notwithstanding the presumed good faith of such arguments, all of them can be repudiated philosophically.[39] More importantly, the Church finds such arguments inadequate because the intentional destruction of innocent life cannot be rationally justified.

> Divine law and natural reason, therefore, exclude all right to the direct killing of an innocent [human being]. However, if the reasons given to justify an abortion were always manifestly evil and valueless the problem would not be so dramatic. The gravity of the problem comes from the fact that in certain cases, perhaps in quite a considerable number of cases[,] by denying abortion one endangers important values to which it is normal to attach great value, and which may sometimes even seem to have priority. We do not deny these very great difficulties.
>
> It may be a serious question of health, sometimes of life or death, for the mother; it may be the burden represented by an additional child, especially if there are good reasons to fear that the child be abnormal or retarded; it may be the importance attributed in different classes of society to considerations of honor or dishonor, of loss of social standing, and so forth. *We proclaim only that none of these reasons can ever objectively confer*

the right to dispose of another's life, even when that life is only beginning.[40]

While the circumstances that give rise to the temptation to destroy a human life in the womb are painfully real, the Church simply cannot acquiesce in the killing of innocents. To do so would sanction a species of unjustifiable homicide and constitute an irreparable trespass on the inalienable right to life possessed by every human being. Failure to denounce abortion also would violate the Church's duty to teach the Christian community and to speak the truth to those entrusted with political power over the life and death of persons in the womb.

Until 1973 the fundamental right to life of the unborn enjoyed widespread moral recognition and substantive legal protection in the United States.[41] To set the context for understanding the public policy of the Church concerning abortion since that time, it will be helpful to examine the legal landscape from which *Roe* v. *Wade* emerged in 1973 and to identify the key aspects of that decision which form the public policy battleground.

THE CONSTITUTIONAL CRISIS IN THE UNITED STATES

Although the degree of the criminality of abortion at common law is disputed,[42] it is clear that English statutory law made the abortion of a quickened fetus a capital crime while imposing a lesser penalty for the felony of aborting a fetus prior to quickening.[43] Criminal sanctions were imposed primarily on the abortionist. Even after the death penalty was abolished for abortion in England in 1837, every abortion was still subject to felony sanction.[44] Connecticut enacted the first abortion legislation in the United States in 1821 and followed the English felony rule for a quickened abortion[45] but did not criminalize abortions prior to quickening until 1860.[46] New York prohibited all abortions in 1828, defining as second-degree manslaughter a quickened abortion but classifying all other abortions as misdemeanors.[47] By 1840 eight States had enacted abortion legislation, the remainder following the common law tradition. With the discovery of the events of conception in the nineteenth century, the quickening distinction was gradually abolished by most States, which increased both the degree of the offense and the penalties for this crime. By the end of the 1950's, the overwhelming majority of States prohibited all abortions with the exception of those therapeutic abortions judged necessary by physicians to save the life of the mother. There were, however, State fights and referenda regarding which abortions, if any, should be legal.

From this historical evidence, it is clear that prior to 1973, there was little dispute regarding the power of a State to restrict, if not to prohibit entirely, the act of abortion.[48] On the day that *Roe* v. *Wade* was decided, thirty States allowed abortion only to save the life of the mother.[49] Alabama, Massachusetts and the District of Columbia permitted abortion only to preserve the life or health of the mother.[50] Mississippi restricted abortion only to save the life of the mother or when the pregnancy resulted from rape.[51] Thirteen States had adopted Section 230.3 of the American Law Institute's Model Penal Code[52] or some variation thereof and allowed abortion to save the life, or physical or mental health of the mother, or when a pregnancy resulted from rape or incest or when the unborn child may be severely disabled either mentally or physically.[53] Only four States allowed abortion on demand, but even those set limits according to the age of the fetus.[54] While efforts were then underway in some States to liberalize abortion laws,[55] a deep moral and legal consensus existed throughout the nation: abortion was a serious moral evil and as such it was a proper object of criminal legislation. The notion that such an act could *not* be prohibited or substantively restricted by public law but could be conceived of as a liberty interest or as a fundamental right within the meaning of the Due Process Clause of the Fourteenth Amendment was therefore a truly revolutionary idea. Furthermore, the scientific and medical community had no doubt that every act of abortion resulted in a death nor doubt about the moral significance of the conceptus, i.e., from the moment of fertilization.[56] Consequently, because the act of taking innocent human life is rarely, if ever, justifiable, the act of abortion had been proscribed radically by the respective States. Religious leaders were not engaged in efforts to repeal state laws which permitted abortion under exceptional circumstances of life of the mother, rape, and incest. While the Church tolerated state law exceptions to abortion, it denounced efforts to liberalize state law restrictions. It also continued to teach the intrinsic evil of the practice[57] and to forbid its members from participating in the knowing procurement of a direct abortion.[58]

9

This socio-political legal framework was radically altered by the Supreme Court in 1973 in *Roe* v. *Wade*. Contrary to common law and to the uniform practice of the respective States, Justice Harry A. Blackmun, writing for the seven person majority, announced without further explanation that "[the] right of privacy . . . founded in the Fourteentth Amendment's concept of personal liberty . . . is broad enough to encompass a woman's decision whether or not to terminate her pregnancy."[59] The Court held that a fetus is not a "person" within the meaning of the Fourteenth Amendment and that "the unborn have never been recognized in the law as persons in the whole sense."[60] Regarding the nonconstitutional sense of personhood, Justice Blackmun argued:

> We need not resolve the difficult question of when life begins. When those trained [in] medicine, philosophy, and theology are unable to arrive at any consensus, the judiciary, at this point in the development of [human] knowledge, is not in a position to speculate as to the answer.[61]

Having admitted an uncertainty about that crucial question, the Court still did not defer to the State of Texas which had concluded that human life begins at conception.[62]

The Court then embraced an extremely radical position that precipitated the constitutional crisis surrounding abortion. Notwithstanding its admitted lack of moral or philosophical certainty, the *Roe* majority acted as if it *knew* that the unborn were *not* human beings. Consequently, as a matter of constitutional principle, human personhood in the context of abortion only begins at birth. The Court announced a rule that accordingly permitted abortion not only in the first few weeks of pregnancy but effectively on demand throughout the entire pregnancy.[63] In the first trimester, the exercise of the abortion right is unconditional and may not be proscribed for any reason. A physician may refuse to perform an abortion; but no State, after *Roe* v. *Wade*, possessed the power to prohibit a first trimester abortion if desired by the mother and agreed to by her doctor. A State may, of course, impose time, place, and manner regulations bearing upon informed consent, majority age, and the health and safety of the medical procedure. During the second trimester, a State may regulate in the interest of ensuring maternal health and safety. With respect to protecting the "potentiality of human life," it becomes "compelling" only when the fetus becomes viable and "capable of meaningful life outside of the mother's womb" (20-24 weeks).[64] But even after viability, the Court decided that a state may not proscribe an abortion "where it is necessary, in appropriate medical judgment, for the preservation of the life or health of the mother."[65] Significantly, the Court, in *Doe* v. *Bolton*[66], decided the same day as *Roe*, broadly construed the "health" of the mother holding that the medical decision about whether or not to abort a pregnancy at any stage of the pregnancy cannot be restricted by narrow legislative criteria but "may be exercised in light of all factors—physical, emotional, psychological, familial and the woman's age—relevant to the well-being of the patient."[67] In light of this principle, a State may not prohibit a woman from obtaining an abortion at any time during her pregnancy, even to proscribe a third trimester abortion should a mother desire to do so.

Roe v. *Wade* represents one of the most sweeping acts of judicial power in American constitutional history. The Supreme Court located the "right" of abortion in a tenuous admixture of privacy and liberty that is at best implicit in the Constitution and at worst has been grafted onto the Constitution by the judicial fiat of the *Roe* majority. It then elevated this new right to equality with such explicit and venerated constitutional rights as the freedom of speech, of the press, and of religious liberty. What had been subject to criminal prohibition was now a *fundamental right* under the Constitution. When read together with *Doe* v. *Bolton*, the right of abortion in the United States is virtually unconditioned.[68] Both because of the radical nature of that reversal of our legal tradition and because the Court begged the questions of the personhood of the human life in the womb and how we ought to regard fetal life, the nation has been in a constitutional crisis since 1973.

THE PUBLIC RESPONSE OF THE CHURCH

Given the nature and scope of what Justice Byron R. White rightly called the Supreme Court's most extraordinary act of raw judicial power,[69] the Church immediately condemned the decision[70] as "a flagrant rejection of the unborn child's right to life."[71] The National Conference of Catholic Bishops' (NCCB) Ad Hoc Committee for Pro-Life Activities (which later became permanently established as the Secretariat for Pro-Life Activities) clearly expressed the official position of the Church:

> [T]he opinion of the Court has established that abortion-on-request is the public policy of this nation. . . . [and] has made the doctor the final judge as to who will live and who will die. . . . Never before has a humane society placed such an absolute and unrestricted power in the hands of an individual.
>
> Although . . . abortion may [now] be legally permissible, it is still morally wrong, and no Court opinion can change the law of God prohibiting the taking of innocent human life. Therefore, as religious leaders, we cannot accept the Court's judgment and we urge people not to follow its reasoning or conclusions.[72]

To counteract this radical turn in American jurisprudence, the Church intensified the deployment of its resources.[73]

In its testimony before the Senate Judiciary Committee in the spring of 1974, for example, the NCCB emphatically announced its collective moral judgment concerning this matter[74] and its full support for a constitutional amendment protecting unborn human life.[75] A brief review of the principle arguments advanced by the Bishops will illustrate the essential elements of the public policy of the Catholic Church in the aftermath of *Roe* v. *Wade*.

Having summarized the competent evidence of the humanity and personhood of fetal life, the Bishops made clear the fundamental question which the American public must ask and answer if it aspires to be a just society in its treatment of the unborn.

> Honesty compels us all to admit that in the abortion debate the question of when human life begins is *not* the central issue in dispute. *Rather, the main question is: how should society value the unborn human life that is present.*[76]

The failure to pose that question directly and to permit a complete exposition of the relevant interdisciplinary evidence contributed to the Court's massive error in judgment. Moreover, the incompetence of the Court regarding the adjudication of competing philosophical and theological arguments should have increased the Court's deference to the unborn and to the legislative decision of Texas to restrict the availability of a direct abortion to life threatening circumstances. The Court's suppression of "a full and open discussion of the question of the objective humanity of the unborn child"[77] and, more importantly, of how this developing human life should be regarded by civil society had done as much harm as the purposeful misrepresentation of the nature of the act of abortion by otherwise responsible medical associations.[78] In this regard the Court had joined the ranks of those persons and institutions who were actively engaged in a kind of semantic distortion of the nature, meaning, and public value of human life and personhood.[79] Given this state of affairs, the NCCB warned the Senate of the foreseeable consequences.

> [W]hen the objective reality of individual human life is either denied or reduced to simple factuality, those values that [are] commonly perceive[d] to flow from the personal transcendence that inheres in the individual (e.g. an inalienable right to life, liberty, pursuit of happiness) are replaced by other values ("meaningfulness," "a biologically oriented world society") that tend to possess a high degree of arbitrariness, caprice, or personal or group bias.[80]

In making their case for the right to life of the unborn, the Bishops then drew upon the explicit language of the Declaration of Independence,[81] The United Nations Declaration of Human Rights,[82] and modern principles of Catholic social teaching.[83] In addition they argued that both at common law and in American jurisprudence prior to *Roe*, there was ample evidence of the moral value and legal recognition of fetal life even prior to viability.

> If the unborn can inherit, be compensated for pre-natal injuries, . . . can have [their] right to continued existence preferred even to the [fundamental constitutional] right of the mother to the free exercise of her religion as in the blood transfusion cases, and enjoy such other rights, then the law would be schizophrenic to allow the unlimited destruction of that child.[84]

To disregard the weight of this legal tradition and to engage in speculation about "meaningful life" and "the potentiality of human life" was deeply troubling. Accordingly, the Bishops warned that:

> [T]he Court has set the stage for society—or government—to decide that some lives are "devoid of value," are lacking in "meaningfulness," or are unworthy of protection because their continuation is a threat to the convenience of others.[85]

Furthermore, the NCCB objected to the lexical priority of the right of privacy, which, if it exists at all, is implicit in the penumbras of parts of the Bill of Rights or in substantive due process concepts, over the right to life which is explicitly guaranteed by the Founders and by the Framers of the Fourteenth Amendment.[86] In fact the Bishops found the Supreme Court's overall treatment of the moral value of fetal personhood and its constitutional status to be "reminiscent of the infamous decision in *Dred Scott* v. *Sanford*."[87]

The NCCB then presented an even more detailed exposition of its reasons for rejecting the holdings and rationales of *Roe* v. *Wade* and *Doe* v. *Bolton*. Of that testimony, several points are especially noteworthy. First, the NCCB criticized the Court's unprincipled construction of the Constitution. While the right of privacy and the right of abortion are construed liberally and held to be consistent "with the demands of the profound problems of the present day,"[88] the right to life of the unborn and the question of legal personhood were construed strictly. Although the Constitution is silent about both a putative right of abortion rooted in privacy and the scope of personhood within the meaning of the Due Process Clause of the Fourteenth Amendment, the Court nevertheless interpreted the silence of the Framers against fetal civil rights in favor of what had been a criminal act at common law and in all States at some stage of pregnancy prior to 1973. In so doing the Court revealed an internal inconsistency which has not escaped the critical eye of constitutional scholars, even among those otherwise committed to the liberalization of abortion regulation.[89] Second, the Bishops' Conference noted that the Supreme Court had no constitutional difficulty in declaring corporations to be "persons" within the meaning of the Fourteenth Amendment nor in entertaining arguments to extend the protection of the Due Process Clause therein to certain classes of natural

14

flora involved in environmental litigation. The refusal to recognize fetal life as legal persons betrayed a disturbing bias in the Court against the unborn. Incredible as it may seem, even *trees* have been recognized by at least one member of the Supreme Court as "persons" within the meaning of the Fourteenth Amendment, thereby according a higher constitutional dignity than human life in the womb.[90] Third, and perhaps most importantly, the Bishops objected to the Court's almost cavalier evaluation of human life. By using such terms as capable of "meaningful life," the Court sounded too much like propagandists who sought to justify abortion, euthanasia, and eugenic experiments on persons whose lives were judged "devoid of value."[91]

Following this careful parsing of their reasons for repudiating these revolutionary decisions of the Supreme Court, the Bishops finally turned their attention to the matter of an appropriate constitutional remedy. Given the depth of the constitutional injury to the right to life of the unborn, the Bishops unanimously urged the Senate to approve and submit to the States for ratification an amendment to the Constitution which not only would reverse *Roe* v. *Wade* and *Doe* v. *Bolton* but which would forever protect the right to life of the unborn from the abuse of federal legislative, judicial, or executive power or by any similar State action. In particular the Bishops' Conference urged the Senate to approve language which reflected four points.

1. Establish that the unborn child is a person under the law in the terms of the Constitution from conception on.

2. The Constitution should express a commitment to the preservation of life to the maximum degree possible. The protection resulting therefrom should be universal.

3. The proposed amendment should give the states the power to enact enabling legislation, and to provide for ancillary matters such as record-keeping, etc.

4. The right of life is described in the Declaration of Independence as "unalienable" and as a right with which all men [and women] are endowed by their Creator. The amendment should

restore the basic constitutional protection for this human right to the unborn child.[92]

After making these recommendations, they concluded their testimony before the Senate by placing their support for a constitutional amendment to restore the civil rights of the unborn within a broader social context. This struggle against abortion on demand is but one aspect of the NCCB's legislative agenda "to build up a more just and loving society."[93] Accordingly, even were a Human Life Amendment to be ratified, the labor necessary to achieve social justice for pregnant women and their unborn children would not be complete until a wide variety of other services such as "nutritional, pre-natal, childbirth and post-natal care for the mother"[94] and appropriate nutritional and pediatric care for the newborn infant were made available to support the procreation of each new generation.[95] Thus the Bishops made clear to the Senate their commitment of the Catholic resources within their power to the human development of both mother and child.

In 1975 the NCCB released its "Pastoral Plan for Pro-Life Activities."[96] This document set forth the comprehensive strategy of the Church to meet the challenge posed by the Supreme Court's unjust abrogation of the civil rights of the unborn. Significantly, the Bishops began by emphasizing the interrelationship of the abortion controversy with other violations of civil rights.

Basic human rights are violated in many ways: by abortion and euthanasia, by injustice and the denial of equality to certain groups and persons, by some forms of human experimentation, by neglect of the underprivileged and disadvantaged who deserve the concern and support of the entire society. Indeed, the denial of the God-given right to life is one aspect of a larger problem. But it is unlikely that efforts to protect other rights will be ultimately successful if life itself is continually diminished in value.[97]

After placing the abortion controversy in this broader civil rights context, the Bishops then outlined the essential features of their three-fold effort—*educational* (with an emphasis on public information), *pastoral*, and *law reform*—to combat the violation of the dignity and personhood of fetal human life.[98] In specifying further the scope of its combined

16

public policy and legal strategy, the Bishops' Conference underscored the relationship between law and morality. They then announced a four point law reform initiative which continues to guide the Church today.

1. Passage of a constitutional amendment providing protection for the unborn child to the maximum degree possible.

2. Passage of federal and state laws and adoption of administrative policies that will restrict the practice of abortion as much as possible.

3. Continual research into and refinement and precise inter- pretation of *Roe* and *Doe* and subsequent court decisions.

4. Support for legislation that provides alternatives to abortion.[99]

Recognizing the enormity of the political and legal challenge and given the moral imperative to redress this systemic injustice, the Bishops' Conference called upon all Catholics, in partnership with all other citizens, to engage in "well-planned and coordinated political action . . . at the national, state and local levels."[100]

In the "Pastoral Guidelines for Catholic Hospitals" the Bishops reaffirmed unequivocally the moral teaching of the Church in regard to abortion.

The opinion of the Court is wrong and is entirely contrary to the fundamental principles of morality. . . . Whenever a conflict arises between the law of God and any human law we are held to follow God's law. . . . Catholic hospitals must witness to the sanctity of life, the integrity of the human person, and the value of human life at every stage of its existence.[101]

Defending the sanctity of life involves two claims: [1] that human life because of its very existence is sacred, and hence its value does not depend on particular medical or developmental conditions; and [2] that because all human lives have dignity and are of equal value they share the same right to life. The teaching of the Church against abortion fully embraces both claims.[102]

SOME MEASURE OF SUCCESS

This call to action was answered zealously by the Catholic community and has been sustained with admirable perseverance. At every level of civil society Catholic action on behalf of the unborn has been visible and vocal. Within the National Conference of Catholic Bishops, the Secretariat for Pro-Life Activities was established permanently to coordinate the development and communication of NCCB public policy. The National Right to Life Committee, a grass-roots organization formed in 1968 by Catholic lay men and women for the purpose of opposing the liberalization of abortion restrictions, was further mobilized to political action at the federal and state level.[103] Organizations such as Birthright and Americans United for Life, founded respectively in 1968 and 1971 to offer alternatives to abortion and to resist the liberalization of abortion laws, have continued to work with other pro-life groups to redress this systemic injustice to the unborn. In almost every diocese throughout the nation, there exists a diocesan pro-life committee whose mission is "to coordinate groups and activities within the diocese to restore respect for human life, particularly efforts to effect passage of a constitutional amendment to protect the unborn child."[104] Most parishes also have a pro-life committee. These diocesan efforts regularly are coordinated by a committee within the State Catholic Conference or its equivalent. Although these Conferences address all relevant social issues, the primary relevance of their committees regarding abortion is three-fold:

1. to monitor the political trends in the state and their implications for the abortion effort;

2. to coordinate the efforts of various dioceses and to evaluate progress in the dioceses and congressional districts; and

3. to provide counsel regarding the specific political relationships within the various parties at the state level.[105]

These state and local organizations are assisted at the national level by the NCCB's Secretariat for Pro-Life Activities. These lay and diocesan organizations also work with the National Committee for a Human Life

Amendment, which has the primary task of grass-roots organizing and mobilizing in connection with federal legislation on abortion. Given the presence and energy of these organizations, and their ecumenical counterparts, pro-life issues and activities are now a permanent feature of the political landscape and will remain so until social justice for fetal human life is secured by public law.

The success of their collective efforts has been quite impressive. Although the United States Senate has yet to approve a Human Life Amendment,[106] Congress enacted and the Supreme Court upheld the Hyde Amendment which withheld from States federal funds under the Medicaid program to reimburse the costs of abortions "except where the life of the mother would be endangered if the fetus were carried to term."[107] The Alan Guttmacher Institute reports that "[a]s a result of the Hyde Amendment, the number of federally funded abortions plummeted, from 294,000 in 1977 before the federal restrictions to 165 in 1990."[108] This restriction upon the use of federal funds was renewed even by the Democratically-controlled 103rd Congress; similar spending limitations have been adopted by a large number of States as well.[109] During the Reagan and Bush administrations, the pro-life movement, with the full support of the Catholic Bishops, successfully urged those Presidents to prohibit by Executive Order the use of federal monies and facilities within the jurisdiction of the Executive Branch to procure a direct abortion, except under circumstances like those specified in the latest version of the Hyde Amendment.

Success also has occurred in the legislative and judicial campaign to undermine the rationale and constitutional status of the right of abortion. In rejecting *Roe*'s constitutionalization of the act of abortion, the Church has attacked repeatedly the plausibility of the right of privacy rationale because it created a rule of law which separates human sexuality, human generation, the complex question of human personhood, and paternity even within marriage from the social nature of the public good.[110] Although abortion on demand is still available in all fifty States, this public policy strategy has borne good fruit at least at the level of rights discourse. The Supreme Court, for example, has abandoned strict judicial review of abortion regulations and hence the notion of the act of abortion as a fundamental constitutional right [111] and has replaced the *Roe* trimester framework of analysis with one dependent upon the viability of the fetus.[112] Although the Court has yet to sustain a substantive prohibition upon a pre-viability abortion, it has upheld a twenty-four-hour waiting period for adult women[113] and a forty-eight-hour waiting period for minors[114] when such temporal restrictions include a medical emergency exception. Statutes requiring a minor to obtain the consent of one of her parents and statutes requiring the notification of both parents have passed constitutional muster, so long as the minor has recourse to a judicial forum in exceptional circumstances.[115] Detailed informed consent statutes have been enacted by twenty-nine States.[116] Furthermore, a substantive state law contradiction of the non-personhood of fetal life exists in those twenty-four States which cannot prohibit abortion at any stage of pregnancy but which define the killing of an unborn child as a form of homicide. Nine of those States prohibit fetal homicide regardless of the stage of pregnancy,[117] while the remaining fifteen States prohibit the killing at different times ranging from seven weeks[118] to quickening[119] to viability.[120] With respect to proposed Congressional legislation, the Bishops made clear their firm opposition to the Freedom of Choice Act,[121] which failed to become law during the 103rd Congress, and to the inclusion of direct abortion as a component of any governmental health care program.[122]

In addition to its legislative and judicial efforts, the Church has tried to heighten public consciousness of the tragic nature and consequences of abortion through its educational system and its vocal presence in public discourse concerning human life issues. Part of the struggle has demanded confrontation with the pro-choice bias of the print and electronic media, which have inadequately informed the public about the nature and practice of abortion. For example, details on the death of the unborn as well as the physical suffering and adverse medical complications of women who have aborted have remained largely unreported.[123] Similarly, there has been an almost irrational denial of the evidence of the psychological trauma suffered by women who have aborted their children.[124] Regarding the state of the law of abortion, a very small percentage of the public actually understands the frequency of abortions in the United States or recognize that an abortion can be procured after the first trimester.

Catholic efforts to counteract this "abortion distortion"[125] and those activities of sister churches, synagogues and other pro-life organizations have tried to help make the public more aware of the nature and practice of abortion since 1973. But even after twenty-two years of public controversy, a large segment of the public still does not understand what *Roe* v.

Wade actually held,[126] and there is great misperception concerning even the number of abortions performed in the United States.[127] Most people, for example, underestimate the number of abortions and mistakenly believe abortions are illegal after the first trimester. Contrary to that perception, over 4400 abortions are performed each day aggregating over 1.6 million per year. Well over 150, 000 of those performed each year are obtained after the twelfth week of pregnancy and more than 10,000 after the twenty-first week.[128]

Notwithstanding this ignorance, the concerted efforts of the Church and the pro-life movement are succeeding in making significant headway in public understanding regarding the nature and extent of legal abortion.[129] The 1991 Gallup/Americans United for Life [AUL] public opinion poll, for example, revealed the moral abhorrence of the vast majority of the electorate to nontherapeutic abortions.[130] Laura Anne Ramsey, AUL vice president for public affairs, reported the pertinent findings:

Although a majority of respondents indicated they would permit abortions during the first three months of pregnancy in cases of rape and incest, "if there is a strong chance of serious deformity in the baby," and if the mother's health would suffer from the pregnancy, *there was solid opposition to abortion in most other circumstances, and virtually under all circumstances after the first three months of pregnancy.* . . . For example: By a margin of 66% to 29%, the respondents . . . [disapproved] of abortion for financial reasons, even in the case of a low-income woman for whom another child would create a heavy financial burden. By a margin of 68% to 27%, they opposed abortion for a woman who has been "abandoned by her partner." And by a margin of 66% to 28%, they oppose abortion in those cases where having a baby would cause a teenage mother to drop out of school.

Disapproval of abortion, even in the first trimester, increases dramatically in most other circumstances: Seventy-seven percent disapprove of abortion in cases where "pregnancy is unplanned and would interrupt a professional woman's career"; [88%] per cent disapprove of abortion "as a means of repeated birth control;" [and] [91%] disapprove of abortion if the tests reveal the baby is not the sex the couple wants.[131]

Seventy-five percent of Americans believe that abortion is "taking . . . [a] human life."[132] Fifty-two percent of women, and forty-eight percent of men, believe "the unborn child's 'right to be born' outweighs, at the moment of conception, the woman's 'right to choose' whether she wants to have a child."[133] Parental consent and notice statutes have overwhelming public support (seventy-four percent favor; twenty-three percent oppose)[134] as does a policy preference for detailed informed consent statutes and alternatives to abortion such as adoption and increased public support for childbearing. Even sixty-seven percent of women and sixty-eight of men favor "a law requiring that the husband of a married woman be notified before she is allowed to have an abortion."[135] Based upon this polling data, one can say unhesitatingly that *the right to choose to kill* a preborn human being by means of abortion is rejected by a supermajority in the electorate whenever the reason is not perceived as life threatening or the consequence of a criminal act such as rape or incest. Such was the state of the law in many States before *Roe* v. *Wade*. Absent a constitutional amendment to restore and secure the civil rights of the unborn, the public appears to be opposed to liberal abortion regulation and supportive of a return to the traditional prohibitions.

NEW DEVELOPMENTS

Perhaps the most significant events which are now shaping the public policy strategy of the Church in the United States concerning abortion are the Clinton Presidency and the 104th Congress. On January 22, 1993, the twentieth anniversary of *Roe* v. *Wade*, President Clinton rescinded longstanding Executive Orders which successfully had restricted the use of federal monies and institutional support for a variety of abortion related activities. These five executive orders specifically lifted the ban on abortion counseling in federal family planning clinics; cancelled the moratorium on federally-funded fetal tissue research; revoked the prohibition on abortions in military hospitals; rescinded the policy which denied foreign aid funding for agencies promoting abortions; and commissioned a study of the personal use of RU-486, the French abortion pill, which had been banned from importation.[136] These actions clearly increased both the availability and the frequency of abortions. Contrary to his predecessors, he nominated and gained Senate confirmation for two

22

new members of the Supreme Court who were veted at least in part to ensure the survival of *Roe* and its progeny.[137] President Clinton also gave his full support in the national health care debate to provide public funds for direct abortions in his proposed National Health Security Act.[138] The delegation of the United States to the International Conference on Population and Development held in Cairo, Egypt during September 1994, led by Assistant Secretary Timothy Wirth, seemed to have embraced the proposition that abortion is an acceptable way to respond to pregnancy which is caused by contraceptive failure.[139] Moreover, the United States continues to support family planning programs throughout the world which use abortion as a population control tool.[140] Most recently, President Clinton vetoed the "Partial-Birth Abortion Ban Act of 1995," which made a specific late-term abortion procedure a federal felony.[141] This bill marked the first time since *Roe* v. *Wade* that Congress had acted to prohibit and criminalize any abortion procedure.[142] The President of the National Catholic Conference of Bishops, in an unprecedented letter addressed to President Clinton signed by all of the Roman Catholic Cardinals in the United States, condemned the veto as "beyond comprehension."[143] They pledged concerted action "to urge Catholics and other people of good will . . . to do all they can to urge Congress to override this shameful veto" and characterized the President's action as "moving our society ever more rapidly to embrace a culture of death."[144]

The mid-term elections of 1994 undoubtedly will have a significant impact on the success of the Church concerning its legislative strategies at all levels of government. More pro-life legislators are now in office throughout the nation than at any time since 1973. Given the Republican Party's plank on abortion and its control of Congress, it is unlikely that any substantive pro-choice legislation will be enacted by the 104th Congress. This will free substantial resources among pro-life organizations to focus on state legislative goals. However, the recent welfare reform debate over those provisions in the Personal Responsibility Act which prohibits States from distributing federal block grant monies to pregnant women under eighteen[145] may have the unintended effect of increasing the number of abortions. This aspect *inter alia* of the proposed legislation was opposed by the NCCB and was removed from the Senate version of the Welfare Reform bill.[146]

CONCLUSION

The teaching of the Church on abortion is the result of a reflective understanding and judgment regarding the experience of human personhood in the light of faith and reason. It presents an intelligent, rational, and responsible assessment of the act of abortion. It demonstrates an unequivocal respect for human life at all stages of pregnancy and after birth as well. It's teaching is based upon what is known from science and upon the moral value, dignity, and fundamental equality of every human person, including the unborn, regardless of age, sex, physical condition or level of dependency. Accordingly, the Church teaches that every person and every civil society are bound by the moral duty to protect unborn human life; any law that permits the willful destruction of human life in the womb is therefore an unjust law. This teaching shapes the contours of the public policy of the Church concerning the law of abortion and guides the political action and advocacy of Catholics throughout the world. Hence, the Church seeks to secure the full legal recognition and constitutional restoration of the right to life of the unborn. It is a demand of fundamental equality and social justice.

While condemning the moral evil of abortion, the Church desires to influence the development of law and public policy to reduce the evil of abortion and its pervasive social causes.[147] To that end the Church exhorts the political community to shape public policy to alleviate the deprivations in the social order which contribute to the culture of abortion in our country, especially addressing the needs of children and families together.[148] Moreover, it engages in this reasoned public discourse knowing that its voice may only succeed in the effort to diminish the evil of abortion. Nevertheless, the Church will continue its effort to eradicate entirely this moral tragedy in our society.

The papers in this collection discuss these issues in an effort to explain, develop, and refine a Catholic stance regarding public policy toward abortion. In convening the conference in which these papers were presented, Saint Louis University, with the generous financial support of the Webb Foundation and the Donahue Family Foundation, Inc., sought to advance that mission by presenting original interdisciplinary scholarship exploring the scientific, moral, theological, and legal issues which bear upon the development of sound public policy. We believe we have accomplished that goal in this volume. The articles herein are offered to

24

the citizen reader and to those entrusted with political and judicial power
to provide a fresh examination of the public policies of the United States
and the respective States regarding the act of abortion.

NOTES

1. 410 U.S. 113 (1973).

2. See *Catechism of the Catholic Church* (Washington, D.C.: United States
Catholic Conference, 1994), no. 2271 and Pope John Paul II *The Gospel of Life:
The Encyclical on Abortion, Euthanasia, and the Death Penalty in Today's World*
(New York: Times Books, 1995), no. 61.

3. See *Didache Apostolorum*, V, 2 (edition Funk, *Patres Apostolici*, I, 17).

4. See, for example, *The Epistle of Barnabas*, XIX, 5 (edition Funk, *Patres
Apostolici*, V, 91-93), and Tertullian, *Apologeticum*, IX, 8 (*PL*, I, 371-72). See also
the Congregation of Doctrine of the Faith (CDF), "Declaration on Abortion,"
4:25 *Origins* (December 12, 1974): 385, 387-92, no. 6, notes 6 and 8.

5. Thomas Aquinas, *Commentary on the Sentences*, book IV, dist. 31; and
Summa Theologiae, I-II, q. 93, a. 3, and q. 95, a. 2; see also, CDF, "Declaration on
Abortion," no. 7, note 11 and John Paul II, *The Gospel of Life*, no. 72, nn. 96-97.

6. John Paul II, *The Gospel of Life*, no. 62, 70, and 71 (emphasis original).

7. Any references to "the unborn" or to "human life in the womb" in this
article include human life from the moment of conception which occurs at
nidation or syngamy. Hence, for example, at the beginning of *Donum Vitae* we
read: "The inviolability of the innocent human being's right to life 'from the
moment of conception until death' is a sign and requirement of the very
inviolability of the person to whom the Creator has given the gift of life," (The
Congregation of Doctrine of the Faith [CDF], "Instruction on the Respect for
Human Life in Its Origin and on the Dignity of Procreation," *Origins* 16:40
[March 19, 1987]: Introduction, no. 4, citing, Pope John Paul II, "Discourse to
those taking part in the 35th General Assembly of the World Medical Association," 29 October 1983: *Acta Apostolicae Sedis* 76 [1984]: 390). The revised
directives for Catholic health care cite the same discourse to emphasize Catholic
responsibilities in this matter: "Catholic health care ministry witnesses to the
sanctity of life 'from the moment of conception until death'" (NCCB, *Ethical
and Religious Directives for Catholic Health Care Services* [Washington, D.C.:
USCC, Inc, 1994], part four, introduction).

8. *Gaudium et Spes*, in Walter M. Abbott, S.J., editor, *Vatican Council II*
(Geoffrey Chapman: London, 1972), no. 51.

9. CDF, "Declaration on Abortion," no. 12.

10. John Paul II, *The Gospel of Life*, no. 60 (emphasis original), citing CDF, "Instruction on the Respect for Human Life," *Origins* 16:40 (March 19, 1987): 697, 699-711, no. I, 1.

11. John Paul II, *The Gospel of Life*, no. 12.

12. John Paul II, *The Gospel of Life*, no. 28 (emphasis original).

13. John Paul II, *The Gospel of Life*, no. 73 (emphasis original).

14. "Abortion (that is, the directly intended termination of pregnancy before viability or the directly intended destruction of a viable fetus) is never permitted" (NCCB, *Ethical and Religious Directives*, no. 45). See also: John Connery, S.J., *Abortion: The Development of the Roman Catholic Perspective* (Chicago, IL: Loyola University Press, 1977), 304-13; John T. Noonan, Jr., "An Almost Absolute Value in History," in John T. Noonan, Jr., ed., *The Morality of Abortion: Legal and Historical Perspectives* (Cambridge, MA: Harvard University Press, 1970), 1-59; and Germaine G. Grisez, *Abortion: The Myths, The Realities, and the Arguments* (New York: Corpus Books, 1970), 165-84.

15. See, CDF, "Declaration on Abortion," no. 8. Because "the life of the body in its earthly state is not an absolute good" (John Paul II, *The Gospel of Life*, no. 47) the Catholic tradition at times has found the indirect killing of innocent life to be morally justifiable based on the principle of double effect, see, David F. Kelly, *The Emergence of Roman Catholic Medical Ethics in North America* (New York: The Edwin Mellen Press, 1979), 275, and Benedict M. Ashley, O.P., Kevin D. O'Rourke, O.P., *Ethics of Health Care* (Washington, D.C.: Georgetown University Press, 1994), 144.

16. See, CDF, "Instruction," Introduction, no. 5. Also, see *Summa Theologiae*, II-II, q. 64, a. 6. By "innocent" life the Catholic tradition includes not only the lack of aggression against another but also the defenselessness of the unborn: "In no way could this human being ever be considered an aggressor, much less an unjust aggressor! He or she is *weak*, defenseless, even to the point of lacking that minimal form of defense consisting in the poignant power of a newborn baby's cries and tears. The unborn child is *totally entrusted* to the protection and care of the woman carrying him or her in the womb" (John Paul II, *The Gospel of Life*, no. 58, emphasis original).

17. For an account of the debate on ensoulment, see Connery, S.J., *Abortion*, 105-23. However, even in the era when the beginning of human life was posited by some theologians to occur as much as six weeks after fertilization, the act of directly killing an "unsouled" fetus was considered a serious moral evil, mainly because of what the unsouled fetus would become, if it were allowed to develop in its natural environment (see, CDF, "Declaration on Abortion," no. 7). While the question of ensoulment is pertinent to human personhood, its relevance presupposes a philosophical commitment to an anthropology that understands body and soul as integrally united (see, John Paul II, *The Gospel of Life*, no. 60). For many moderns human personhood need not be understood exclusively in

26

such terms. Accordingly, the unity of being that exists between an adult human being and his or her syngamus self is sufficient to affirm the moral significance and personal identity of the conceptus from fertilization through adult maturation. See, for example, Frederick E. Crowe, S.J., "The Life of the Unborn: Notions from Bernard Lonergan," in *Appropriating the Lonergan Idea*, ed. Michael Vertin (Washington DC: Catholic University of America Press, 1989), 360-69.

18. See also, *Gaudium et Spes*, no. 51 and *Humanae Vitae* (Washington, D.C.: USCC, 1968), no. 14, and CDF, "Declaration on Abortion," no. 7. Connery demonstrates the historical continuity of Jewish and Christian teaching regarding abortion and notes that the condemnation of abortion in Christian moral reflection at no point focused upon animation as a decisive criterion (see, *Abortion*, 303-4).

19. This does not mean we can be philosophically certain about ensoulment in human life. See, Joseph F. Donceel, "Animation and Hominization," *Theological Studies* 31 (1970): 76-105. Whether a human being exists from the first moment of conception requires distinguishing between two views: we cannot be certain that such is not the case; and we can be certain that such is the case, for example the argument of Aquinas on delayed animation in *Summa contra Gentiles*, II, 88-89 and *Summa Theologica*, I, q. 118, a. 1-3. Also see Joseph F. Donceel, "A Liberal Catholic's View," in Patricia Beattie Jung and Thomas A. Shannon, eds. *Abortion and Catholicism: The American Debate* (New York: Crossroad, 1988), 48-53, at 48.

20. Andre E. Hellegers, "Fetal Development," in *Biomedical Ethics*, eds. Thomas A. Mappes and Jane S. Zembaty (New York: McGraw-Hill, 1981), 405 ff.

21. See Harold J. Morowitz and James S. Trefil, *The Facts of Life: Science and the Abortion Controversy* (New York: Oxford University Press, 1992), 46. See also James J. McCartney, *Unborn Persons: Pope John Paul II and the Abortion Debate* (New York: Peter Lang, 1987), 141-48.

22. The Church does not maintain that it has certitude regarding the question of ensoulment. But it acts responsibly when, given the reasonable probability of its judgment, it insists upon the moral recognition and legal protection of human life from the moment of fertilization.

This declaration expressly leaves aside the question of the moment when the spiritual soul is infused. There is not a unanimous tradition on this point and authors are as yet in disagreement. For some it dates from the first instant, [i.e., at syngamy, the successful completion of fertilization], for others it could not at least precede nidation [i.e., implantation of an embryo in the lining of the uterus]. It is not within the competence of science to decide between these views, because the existence of an immortal soul is not a question in its field. It is a philosophical problem from which our moral affirmation remains independent for two reasons: (i) supposing a later animation, there is still nothing less than a *human* life, preparing for and calling for a soul in which the nature received from parents is completed; (ii) on the other hand it suffices that this presence of the soul be probable (and one can never prove the contrary) in order that the taking of life involve[s] accepting the risk of killing a [human being], not only waiting for, but already in possession of his [or her] soul (CDF, "Declaration on Abortion," note 19, emphasis original).

23. Of course, even if the personal status of unborn human life could be ascertained from the earliest moment, with according moral and legal rights, the abortion debate would not be resolved. Scholars argues that determining the status of unborn life as personal with human rights does not resolve potential clashes of rights between the mother and the unborn. See, for example, Francis J. Beckwith, "Arguments from Bodily Rights: A Critical Analysis," in *Politically Correct Death: Answering the Arguments for Abortion Rights* (Grand Rapids: Baker Book House, 1993), chap. 7; James Keenan, "Reply to Beckwith: Abortion—Whose Agenda Is It Anyway?" *International Philosophical Quarterly* 32 (June 1992): 239-45. Nevertheless, as society tries to protect the rights of the mother it must occur by honoring our responsibilities to one another, including the unborn. See, Baruch Brody, *Abortion and the Sanctity of Human Life: A Philosophical View* (Cambridge, MA: M.I.T. Press, 1975), 30. Pope John Paul II argues that attacks "directly against respect for life ... represent a *direct threat to the entire culture of human rights*" (*The Gospel of Life*, no. 18, original emphasis). He adds later: "as far as the right to life is concerned, every innocent human being is absolutely equal to all others. This equality is the basis of all authentic social relationships" (ibid., 57).

24. The Church perceives its involvement with the divine and the human as inseparable. Thus, the vision of two cities popularized by Saint Augustine doesn't imply that they are to exist as completely separate entities. "The Church, . . . is to be a leaven and, as it were, the soul of human society in its renewal by Christ and transformation into the family of God," *Gaudium et Spes*, no. 40.

25. See NCCB, *Economic Justice for All: Pastoral Letter on Catholic Social Teaching and the U.S. Economy* (Washington, D.C.: USCC, 1986), no. 28.

26. Pope John XXIII explained the responsibility of Catholics in the modern world more fully when he wrote:

Nevertheless in order to imbue civilization with sound principles and enliven it with the spirit of the gospel, it is not enough to be illumined with the gift of faith and enkindled with the desire of forwarding a good cause. For this end it is necessary to take an active part in the various organizations and influence them from within. Pope John XXIII, *Peace on Earth: Pacem In Terris* (Boston, MA: St. Paul Editions, 1963), no. 147. See also, NCCB, *Economic Justice for All*, no. 27.

27. See, Archbishop John Roach, "The Need for Public Dialogue on Religion and Politics," 11:25 *Origins* (December 3, 1981): 389, 391-93.

28. John Courtney Murray, S.J. *We Hold These Truths: Catholic Reflections on the American Proposition* (Kansas City: Sheed and Ward, 1960), 79-123. Also see, J. Leon Hooper, S.J. *The Ethics of Discourse: The Social Philosophy of John Courtney Murray* (Washington, D.C.: Georgetown University Press, 1986), 14-17, 93-99, and Cardinal John Dearden, "The Challenge of Religious Pluralism," *Origins* 6:19 (October 28, 1976): 295.

29. See the emphasis upon the human reasoning of natural law argument in the "Declaration of Abortion," no. 8-13. For another example of natural law reasoning (with regard to the contraception debate) see the *Instruction on Respect for Human Life*, II, B, 4. Also see note 5 above. For a comparative analysis of natural law with other approaches in moral theory with regard to the abortion debate, see L. W. Sumner, *Abortion and Moral Theory* (Princeton, NJ: Princeton University Press, 1981).

30. See, for example, Thomas A. Shannon, "Abortion: A Challenge for Ethics and Public Policy," in Patricia Beattie Jung and Thomas A. Shannon, *Abortion and Catholicism*, 185-201. Pope John Paul II explains in his recent encyclical that it may be legitimate to vote for laws that decrease abortion when it cannot be eliminated: "when it is not possible to overturn or completely abrogate a pro-abortion law, an elected official, whose absolute personal opposition to procured abortion was well known, could licitly support proposals aimed at *limiting the harm* done by such a law and at lessening its negative consequences at the level of general opinion and public morality" (*The Gospel of Life*, no. 73, emphasis original). However, public officials must avoid separating "the realm of private conscience from that of public conduct;" when that occurs "individual responsibility is thus turned over to the civil law, with a renouncing of personal conscience, at least in the public sphere" (ibid., 69).

31. See, for example, Cardinal Joseph Bernardin, "The Consistent Ethic: What Sort of Framework?" *Origins* 16 (October 30, 1986): 345, 345-50. For a philosophical analysis of the appeal to consistency in the abortion debate, see Harry J. Gensler, "A Kantian Argument Against Abortion," *Philosophical Studies* 49 (1986): 83-98.

32. *Catechism*, no. 2273 at 548 (emphasis original). John Paul II writes: "A civil law authorizing abortion or euthanasia ceases by that very fact to be a true, morally binding civil law" (*The Gospel of Life*, no. 72).

33. The Founders of the United States fully embraced this insight by asserting in the Declaration of Independence that "all men are created equal." On that basis alone the Founders invoked the moral right to political liberty and

self-governance.

34. Lisa Cahill explains that G. E. M. Anscombe adopted from Aristotle the phrase "human flourishing" to describe what grounds, defines, and constitutes the virtues that human beings ought to cultivate. See Lisa Cahill, "Abortion, Autonomy, and Community," in Patricia Beattie Jung and Thomas A. Shannon, eds. *Abortion and Catholicism: The American Debate* (New York: Crossroad, 1988), 85-97, at 95, referring to G. E. M. Anscombe, "Modern Moral Philosophy," *Philosophy* 33 (1958): 18.

35. Defending the right of the unborn to life is not a matter of privacy. There is, however, in Church teaching a proper sphere of reproductive privacy of parents to decide when and how many children to have (in conformity to Divine law and Church teaching). Vatican II refers to this sphere of reproductive privacy as the "Christian sense of responsibility" (*Gaudium et Spes*, 50) and *Humanae Vitae* refers to it as "responsible parenthood" (no. 10).

36. For a feminist, pro-choice critique of pursuing the right to abortion under the law of privacy, see Catherine A. MacKinnon, *Feminism Unmodified: Discourses on Life and Law* (Cambridge, MA: Harvard University Press, 1987), 93-102. Although feminism is associated usually with defending women's privacy in the abortion debate, not all feminists are pro-choice. For example, the pro-life feminist Sidney Callahan contests her opponents arguments. Callahan shifts the discussion on abortion from: focusing on the moral right of a woman to control her own body to a more inclusive idea of justice; focusing on the autonomy and choice of the woman to an expanded sense of personal responsibility; focusing on fetal life as having merely contingent value to the moral claim for the intrinsic value of human life; focusing on the woman's right to full social equality from a pro-choice perspective to making the same claim from a pro-life perspective. See Sidney Callahan, "Abortion and the Sexual Agenda: A Case for Pro-Life Feminism," *Commonweal* 123 (April 25, 1986): 232-38.

37. See NCCB, *Economic Justice for All*, no. 71.

38. See David C. Reardon, *Aborted Women: Silent No More* (Chicago: Loyola University Press, 1987). Having interviewed 252 women in 42 states, he reported that "women who abort in the 'hard' case—for rape, incest, when pregnant with a handicapped child, or for reasons of physical or mental health—are much more likely to suffer from severe emotional and psychiatric stress after their abortion than are those who abort purely for reasons of convenience" (Id., xxv).

39. See, e.g. Francis J. Beckwith, *Politically Correct Death: Answering Arguments for Abortion Rights* (Grand Rapids, MI: Baker Books, 1993), chapters 3-8.

40. CDF, "Declaration on Abortion," no. 14 (emphasis added). Also, the values of the freedom and dignity of women have limits within the relational context of justice, see CDF, "Declaration on Abortion," no. 15.

41. In 1789 when the Constitution was ratified and in 1791 when the Fifth Amendment was ratified along with the other nine amendments in the Bill of Rights, William Blackstone's *Commentaries on the Laws of England* (London 1765) guided the practice of bench and bar alike in construing both the common law and positive law expressed in written constitutions and legislative enactments. Blackstone reports that the word "person" in the common law meant one "like us" who had been "formed by God" in their mothers womb. See *Commentaries*, Book 1, ch. 1, 125-26, and Book 4, ch. 14. Because the Fifth Amendment provides in pertinent part that "nor shall any person be deprived of life, liberty or property without due process of law," and because the trend in American law had been to criminalize all abortions, human life in the womb was protected by the criminal laws of the United States in the federal territories of Arizona, Colorado, Idaho, Montana and Nevada. See James C. Mohr, *Abortion in America: The Origins and Evolution of National Policy, 1800-1900* (New York: Oxford University Press, 1978), 200.

The Fourteenth Amendment was ratified in 1868 which expressly prohibited the respective States "[to] deprive any person of life, liberty or property without due process of law." At that time, a direct abortion procured after quickening was a crime at common law and hence in all states in which the common law was in effect. In addition, states like Connecticut and Pennsylvania, which voted for ratification, made it a statutory crime to procure a direct abortion after conception (Id., 301).

42. At common law, abortion of a quickened fetus was subject to criminal indictment. But the great common-law scholars are divided on the degree of criminality. Bracton, for example, described abortion as a species of homicide early in the 13th century. See Henrici de Bracton, *De Legibus et Consuetudinibus Angliae* (1879), ed. T. Twiss (Buffalo, NY: W. S. Hein, 1990), 279 ("if the foetus be already formed and animated, and particularly if it be animated"). However, Coke argued that a quickened abortion was a great misprison, and no murder. See Lord Coke, *The Third Part of the Institutes of the Laws of England* (London: W. Clarke, 1817), 50. Blackstone distinguished between the completed abortion of a quickened child, in which case it had been considered manslaughter, but not murder, and the abortion of quickened child that was born alive and subsequently died, in which case it was murder. See William Blackstone, *Commentaries on the Laws of England* (London, 1765), Book 1, ch. 1, 125-30, and book 4, ch. 14.

43. Lord Ellenborough's Act, 43 Geo. 3, c.58 §§ 1-2 (1803).

44. Offense Against the Persons Act of 1861, 24 & 25 Vict., c. 100, § 59. Even after the liberalizing reforms of 1967, the British Parliament still made the destruction of the life of a child capable of being born alive a felony. See also, The Infant Life Preservation Act, 19 & 20 Geo. 5, c. 34 (1967).

45. Conn. Stat., Tit. 20, § 14 (1821).

46. Conn. Pub. Acts, c. 71, § 1 (1860).

47. N.Y. Rev. Stat., pt. 4, c. 1, Tit. 2, Art. 1, § 9, p. 661, and Tit. 6, §21, p.694 (1829).

48. For a comprehensive examination of the state of the law of abortion both prior to and after *Roe* v. *Wade*, see Paul Benjamin Linton, "Enforcement of State Abortion Statutes After Roe: A State by State Analysis," 67 *University of Detroit Law Review* 157-259 (1990).

49. Ariz. Rev. Stat. Ann. §§ 13-211, 13-212 (1956); Conn. Gen. Stat. Ann. § 53-29 *et seq.* (West Supp. 1972); Idaho Code §§ 18-601, 18-602 (Supp. 1972); Ill. Rev. Stat. ch. 38, para. 23-1(1971); Ind. Code Ann. §§ 35-1-58-1, 35-1-58-2 (Burns 1971); Iowa Code § 701.1 (1950); Ky. Rev. Stat. Ann. § 436.020 (Michie/Bobbs/Merrill 1962); La. Rev. Stat. Ann. § 14:87 (West 1964); Me. Rev. Stat. Ann. tit. 17, § 51 (1964); Mich. Comp. Laws Ann. § 750.14 (West 1968); Minn. Stat. Ann. §§ 617.18, 617.19 (West 1971); Mo. Ann. Stat. § 559.100 (Vernon 1969); Mont. Code Ann. §§ 94-401, 94-402 (1969); Neb. Rev. Stat. §§ 28-404, 28-405 (1964); Nev. Rev. Stat.§§ 200.220, 201.120 (1967); N.H. Rev. Stat. Ann. §§ 585.13 (1955); N.J. Stat. Ann. § 2A.87-1 (West 1969); N.D. Cent. Code §§ 12-25-01, 12-25-02, 12-25-04 (1970); Ohio Rev. Code Ann. § 2901.19 (Baldwin 1953); Okla. Stat. Ann. tit. 2, §§ 861, 862 (West 1971); Pa. Stat. Ann. tit. 18, §§ 4718, 4719 (Purdon 1963); R.I. Gen Laws § 11-3-1 (1956); S.D. Codified Laws Ann. §§ 22-17-1, 22-17-2 (1967); Tenn. Code Ann. §§ 39-301, 39-302 (Supp. 1956); Tex. Penal Code Ann. art. 1191 *et seq.* (Vernon 1961; Utah Code Ann. §§ 76-2-1, 76-2-2 (1953); Vt. Stat. Ann. tit. 13, §101 (1958); W. Va. Code § 61-2-8 (1966); Wis. Stat. § 940.04 (1969); Wyo. Stat. §§ 6-77, 6-78 (1957).

50. Ala. Code tit. 14, § 9 (1958)(statutory health exception added in 1951 Ala. Acts 1630); Mass. Gen. Laws Ann. ch. 272, §19 (1968)(judicially created health exception announced in *Kudish* v. *Bd. of Registration in Medicine*, 356 Mass. 98, 99-100, 248 N.E.2d 264, 266 [1969]); D.C. Code Ann. § 22-201 (1967) (health exception included in original code, 31 Stat. 1322 (1901).

51. Miss. Code Ann. § 2223 (Supp. 1966)(rape exception added by statute in 1966 Miss. Laws, ch. 358, § 1).

52. Model Penal Code 230.3 (American Law Institute, 1962).

53. Ark. Stat. Ann. § 41-303 *et seq.* (Supp. 1969); Cal. Penal Code §§ 187. 274, 275 (West Supp. 1971) & Cal. Health & Safety Code 25950 *et seq.* (West Supp. 1971)(no mental or physical disability exception); Colo. Rev. Stat. § 40-6-101 *et seq.* (Perm. Supp. 1971); Del. Code Ann. tit. 11, §§ 222(22), 651-654 & *id.* tit. 24, §§ 1766(b), 1790-1793; 1972 Fla. Laws 608, ch. 72-196 (1972); Ga. Code Ann. § 26-1201 *et seq.* (1971); Kan. Stat. Ann.§ 21-3407 (Vernon 1971); Md. Ann. Code art. 43, §§ 129A, 137-39 (Supp. 1972); N.M. Stat. Ann. § 40A-5-1 *et seq.* (2nd repl. vol. 1972); N.C. Gen. Stat. § 14-44 *et seq.* (Supp. 1971); Or. Rev. Stat. § 435.405 *et seq.* (1969); S.C. Code Ann.§ 16-82 *et seq.* (Supp. 1971); Va. Code Ann. § 18.1-62 *et seq.* (Supp. 1971).

54. Alaska Stat. §11.15.060 (1970)(prior to viability); Haw. Rev. Stat. § 453-16 (Supp. 1971)(prior to viability); N.Y. Penal Law § 125.00 *et seq.* (McKinney Supp. 1971)(twenty-four weeks); Wash. Rev. Code Ann. § 9.02.010 *et seq.* (Supp. 1971)(before quickening and not more than four lunar months after conception).

55. In 1972 a report of a federal commission (the Rockefeller Report), mentioned that abortion laws should be liberalized in order to provide a legitimate way of controlling the population of the United States, *On Population and the American Future* (New American Library, 1992), 177-78. There was little public acceptance of the report, but in a certain sense, abortion as a possible part of public policy was placed in the public psyche.

56. In 1857 the American Medical Association appointed a Committee on Criminal Abortion to investigate the practice of abortion. In its findings reported in 1859, the Committee condemned the frequency of abortion and detailed three causes of this general demoralization:

> The first of these causes is a wide-spread popular ignorance of the true character of the crime—a belief, even among mothers themselves, that the foetus is not alive till after the period of quickening. The second... is the fact that the profession itself is careless of foetal life....The third reason of the frightful extent of this crime is found in the grave defects of our laws, both common and statutory, as regards the independence and actual existence of the child before birth, as a living being.

See 12 Trans. of the Am. Med. Assn. 75-76 (1859). In 1871, a more detail account of the practice of abortion was released by the Committee which noted that "[w]e had to deal with human life. In a matter of less importance we could entertain no compromise. An honest judge on the bench would call things by their proper names." See 22 Trans. of the Am. Med. Assn. 258 (1971).

In 1967, the AMA adopted the Committee on Human Reproduction's recommended policy of strict opposition to induced abortion except when there is "documented medical evidence" of a threat to the life or health of the mother, where the child may be born with incapacitating physical deformity or mental deficiency or where the pregnancy resulted from legally established statutory or forcible rape or incest [which] may constitute a threat to the mental or physical health of the patient. See Proceedings of the AMA House of Delegates 40-51 (June 1967). Even under those circumstances, no abortion could be obtained unless it were performed in an AMA accredited hospital and not until the medical judgment of the attending physician were confirmed in writing by two competent physicians after they have independently examined the patient (Id.).

57. The nature of the act of abortion is understood by the universal Church as *malum in se* and never morally permissible even under the most trying of circumstances: "no one can, in any circumstances, claim for himself [or herself]

the right to destroy directly an innocent human being" (John Paul II, *The Gospel of Life*, no. 53). Also, John Paul II teaches that "*the direct and voluntary killing of an innocent human being is always gravely immoral. . . .* The deliberate decision to deprive an innocent human being of his [or her] life is always morally evil and can never be licit either as an end in itself or as a means to a good end" (ibid., 57, emphasis original).

58. In the Catholic Church, cooperation in a direct abortion subjects the person to immediate excommunication from the Church which may be removed only after sacramental repentance in accord with special canonical procedures. See, *The Code of Canon Law* (1983), commissioned by the Canon Law Society of America, ed. James A. Coriden, Thomas J. Green, Donald E. Heinteschel (New York: Paulist Press, 1985), cann. 1398, 1323-24. The *Catechism of the Catholic Church*, no. 2272 provides in full:

> Formal cooperation in an abortion constitutes a grave offense. The Church attaches the canonical penalty of excommunication to this crime against human life. "A person who procures a completed abortion incurs excommunication *latae sententiae*,"(can. 1398) "by the very commission of the offense,"(can.1314) and [hence] subject to the conditions provided by Canon Law (cann.1323-1324). The Church does not thereby intend to restrict the scope of mercy. Rather, she makes clear the gravity of the crime, the irreparable harm done to the innocent who is put to death, as well as to the parents and the whole of society.

Pope John Paul II reiterates this teaching but clarifies that excommunication requires knowledge of the penalty: "The excommunication affects all those who commit this crime with knowledge of the penalty attached, and thus includes those accomplices without whose help the crime would not have been committed" (*Gospel of Life*, no. 62). Also, the Pope reiterates the proscription against formal cooperation with abortion: "from the moral standpoint, it is never licit to cooperate formally in evil. Such cooperation occurs when an action, either by its very nature or by the form it takes in a concrete situation, can be defined as a direct participation in an act against innocent human life or a sharing in the immoral intention of the person committing it" (*The Gospel of Life*, no. 74).

59. 410 U.S. 113, 153 (1973).

60. 410 U.S. at 159.

61. 410 U.S. at 159. Justice Blackmun noted but rejected the argument of Texas "that, apart form the Fourteenth Amendment, life begins at conception and is present throughout the pregnancy, and that, therefore, the State has a compelling interest in protecting that life from and after conception" (Id.).

62. In order to avoid the risk of killing an innocent human being, the Court could have resolved its doubt in favor of the humanity of the fetus by recognizing that moral or philosophical certainty in this matter was not necessary for rational legislation or for a sound judicial review of the issue. The unborn *could still be regarded* as fully human in order to avoid the risk of killing an innocent human being.

63. See Laurence H. Tribe, *American Constitutional Law* (2nd ed.) 1341-1342 (Mineola NY: The Foundation Press, 1988).

64. 410 U.S. at 163.

65. 410 U.S. at 165.

66. 410 U.S. 179 (1973)

67. 410 U.S. at 192.

68. In connection with these two opinions, John T. Noonan Jr., now a senior judge of the Ninth Circuit Court of Appeals, concluded the following.

1. Until a human being is "viable" or "capable of meaningful life," a state has no "compelling interest" which justifies it in restricting in any way in favor of the fetus a woman's fundamental personal liberty of abortion. For six months, or "usually" for seven months the fetus is denied the protection of law by virtue of either the Ninth Amendment or the Fourteenth Amendment.

2. After viability has been reached, the human being is not a person 'in the whole sense,' so that even after viability he or she is not protected by the Fourteenth Amendment's guarantee that life shall not be taken without due process of law.

3. A state may nonetheless not protect a viable human being by preventing an abortion undertaken to preserve the health of the mother. Therefore a fetus of seven, eight, or nine months is subordinated by the Constitution to the demand for abortion predicated on health.

4. What the health of a mother requires in any particular case is a medical judgment to be "exercised in the light of all factors—physical, emotional, psychological, familial, and the woman's age—relevant to the well-being of the patient."

John T. Noonan, Jr., "Raw Judicial Power," *National Review* (March, 1973): 259-64.

69. See *Roe* v. *Wade*, 410 U.S. 113, 221 (1973)(White, J., dissenting). See also, Noonan, "Raw Judicial Power."

70. See, National Conference of Catholic Bishops (NCCB), "Statement of the Committee for Pro-Life Affairs" (January 24, 1973), reprinted in NCCB, *Documentation on The Right to Life and Abortion*, vol. I (Washington, D.C.: United States Catholic Conference, 1974), hereinafter *Documents*, 59-60.

71. NCCB, *Documents*, 59.

72. NCCB, *Documents*, 59.

73. Although *Roe* v. *Wade* and *Doe* v. *Bolton* precipitated a constitutional crisis, the NCCB had issued several previous statements denouncing the efforts of those who would liberalize abortion. In its 1968 Pastoral Letter entitled *Humanae Vitae*, for example, the Bishops argued that

[r]everence for life demands freedom from direct interruption of life once it is conceived. Conception initiates a process whose purpose is the realization of human personality. A human person, nothing more and nothing less, is always at issue once conception has taken place. We expressly repudiate any contradictory suggestion as contrary to Judaeo-Christian traditions inspired by love for life, and Anglo-Saxon traditions protective of life and the person (NCCB, *Documents*, 69).

See also NCCB, "Statement on Abortion" (April 17, 1969), "Statement on Abortion" (April 22, 1970) and the "Declaration on Abortion" (November 18, 1970) in NCCB, *Documents*, 61-67.

74. It is important to note not only the unanimity among Catholic Bishops in this matter but also that the Catholic Church was the only religious community immediately to recognize the depth of the problem.

75. For subsequent statements of the Bishops on extending the constitutional right to life to the unborn, see NCCB, "Pastoral plan for Pro-Life Activities: A Reaffirmation," *Origins* 15:24 (November 28, 1985): 401, and NCCB, "Resolution on Abortion," *Origins* 19:24 (November 16, 1989): 395-96.

76. NCCB, *Documents*, 13 (emphasis added).

77. NCCB, *Documents*, 14.

78. See, "A New Ethic for Medicine and Society," *California Medicine* (September, 1970): 67-68. In that official journal of the California Medical Association, from which the Bishops quoted in their written testimony, an editorial admitted the existence of the concerted effort among at least some medical professionals and certain ethicists to depose the traditional western ethic that "has always placed great emphasis on the intrinsic worth and equal value of every human life regardless of its stage or condition" (NCCB, *Documents*, 13, quoting the editorial).

79. This deliberate effort to distort the public mind was quite clearly admitted in a September 1970 editorial of *California Medicine*. There the following strategy was acknowledged:

The process of eroding the old ethic and substituting the new has already begun. It may be seen most clearly in changing attitudes toward abortion....Since the old ethic has not been fully displaced *it has been necessary to separate the idea of abortion from the idea of killing*, which continues to be socially abhorrent. *The result has been a curious avoidance of the scientific fact, which everyone really knows, that human life begins at conception and is continuous whether intra- or extra-uterine until death* (*California Medicine*, 67-68, quoting the editorial, emphasis added).

The intellectual bias in *Roe* against the weight of the scientific, moral and legal evidence in favor of the humanity and personhood of fetal life is surely not unlike what the California Medicine editorial described as: "The very considerable semantic gymnastics which are required to rationalize abortions as anything but taking a human life would be ludicrous if they were not often put forth under socially impeccable auspices" (Id., 68, quoting the editorial). Unfortunately, the "socially impeccable auspices" here was the Supreme Court of the United States.

80. NCCB, *Documents*, 15.

81. In demanding social justice for the unborn, the Bishops relied upon the following argument of the Founders:

We hold these truths to be self evident, that all men are created equal, that they are endowed by their Creator with certain unalienable rights, that among these are life, liberty and the pursuit of happiness. That to secure these rights, Governments are instituted among men, deriving their just powers from the consent of the governed. That whenever any Form of Government becomes destructive of these ends, it is the right of the people to alter or to abolish it, and to institute new government, laying its foundation on such principles and organizing its powers in such form, as to them shall seem most likely to effect their safety and happiness (NCCB, *Documents*, 17, quoting the Declaration of Independence).

82. "Everyone has the right to life, liberty and security of person" (NCCB, *Documents*, 17, quoting the United Nations Declaration on Human Rights).

83. Drawing upon the social teaching of Pope John XXIII found in his encyclical *Pacem in Terris* the Bishops asserted that:

Any human society, if it is to be well-ordered and productive, must lay down as a foundation this principle, namely, that every human being is a person, that is, his nature is endowed with intelligence and free will.

By virtue of this, he has rights and duties of his own, flowing directly and simultaneously from his very nature. These rights are therefore universal, inviolable and inalienable. [no.9]

[Among these]....[e]very man has the right to life, to bodily integrity, and to the means which are necessary and suitable for the proper development of life. [no.11]. NCCB, *Documents*, 17-18.

84. NCCB, *Documents*, 19. The Bishops were prescient regarding schizophrenia in the law of abortion. In all states today, a woman may kill her fetus throughout the entire term of pregnancy. But in many states today, if a pregnant woman is attacked by a criminal assailant, and if that attack results in the death of the fetus, the defendant may be charged with the homicide of the fetus, even if the woman survives the attack (see *infra* notes 117-20, and accompanying text). To admit the personhood of the fetus in one context and not in the other creates a noteworthy contradiction in public law. See Clarke D. Forsythe, "Homicide of the Unborn Child: The Born Alive Rule and Other Legal Anachronisms," 21 *Valparaiso University Law Review* 563-629 (1987) (presenting a critical analysis of the misuse of the common law defense to homicide known as the born alive rule; demonstrating that the use of this archaic rule of evidence is obsolete in the face of modern science; and offering a model penal statute creating a variety of offenses against the unborn child).

85. NCCB, *Documents*, 21.

86. NCCB, *Documents*, 21. The right of privacy had been raised to the status of a fundamental constitutional right in *Griszwold* v. *Connecticut*, 381 US 479 (1965). There the Court recognized a privacy right which inhered in the penumbras or emanations of several aspects of the Bill of Rights. The Court held that this new right of privacy placed substantive restriction upon the power of government to regulate the contraceptive practices of a married couple and accordingly struck down Connecticut's criminal prohibition on the use of contraceptives. In *Roe* the Court ambiguously declared:

[t]his right of privacy, whether it be founded in the 14th Amendment's concept of personal liberty [as] we feel it is, or, as the District Court determined, in the [Ninth Amendment], is broad enough to encompass a woman's decision whether or not to terminate her pregnancy.

Roe, 410 US at 153.

87. NCCB, *Documents*, 21.

88. NCCB, *Documents*, 22 (citing *Roe* v. *Wade*).

89. See e.g., John Hart Ely, "The Wages of Crying Wolf: A Comment on Roe v. Wade," 82 *Yale Law Journal* 920 (1973).

90. See e.g., *Sierra Club* v. *Morton*, 405 U.S. 727, 741-43 (1972) (Douglas, J., dissenting)(arguing for the personhood of trees to establish standing in federal court). See also, Stone, "Should Trees have Standing? Toward Legal Rights for Natural Objects," 45 *S. Cal.L.Rev.* 450 (1972).

Problems with the privacy rationale and with the viability criterion were also demonstrated. For example, although the Court claimed the woman's right of privacy was fundamental and broad enough to encompass the right of abortion, this right cannot be exercised without consultation with a physician. To give such power to physicians was anomalous especially given the breadth of the privacy claim. After objecting again to the radical scope of the decision which effectively created abortion, the Bishops found the Court's reliance upon "viability" to be an equivocation since the fetus remains viable within the womb absent some disease pathology or the deadly violence of abortion.

91. NCCB, *Documents*, 27.
92. NCCB, *Documents*, 29.
93. NCCB, *Documents*, 29.
94. NCCB, *Documents*, 30.
95. The full text of the paragraph concluding the Bishops' testimony is noteworthy.

However, we do not see a constitutional amendment as the final product of our commitment or of our legislative activity. It is instead the constitutional base on which to provide support and assistance to pregnant women and their unborn children. This would include nutritional, pre-natal, childbirth, and post-natal care for the mother, and also nutritional and pediatric care for the child through the first year of life. Counseling services, adoption facilities, and financial assistance are also part of the panoply of services, and we believe that all of these should be available *as a matter of right to all pregnant women and their children.* Within the Catholic community, we will continue to provide these services through our professional service agencies to the best of our ability to anyone in need (NCCB, *Documents*, 30, emphasis added).

96. NCCB, *Documents*, vol. II, 45-57.
97. NCCB, *Documents*, vol. II, 46.
98. The Bishops announced:

Thus this Pastoral Plan seeks to activate the pastoral resources of the Church in three major efforts: [1] an educational/public information effort to inform, clarify and deepen understanding of the basic issues; [2] a pastoral effort addressed to the specific needs of women with problems related to pregnancy and to those who have had or have taken part in an abortion; [3] a public policy effort directed toward the legislative, judicial and administrative areas so as to ensure effective legal protection for the right to life (NCCB, *Documents*, vol. II, 46).

99. NCCB, *Documents*, vol. II, 52.

100. NCCB, *Documents*, vol. II, 52. On March 26, 1976, the United States Catholic Conference offered similar testimony before the Subcommittee on Civil and Constitutional Rights of the House Committee on the Judiciary. See NCCB, *Documents*, vol. II, 1-36.

101. Ad Hoc Committee on Pro-Life Activities of the National Conference of Catholic Bishops, "Pastoral Guidelines for the Catholic Hospital and Catholic Health Care Personnel," NCCB, *Pastoral Letters of the United States Catholic Bishops*, vol. III (Washington, D.C.: 1983), 370-74.

102. See Leonard J. Weber, "Who Shall Live?" in James J. Walter and Thomas A. Shannon, eds. *Quality of Life: The New Medical Dilemma* (New York: Paulist, 1990), 111-18, at 111. John Paul II explains that "the sacredness of life gives rise to its *inviolability*" (*The Gospel of Life*, no. 40). The revised *Ethical and Religious Directives* explain that "the Church's commitment to human dignity inspires an abiding concenr for the sanctity of human life from its very beginning" (part four, introduction).

103. See S. L. Markson, "The Roots of Contemporary Anti-Abortion Activism," in P. Sachdev, ed., *Perspectives on Abortion* (Metuchen, NJ: Scarecrow Press, 1985), 33-43.

104. "Pastoral Plan for Pro-Life Activities" in NCCB, *Documents*, vol. II, 53. These activities are overseen by the Diocesan Pro-Life Director who is appointed by the local ordinary.

105. NCCB, *Documents*, vol. II, 53.

106. In 1981, passage of a Human Life Amendment failed by two votes in the Senate. Notwithstanding continued resistance to this effort, the NCCB remains committed to this constitutional remedy.

107. The Supreme Court upheld the constitutionality of the original Hyde Amendment in 1976. *Harris* v. *McRae*, 448 U.S. 297, 325 n. 27 (1980)(quoting Pub.L. 94-439, §209, 90 Stat. 1434(1976)). This language was modified in 1993 through an appropriations rider to include rape and incest. The Supreme Court also upheld the power of state governments to make "a value judgment favoring childbirth over abortion, and . . . implement that judgment by the allocation of public funds." *Maher* v. *Roe*, 432 U.S. 464, 474 (1977). See also *Poelker* v. *Doe*, 432 U.S. 519 (1977)(pre curiam)(sustaining the power of municipal hospitals to refuse to provide nontherapeutic abortions even where such refusal may create an insurmountable obstacle to the exercise of the right of abortion).

108. Stanley K. Henshaw and Jennifer Van Vort, eds., *Abortion Factbook* (New York: The Alan Guttmacher Institute, 1992), 128.

109. Only thirteen states "continue to fund all or most medically necessary abortions". See, Henshaw and Van Vort, *Abortion Factbook*, 127. "Thirty states

INTRODUCTION

and the District of Columbia have a "life-only" exception similar to the federal restrictions (Id.). See e.g., Mo. Rev. Stat. Ann. 188.21 (1986)(prohibiting public employees "[acting] within the scope of their employment to perform or assist an abortion, not necessary to save the life of the mother") and Mo. Rev. Stat. Ann. 188.215 (1986)(prohibiting the use of any public facility "for the purpose of performing or assisting an abortion not necessary to save the life of the mother." These provisions were upheld by the Court in *Webster* v. *Reproductive Health Services*, 109 S.Ct. 3040, 3053 (1989).

110. The Bishops argue, for example, that to claim the right to kill the preborn at will is itself a radical departure from the common law, the practice of the states, and sound moral judgment. But to claim further that it is a *private* right possessed solely by the pregnant woman in consultation with her physician is truly revolutionary in Western democratic thought. For the power to kill has always been held only by the state subject to self-defense exceptions. In addition, the NCCB asserted that the right of privacy justification for the right of abortion not only degrades the human life and dignity of the unborn but also effectively removes human sexuality and the act of childbearing from its proper social context. The right of privacy rationale also laid the foundation for the father of the unborn child to be stripped of his paternal rights, even within a valid marriage. To privatize such a fundamental dimension of the human community would seed alienation precisely because it denies human sociality.

111. In *Webster* v. *Reproductive Health Services*, 492 U.S. 490 (1989), a plurality of the Court (Justices Rehnquist, White and Kennedy) rejected the *Roe* trimester distinction and disclosed their view that the abortion right was a "liberty interest" under the Fourteenth Amendment. In her concurrence, Justice O'Connor indicated her willingness to evaluate abortion legislation under an "undue burden" test, which would fall between strict judicial review (required for fundamental rights as in *Roe*) and rational basis review held by the Rehnquist plurality. Justice Scalia indicated his desire to overrule *Roe* outright.

112. See *Planned Parenthood of Southeastern Pennsylvania* v. *Casey*, 112 S.Ct. 1291 (1992).

113. Eleven states currently require a 24 hour waiting period: Delaware, Idaho, Massachusetts, Michigan, Mississippi, Nebraska, North Dakota, Ohio, Pennsylvania, South Dakota and Utah. Three states require lesser periods: Kansas (8 hours); Kentucky (2 hours); and South Carolina (1 hour). Tennessee's two day reflection period, which excludes the day the information was given, is currently in litigation. See *Woman's Right-to-Know State Statutes*, (Chicago: Americans United For Life) (December 1994).

114. *Hodgson* v. *Minnesota*, 110 S.Ct. 2972, 2941,44 (opinion of Stevens, J.), 2969 (Kennedy, J., concurring in part and dissenting in part).

115. See *Planned Parenthood Association of Kansas City, Mo.* v. *Ashcroft*, 462 U.S. 476 (1983) (one-parent written consent with judicial bypass); *Hodgson* v.

41

Minnesota, 110 S.Ct. 2629 (1989) (two-parent notice with judicial bypass). See generally, State Parental-Involvement Statutes (Chicago: Americans United for Life) (September 1994).

116. See Woman's Right-to-Know State Statutes (Chicago: Americans United For Life) (December 1994)

117. Ariz.Rev.Stat. § 13-1103(A)(5) (West 1989 & 1993 Supp.) (manslaughter); Ill. Comp.Stat. Ann. ch. 720, §§ 5/9-1.2, 5/9-2.1,5/9-3.2 (1993)(murder, manslaughter); Ind.Code Ann. § 35-42-1-6 (Burns 1994) (feticide); La. Stat. Ann.§§4:2(7),14:32.5-14:32.8 (West1986&1994 Supp.)(murder, feticide); Minn. Stat.Ann. §§609.266, 609.2661-609.2665,609.268(1) (West 1987 & 1994 Supp.) (murder, manslaughter); Mo. Rev.Stat. §§1.205,565.024 (Vernon's 1994 Supp.) (involuntary manslaughter); N.D.Cent.Code §§12.1-17.1-01 to 12.1-17-04(1993 Supp.)(murder, manslaughter); S.D. Cod. Laws Ann. §22-17-6 (1988) (intentional killing of human fetus); Utah Code Ann.§ 76-5-201 *et seq.* (1990 & 1994 Supp.) (any form of homicide).

118. Cal. Pen. Code § 187(a)(1988)(murder)(post-embryonic stage, seven to eight weeks' gestation).

119. Fla.Stat.Ann. §782.09 (West 1992)(manslaughter); Off. Code.Geo.Ann. §16-5-80 (1991)(feticide); Mich.Comp.Laws Ann. §750.322 (West 1991) (manslaughter) (limited by judicial decision to viability, see *Larkin* v. *Callahan,* 389 Mich. 533, 208 N.W.2d (1973)); Miss. Code Ann.§ 97-3-37(1993) (manslaughter); Nev. Rev.Stat. §200.210 (1993) (manslaughter); Okla. Stat.Ann.tit.21, §713 (West1988)(manslaughter); Wash. Rev.Code Ann. § 9A.32.060(1)(b)(1986) (manslaughter); Wis. Rev.Stat. §940.04.(2)(a) (feticide).

120. Iowa CodeAnn. §707.7(West 1993)(feticide); *Commonwealth* v. *Cass,* 392 Mass. 799, 467 N.E.2d 1324 (1984)(vehicular homicide) (eight and one-half months pregnant); *Commonwealth* v. *Lawrence,* 404 Mass. 378, 536 N.E.2d 571 (1989) (involuntary manslaughter) (twenty-seven weeks pregnant); *State* v. *Horn,* 282 S.C. 444, 319 S.E.2d 703(1984) (homicide)(full term); Tenn. Code Ann.§39-13-214 (Michie 1991) (criminal homicide); R.I.Gen.Laws §11-23-5 (Michie 1981) (manslaughter).

121. See Helen Alvare, "Testimony Opposing Freedom of Choice Act," 21 *Origins* (April 2, 1992): 692-96.

122. The 103rd Congress did enact the Freedom of Access to Clinic Entrances Act which authorizes the criminal prosecution of abortion clinic protestors under certain circumstances. In addition, the Clinton Administration has clearly supported the use of federal anti-racketeering statutes to prosecute alleged criminal conspiracies among pro-life organizations like Operation Rescue.

123. See for example, David Shaw, "Abortion Bias Seeps into News," *Los Angeles Times* (Sunday, July 1, 1990), finding "that the press often favors abortion rights in its coverage even though journalists say they make every effort to be fair" (ibid.).

124. Regarding the physical and psychological consequences of abortion, see David C. Reardon, *Aborted Women: Silent No More* (Chicago: Loyola University Press, 1987). In light of the experience of women who have aborted, Reardon reports that "half of all aborted women express some immediate or long-term physical complication and almost all suffer from emotional or psychological setbacks" (Id., xi).

125. The phrase is borrowed from Ms. Helen Alvare, who serves as the Director of Planning and Information in the Secretariat for Pro-Life Activities in the United States Catholic Conference.

126. In its nationwide Abortion and Moral Beliefs Survey conducted by the Gallup Organization at the request of American United for Life, the pro-life legal and educational organization, the survey results showed that many Americans could not accurately describe the circumstances under which abortions are permitted under *Roe* v. *Wade*. For example, 42% of the people surveyed by Gallup thought the *Roe* decision made abortions legal only during the first three months of pregnancy. Of this group, 38% thought *Roe* made abortion legal during the first three month's of pregnancy "only when the mother's life or health" is in danger. See, Americans United For Life (AUL), News Release, February 28, 1991 (summarizing the Gallup polling data).

127. See Kenneth R. Craycraft, Jr., "Fact and Fiction: What Americans Really Think About Abortion," *Crisis Magazine* (May 1991): 21-23. Reporting and commenting on the results of the Americans United for Life/Gallup and the National Conference of Catholic Bishops/Wirthlin Group pools, Mr. Craycraft, a research associated at the American Enterprise Institute, noted that:

> [T]he Wirthlin Poll found that a startling 85 percent of Americans do not know that between 1 million and 2 million abortions are performed each year. Fifty-eight percent thought that fewer than 1 million abortions are performed yearly; 47 per cent guessed less than 500,000; and a full 31 per cent put the number at less than 100,000 (Id., 22).

This is in marked contrast to the conservative estimates of the Alan Guttmacher Institute and Planned Parenthood of America which "report the abortion rate at 4400 per day, or about 1.6 million per year" (Id.).

128. For example, of 1,590,750 abortions performed in 1988, 167,680 abortions were obtained after thirteenth week of pregnancy. Of that number 10,660 were procured after the twenty-first week. See, Henshaw and Van Vort, *Abortion Factbook*, 179. The 1988 data show the following breakdown of the number abortions during the pregnancy term with the weeks of gestation calculated after the onset of the last menstrual period: <9 weeks: 800,480; 9-10 weeks: 424,270; 11-12 weeks: 198,320; 13-15 weeks: 96,620; 16-20 weeks: 60,400; >21 weeks: 10,660 (Id.).

129. Pro-life programming, which until recently has been systematically blocked by FCC licensees and network executives, finally has been aired in the 1990s. A splendid example is the series of one-minute announcements produced by the deMoss Foundation which depict parental joy over the presence of children who were nearly aborted during pregnancy and the deep sorrow and irrevocable loss experienced by mothers who choose abortion rather than life for their child.

130. For a collection of data on the practice of abortion, on sociological research, and on opinion polls, on the teaching of religious denominations, see Maureen Muldoon, *The Abortion Debate in the United States and Canada: A Source Book* (New York: Garland, 1991).

131. AUL News Release, 2-3 (emphasis added).

132. AUL News Release, 4. Significantly, "[t]his view was shared by 96% of those who consistently disapprove of abortion, 82% of those who often disapprove ([i.e.] disapprove of abortion under most of the circumstances it is currently conducted), and even 47% of those who seldom disapprove of abortion" (Id.).

133. AUL News Release, 4 (emphasis added).

134. See The Gallup Organization, News Release, March 6 1992, detailing results of public opinion poll conducted for Life Magazine. In a 1992 Wirthlin poll, 83% of the public favors parental notification for minors under 18; 74% favor spousal notification; and 85% of Americans favor informed consent statutes. See, National Right to Life Committee, News Release, January 23 1992, 3 (reporting the results of a Wirthlin Group nationwide poll conducted from January 14, 1992 - January 16, 1992).

135. Gallup/AUL poll, 6. Only 30 % of men and 31% of women would oppose spousal notification (Id.).

136. See, "On File," 22 *Origins* (February 4, 1993): 574, no author.

137. In their respective testimony before the Senate Judiciary Committee, nominees Judge Ruth Bader Ginsberg and Judge Stephen G. Breyer both made clear their unambiguous support for a constitutional right of privacy and for the legitimacy of a right to abortion.

138. See NCCB's "Resolution on Health Care Reform" (Approved June 18, 1993) in 23: 7 *Origins* (July 1, 1993): 97, 99-101. There the Bishops outlined their policy priorities for health care reform and disclosed their opposition to the Clinton Administration's attempt to include abortion coverage in any national health care reform proposal (Id., 101).

139. See, "U.S. State Department: Timothy Wirth," 23:43 *Origins* (April 14, 1994): 758-60. (The Statement of Timothy Wirth was delivered on April 4, 1994 to the Preparatory Committee of the International Conference on Population and Development). In addition to making clear the United States' support for a liberal contraceptive policy including voluntary sterilizations, Secretary Wirth

stated that:

> Every effort should be made to prevent unwanted pregnancies, but in the interest of public health and *as a matter of principle* women should have access to safe abortion services and to humane services for complications due to unsafe abortions (Id., 759, emphasis added).

The tenor of this letter prompted separate written responses addressed to President Clinton by Pope John Paul II and by the U.S. Cardinalate, see "Letter to President Clinton," 23 *Origins* (April 14, 1994): 760. In his letter on their behalf, Cardinal Keeler expressed concern "with your administration's promotion of abortion, contraception, sterilization and the redefinition of the family." See, Cardinal William Keeler, "Concerns Expressed to Clinton on Cairo Conference," 24:4 *Origins* (June 9, 1994): 58. He also made clear their collective objections to the direction the conference seemed to be taking.

> The draft final document of the Cairo conference, with the support of the United States,...advocates [abortion and] the world-wide distribution of artificial contraceptives and the increased practice of sterilization which will have the effect of promoting a self-centered and casual view of human sexuality, an approach so destructive of family life and the moral fiber of society (Id., 59).

140. National Right to Life Committee, Inc., "The Clinton Administration's Promotion of Abortion as a Tool of Population Control in Less Developed Nations," June 1, 1994, p. 2 (reporting that in fiscal year 1993 the United States contributed $580 million to such programs).

141. See "Partial-Birth Abortion Ban Act of 1995," H.R. 1833, 104th Cong., 1st Sess. (1995). This bill was passed by the House of Representatives on November 1, 1995 and by the Senate on December 7, 1995. The House agreed to Senate Amendments on March 27, 1996. In his veto message, the President argued that "[b]y refusing to permit women, in reliance on their doctor's best medical judgment, to use this procedure when their lives are threatened *or* when their health is put into serious jeopardy, the Congress has fashioned a bill that is consistent neither with the Constitution nor with sound public policy." (Partial-Birth Abortion Ban Act—Veto Message of the President of the United States, H. Doc. No. 104-198, 104th Cong., 2nd Sess. 1 (1996) (emphasis original).

142. The proposed legislation punished "[a]ny physician who . . . knowingly performs a partial-birth abortion and thereby kills a human fetus" by fine and up to two years imprisonment (H.R. 1833, 104th Cong., 1st Sess. (1995), Sec. 1531 (a)). It also created a civil damages remedy in favor of the non-consenting father, and maternal grandparents of a minor, (Sec. 1531(c)(1)-(2)) but exempted from prosecution or civil liability the woman upon whom the procedure was

performed. (Sec. 1531(d)).

143. Letter to President Willliam Clinton from the Most Rev. Anthony M. Pilla and Cardinals Bernardin, Bevilacqua, Hickey, Keller, Law, Maida, Mahony, and O'Connor, April 16, 1996, p.1.

144. Id. At 2.

145. See The Personal Responsibility Act, H.R. 4, 104th. Cong., 1st. Sess. (1995). The House version of H.R. 4 prohibited cash aid for unmarried minor mothers and their children and for new babies in families already on Temporary Assistance for Needy Families. The Senate version, styled the Work Opportunity Act, rejected those provisions. The conference bill, renamed the Personal Responsibility and Work Opportunity Act, does not exclude any category of children but does prohibit States from aiding children of unmarried minors unless the mothers live with an adult.

146. By a vote of 87 to 12, the U.S. Senate passed a revised version of the House bill which did not include a provision rendering pregnant minors ineligible for federal block grant monies.

147. See, CDF, *Declaration on Abortion*, no. 26.

148. NCCB, "Putting Children and Families First: A Challenge for Our Church, Nation and World," *Origins* 21:25 (November 28, 1991): 400. NCCB Ad Hoc Committee for a Pastoral Response to Women's Concerns, "One in Christ Jesus: Toward a Pastoral Response to the Concerns of Women for Church and Society," *Origins* 22:9 (December 31, 1992): 489. The American Bishops emphasize that only by relating dignity, solidarity, and justice can we hope to build a healthy community, see NCCB, *Economic Justice*, no. 13.

Keynote Address[1]

Governor Robert P. Casey

I

All of us are joined in our conviction that abortion is a bad thing. And although many of us are Catholics, we are also joined in the conviction that abortion is not simply a Catholic concern. It's a catholic concern with a small "c"—the concern of anyone who rejects the idea of human life as a disposable commodity. The concern of anyone with eyes to see, a mind to reason, and a heart to feel.

It is not an arrogant boast, but a demographic fact, that most Americans share this conviction.[2] Anytime the question is put squarely to them, "Do you oppose abortion on demand?" more than two out of three Americans answer yes.[3] Asked if they favor restrictions on abortion such as we have enacted in Pennsylvania, again a majority of seventy to eighty percent say yes.[4] Perhaps the most telling survey of all found that seventy-eight percent of the people would outlaw ninety three percent of all abortions—all but the familiar hard cases. Even in the 1992 election cycle, in which all sides sought to shelve the issue of abortion, exit polls revealed its central importance in the minds of most voters.[5]

To those who favor liberal abortion policies, this persistent opposition is a mystery, a disturbing sign of something backward and intolerant in our society. Sometimes the abortion lobby pretty much concedes that Americans by and large favor restrictions on abortion—as when Pennsylvania's abortion laws were upheld by the Supreme Court.[6] Such setbacks to their cause leave abortion advocates bewildered and alarmed, convinced that Americans still need to be "educated on the issue."[7]

Other times—like right now—their tactic is to obscure public opinion by marginalizing the pro-life side, dismissing critics of their cause as a handful of fanatics resisting the tide of opinion.[8] A quarter of a million people may gather to protest abortion on the Washington Mall, and if the

47

media notice them at all, they're treated almost in a tone of pity, like some narrow fringe estranged from modern realities.[9] As I discovered, even the governor of a major state, who holds pro-life views, can be denied a hearing at his party's convention without the national media protesting it.[10] The success of this tactic is truly a public relations triumph, only possible in an environment which constantly marginalizes and suppresses the pro-life message. And despite twenty years of brainwashing, the American people have not been fooled. If the majority of Americans support abortion, why have three of the last four presidential elections been won resoundingly by pro-life candidates?[11] If my position is irrelevant, then so, I'm afraid, are the views of some eighty to eight-five percent of the people of Pennsylvania and the United States.[12]

As I read the polls showing our continuing unease with abortion, nothing makes me more proud to call myself an American. Among the "herd of independent minds" who make up our opinion leaders, abortion may be taken as a mark of progress. But most Americans have not followed. In the abortion lobby's strange sense of the word, America has never been a "progressive" nation. For we know—and this used to be the credo of my party—that progress can never come by exploiting or sacrificing any one class of people. Progress is a hollow word unless everyone is counted in and no one written off, especially the most weak and vulnerable among us.

You cannot stifle this debate with a piece of paper. No edict, no federal mandate can put to rest the grave doubts of the American people. Legal abortion will never rest easy on this nation's conscience. It will continue to haunt the consciences of men and women everywhere. The plain facts of biology, the profound appeals of the heart, are far too unsettling to ever fade away.

II

The abortion issue has intersected with my public life from the very beginning. It started in 1966, seven years before *Roe* v. *Wade*.[13]

The occasion was the Pennsylvania Democratic gubernatorial primary. New York had just passed a very liberal abortion law,[14] and the question was: Would I sign such a law in Pennsylvania if it were to pass? My opponent's answer was that this was an issue only women fully understood; that he would appoint a women's commission to study the issue, if elected; and that he would sign such a law, if enacted, in Pennsylvania. My response was simple and unequivocal: If the law were to pass, I would veto it.

I lost that primary by a narrow margin. I am fairly certain that my abortion position hurt me, because in a Democratic primary, where turnout is relatively low, liberal voters turn out in disproportionately large numbers and thus exercise a disproportionate influence on the outcome.[15]

The point I want to make about my decisional process in 1966 is this: I took the position against a liberal abortion law instinctively. I did not consider it to be a position dictated by my Catholic faith. As a matter of fact, the Catholic Church made it clear that it took no position in the primary. And many Catholics worked openly and actively for my opponent.

For me, the imperative of protecting unborn human life has always been a self-evident proposition. I cannot recall the subject of abortion ever being mentioned, much less discussed in depth, in school or at home. My position was simply a part of me from the very beginning.

When I was elected Governor in 1986, both my Democratic primary opponent and general election Republican opponent were pro-choice.[16] The general election was a photo finish.[17] When my opponent and I debated on statewide television shortly before the election, the inevitable question was asked: "If the Supreme Court overruled *Roe* v. *Wade*, and the Pennsylvania Legislature passed a law banning all abortion except to save the life of the mother, would you sign it?" My opponent said that, while there were "too many" abortions in our country, and we should work to reduce that number, he would veto the law banning abortion. My answer was, "Yes, I would sign such a law."

My campaign people thought that my answer, with no qualifiers—no ifs, no ands, and no buts—had lost the election. I won by about 75,000 votes.[18]

When I ran for re-election in 1990, my Republican opponent was stridently pro-choice.[19] The abortion issue was the motivating factor behind her candidacy.[20] She was banking on the conventional wisdom of that period—the post-*Webster* period—when the pro-choice groups tried to convince the country that women, shocked by the *Webster* decision, would rise up and drive all pro-life candidates from public life.[21] And their message was as cruel as it was direct. The leader of the National Organization for Women in Pittsburgh said that I was sick and would probably be dead before the election. (I had open-heart surgery in 1987.) My opponent called me "a rednecked Irishman."[22] The National Abortion Rights Action League released a poll purporting to show the election a dead heat when people were informed of my position on abortion. Pro-choice groups sent several dozen of their supporters to the Governor's residence where they chanted, "Get your rosaries off my ovaries," as the television cameras whirred. And my opponent, who spent two million dollars, ran a television commercial purporting to depict a rape—to dramatize my position of refusing to recognize an exception for rape—in which it was difficult to distinguish me from the rapist.[23]

I won by over one million votes, the largest winning margin in Pennsylvania gubernatorial political history.[24] I am convinced the abortion issue was a key factor in that victory.

But, in between the 1986 and 1990 campaigns, I came face to face for the first time with a conflict between my personal and public position on abortion, and what I regarded as the duty imposed by my oath of office to "support, obey, and defend" the Constitution of the United States. As a lawyer, I was trained to believe that the Constitution means what the United States Supreme Court says it means.[25] The consequence of that line of reasoning was that I could not sign a law which was, on its face, in direct conflict with what the Supreme Court had decided, even when I personally did not agree with the Court's ruling.

That issue was squarely presented when our legislature, in December 1987, and before the *Webster* ruling, passed an abortion control law which required a woman seeking an abortion to notify the father of the child. This meant the biological father, whether or not he was the spouse of the woman. The Supreme Court had already struck down as unconstitutional a spousal notification requirement, where the biological father was the woman's husband and the two were living together in a normal domestic relationship.[26]

I vetoed the law, pointing to my constitutional duty, under my oath, and the futility—from the standpoint of protecting unborn human life—of passing laws which had no chance of ever taking effect to help the unborn.[27]

This is what I said in my veto message:

Let me restate in summary the distinction between personal belief and constitutional duty as it applies to this legislation. I believe abortion to be the ultimate violence. I believe strongly that *Roe* v. *Wade* was incorrectly decided as a matter of law and represents a national public policy both divisive and destructive. It has unleashed a tidal wave that has swept away the lives of millions of defenseless, innocent unborn children. In according the woman's right of privacy in the abortion decision both exclusivity and finality, the Supreme Court has not only disregarded the right of the unborn child to life itself, but has deprived parents, spouses, and the state of the right to participate in a decision in which they all have a vital interest. This interest ought to be protected, rather than denied, by the law. This policy has had, and will continue to have, a profoundly destructive effect upon the fabric of American life. But these personal beliefs must yield to the duty, imposed by my oath of office, to follow the Constitution as interpreted by the Supreme Court of the United States . . . .

Most importantly, I emphasize again that we must—and we will—enact a strong and sustainable Abortion Control Act that forms a humane and constitutional foundation for our efforts to ensure that no child is denied his or her chance to walk in the sun and make the most out of life. I will sign this bill when it reaches the end of the legislative process and attains those standards.

Following the veto, my staff and I worked closely with pro-life groups and legislative leaders to draft the Abortion Control Act of 1989 within the framework of the Supreme Court cases, including the *Webster* decision.[28] The law requires parental consent for minors, informed consent, and a 24-hour waiting period.[29] These limitations were upheld in *Planned Parenthood of Southeastern Pennsylvania* v. *Casey*.[30] A spousal notification requirement in the law was struck down.[31]

Thus, while concluding that my oath of office precluded me from signing an unconstitutional law, I also recognized a right, if not a duty, to work to change the law within the democratic process. First, by enacting a law that was designed to limit and reduce abortions within the constitutional authority of the states. Second, to speak out in favor of the protection of human life so as to influence others, including federal and state policy makers, so that they too would adopt this view.

I have described how I understood my position in 1987. But now, six years later, I feel compelled to inquire further: What exactly *is* the relationship between the rulings of the United States Supreme Court and the Constitution I am bound to uphold?

As everyone knows, the Court can be—and has been—seriously wrong. The Court erred in the case of *Dred Scott*.[32] And I believe that the Court erred in the case of *Roe* v. *Wade*.[33]

In this context, in this place, one cannot help but recall Abraham Lincoln's attitude toward the Supreme Court's *Dred Scott* decision, which he and so many others believed to be disastrously wrong.

Lincoln viewed the *Dred Scott* decision as "not having yet quite established a settled doctrine for the country."[34] A year after the decision, he said, "If I were in Congress, and a vote should come up on a question whether slavery should be prohibited in a new territory, in spite of the *Dred Scott* decision, I would vote that it should."[35] Several years later, Congress did precisely that.[36] In open defiance of *Dred Scott*, Congress outlawed slavery in the territories.[37]

In his first inaugural address, Abraham Lincoln, in referring to the *Dred Scott* case, expressed the view that other officers of the government could not be obligated to accept any new laws created by the Court unless they, too, were persuaded by the force of the Court's reasoning.[38] Any other position would mean, in his view, that "the policies of the government upon vital questions, affecting the whole people, (could) be irrevocably fixed by decisions of the Supreme Court, the instant they are made, in ordinary litigation between parties, in personal actions."[39] If that were to occur, said Lincoln, "the people will have ceased to be their own rulers, having to that extent practically resigned the government into the hands of that eminent tribunal."[40]

After much thought and reflection since 1987, I must confess that I am more and more persuaded that Lincoln's view should be the standard for pro-life elected officials in 1993 and beyond.

III

The question I want to address tonight, then, is this: What are the responsibilities of a pro-life politician?

For no matter what the majority sentiments may be, the drift of law favors abortion.[41] Our courts, which do not operate on majority rule, say abortion is legal, an implied constitutional right to privacy found nowhere in the text of the Constitution.[42] For a politician like myself, opposition to abortion may thus become opposition to the existing laws one is sworn to uphold.

What then do conscience and duty require?

I believe the first step is to understand that such dilemmas are not new to our day. Any citizen who has ever tried to use political power for the common good has felt an awful sense of powerlessness. There are always limits on what we can do, always obstacles, always frustrations and bitter disappointments. This was the drama a future president once studied in *Profiles in Courage*,[43] a book that now seems quaint in its simple moral idealism. The founders of our country understood the limits of political power when they swore allegiance to something higher, their "sacred honor."[44] Lincoln felt this tension when he sought to uphold the equality of men.[45] His real greatness was in seeing that political reform alone wasn't enough; not only the slave had to be freed, but the slave owner from the bonds of his own moral blindness.[46] Likewise, Thomas More expressed the dilemma when, faced with the raw power of the state, he declared, "I die the king's good servant but God's first."[47] Far from being a new problem, this tension goes all the way back to the Pharisees and their challenge to declare for or against Caesar.[48]

Just as the problem is an old one, so are the alternatives. One of these alternatives is accommodation with power, a pragmatic acceptance of "the facts." In the abortion question, this position is summed up in familiar disavowal, "I'm personally opposed, but . . . ."

The hard facts—so runs this view—are against us. However we might oppose it, abortion is a sad feature of modern life. Tolerance is the price we pay for living in a free, pluralistic society. For any Catholic politician to "impose" an exclusively sectarian moral viewpoint would be an act of theocratic arrogance, violating our democratic trust. The proper and prudent course is therefore to bring change by "persuasion, not coercion." Absent a "consensus," it is not the place of any politician to change our laws permitting abortion.

I want to be careful here not to misrepresent this position. Some very honorable people hold it, and it is not my purpose to challenge their motives. Yet, as some politicians advance this view it does seem an evasion, a finesse rather than an honest argument. But that, so far as I am concerned, is the secret of their own individual hearts. Here I mean only to challenge the argument on its own intellectual grounds, with the presumption of good faith extended all around.

We can dispense easily with the charge of theocratic arrogance. That would certainly apply if we were trying to impose some uniquely Catholic stricture like church attendance or fast days on the general population. But the stricture to refrain from killing is not uniquely Catholic.[49] And that, as a purely empirical assertion, is how nearly all people of all faiths at all times have regarded abortion—as killing.[50] For example, Frank Sussman, the lawyer who represented Missouri abortion clinics in *Webster*, claimed that "Neither side in this debate would ever disagree on the physiological facts. Both sides would agree as to when a heartbeat can first be detected. Both sides would agree as to when brain waves can first be detected. But when you try to place the emotional labels on what you call that collection of physiological facts, that is where people part company."

Or New York Mayor Ed Koch, a fellow Democrat, wrote in a column that "I support *Roe* v. *Wade* wholeheartedly. And I do it even while acknowledging to myself that at some point, perhaps even after the first trimester, abortion becomes infanticide."

Or President Clinton explained when speaking in Chillicothe, Ohio: "Very few Americans believe that all abortions all the time are all right. Almost all Americans believe that abortions should be illegal when the children can live without the mother's assistance, when the children can live outside the mother's womb."[51]

By referring to the unborn as "children," the President was not making a theological claim; he was just putting all the physiological facts together. The same is true when we say abortion "kills." We don't say it in meanness. It's a unique kind of killing, for the motive may not be homicidal; it may be done in ignorance of what actually is occurring. We reserve a special compassion for women who find themselves contemplating abortion. But as an objective fact, that is what abortion is, and so humanity has always regarded it. Science, history, philosophy, religion, and common intuition all speak with one voice in asserting the humanity of the unborn. Only our current laws say otherwise.[52]

So much for theocratic arrogance. But I believe the more important fallacy underlying the "personally opposed, but . . . " line of reasoning arises from a deeper intellectual confusion. It confuses prudence with pragmatism and mistakes power for authority.

Prudence we all know to be a virtue. Classical thinkers rated it the supreme political virtue. Roughly defined, it's the ability to distinguish the desirable from the possible.[53] It's a sense of the good, joined with a practical knowledge of the means by which to accomplish the good. A world in which every unborn child survives to take his first breath is desirable. But we know that such a world has never been. And prudence cautions us never to expect such a world. Abortion is but one of many evils that, to one extent or another, is to be found at all times and places.[54] While we may make good laws, those laws cannot make us good.

But the point is that after facing up to such facts, the basic facts of our human condition, prudence does not fall silent. It is not an attitude of noble resignation; it is an active virtue. The voice that says, "Ah, well, there is no consensus. We must take the world as it is. There is nothing further to be done"—that is not the voice of prudence. It is the voice of expediency.

Prudence compromises—it doesn't capitulate. It's tolerant, but not timid.

Prudence asks: "If there is no consensus, how do we form one? What means of reform are available to us? How, lawfully, can we change the law?"

And here is where the difference between power and authority comes in. In the best of worlds, the law commands both. The law confers power on rightful authority, and invests authority with power. The integrity of our laws rests on a continuity, a *corpus juris* reflecting the accumulated experience of our civilization. Laws are the conventional application of permanent principles. And if democratic government depends on any one central idea, it's that raw power alone, laws that flout those permanent principles, cannot command our respect. Our obedience, yes. Our allegiance, no.

Alexander Hamilton put it this way: "The sacred rights of mankind are not to be rummaged for among old parchments or musty records.

They are written, as with a sunbeam, in the whole volume of human nature, by the hand of Divinity itself; and can never be erased or obscured by mortal power."[55] Even the more secular minded Thomas Jefferson agreed: The "only firm basis" of freedom, he wrote, is "a conviction in the minds of people that their liberties are the gift of God."[56]

American history has had its dark moments, but only twice has this principle been radically betrayed. Only twice has mortal power, using the instrument of the law itself, sought to exclude an entire class of people from their most sacred human rights.

This place in which we meet today marks the first time.

One hundred and thirty six years ago, a human being was declared a piece of property, literally led off in chains as people of good conscience sat paralyzed by a ruling of the court.[57]

The other time was January 22, 1973.[58] An entire class of human beings was excluded from the protection of the state, their fate declared a "private" matter.[59] That "sunbeam" Hamilton envisioned, the Creator's signature on each new life, was deflected by human hands. No one has ever described what happened more concisely than Justice Byron R. White in his dissent.[60] It was an act of "raw judicial power"—power stripped of all moral and constitutional authority.[61]

Roe v. Wade was not, then, one more natural adaptation in our constitutional evolution. It was not like Brown v. Board of Education,[62] a refinement extending law and liberty to an excluded class. Just the opposite: It was an abrupt mutation, a defiance of all precedent, a disjuncture of law and authority. Where we used to think of law as above politics, in Roe law and politics became indistinguishable. How strange it is to hear abortion now defended in the name of "consensus." Roe itself, the product of a contrived and fraudulent test case, was a judicial decree overruling a consensus expressed in the laws of most states.[63] It arose not from the wisdom of the ages or from the voice of the people, but from the ideology of the day and the will of a determined minority. It compels us to ignore the consensus about the treatment of the unborn. It commands us to disregard the clearest of Commandments.[64] After twenty long years, the people of the United States have refused to heed that command.[65]

Roe v. Wade is a law we must observe but never honor. In Hamilton's phrase, it's a piece of "parchment,"[66] a musty record bearing raw coercive power and devoid of moral authority. It has done its harm and will do much more. But those who say we must learn to live with it still don't get it. Ultimately, *Roe* cannot survive alongside our enduring, unshakable sense of justice. It is no more permanent than any other act of human arrogance. It is no more unchangeable than the laws which sent Dred Scott back to his master.

This has been the generation of what Malcolm Muggeridge called "the humane holocaust."[67] The loss can never be recovered. Indeed, it can't even be calculated. Not even the familiar statistic—1.6 million a year[68]—begins to express the enormity of it. One person's life touches so many others. How can you measure the void left when so many people aren't even permitted to live among us?

The best we can do is change what can be changed, and, most importantly, stay the course.

And there is no need to wait for some political consensus to form. That consensus is here, and it grows every time someone looks for the first time at a sonogram. It needs only leaders—prudent, patient leaders. It doesn't need apologists to soothe us into inaction. It needs statesmen who will work for change—change here and now.

So, we must ask ourselves, what must the role of the pro-life public official be in 1993 in the face of the catastrophic human carnage of abortion?

Let me be specific.

First, relentless, outspoken opposition to passage of the so-called Freedom of Choice Act.[69]

Second, continuous effort to expand and enlarge the protection of human life in state and national laws and policies.

Third, a continuous drumbeat of public expression which makes the American people confront the facts about abortion in all of its evil.

Fourth, advocacy of a New American Compact in this country which seeks to involve all public and private institutions in a fight for policies and programs to offer women meaningful alternatives to abortion and to offer children and families the help they need to live decent, healthy, and happy lives.

Fifth, political action which challenges both major parties and their candidates to protect human life and works for change in national elections.

The need for constancy, activism and relentless effort cannot be overstated. In light of recent events, there is no doubt that this country faces a crisis of awesome dimensions.

National commentators want to treat this issue as settled.[70] We can never let them get away with that. This issue will never die. It will never be "over."

We live in a time when many of those who claim *the right to choose* deny pro-life advocates *the right to speak*. Our voices must be even more determined in response to every such effort to silence us.

In summary, the role of the public official must be to lead—to stand up and say to the people of this country who believe in protecting human life: Press On!

Let this, then, be our clarion call, our call to arms, the keynote of this gathering: Press On!

NOTES

1. This address originally was written for and presented at the conference on abortion at Saint Louis University. Permission was granted by the Conference Committee to publish it in the *Saint Louis University Public Law Review* XIII (1993).

2. George Gallup, Jr., *The Gallup Poll: Public Opinion* (Wilmington, DE: Scholarly Resources, Inc., 1993).

3. George Gallup, Jr., *The Gallup Poll*, 7.

4. George Gallup, Jr., *The Gallup Poll*, 8. The Pennsylvania statute has such restrictions as requiring informed consent of the patient, a 24-hour waiting period so the woman can be provided with information, and parental consent for minors. Abortion Control Act, 18 Pa. C.S. §§ 3201-3220 (1982).

5. Karlyn H. Keene et al., "The Pro-Choice Label," *Public Perspective* (Sept./Oct. 1992): 98.

6. *Planned Parenthood of Southeastern Pennsylvania* v. *Casey*, 112 S. Ct. 2791 (1992).

7. Robin Toner, "Political Memo: Success Spoils Unity of Abortion Rights Groups," *New York Times* (Apr. 20, 1993): A18.

8. Anthony Lewis, "Abroad at Home; Right to Life," *New York Times* (March 12, 1993): A29.

9. See Paul Richter, "Anti-Abortion Activists Mark Roe vs. Wade," *Los Angeles Times* (Jan. 23, 1991): A4.

10. John Leo, "Here Come the World Creatures," *U.S. News & World Report* (Oct. 19, 1992): 27; and Mary McGrory, "Looking Over Their Shoulders," *Washington Post* (Aug. 20, 1992): A2.

11. Ralph Hallow, "GOP Set to Make Crime Its Issue," *Washington Times* (Jan. 31, 1993): A1.

12. See George Gallup, Jr., *The Gallup Poll*, 8.

13. 93 S. Ct. 705 (1973).

14. Vivienne Walt, "New York Groups Gearing Up for Battle," *Newsday* (July 6, 1989): 4.

15. Chris Black, "Abortion Low-Profile. Issue in Mayor Race: The Race for City Hall," *Boston Globe* (Aug. 17, 1993): 12.

16. Paul Taylor, "Scranton Drops Ads and His Mitts," *Washington Post* (Oct. 24, 1986): A3.

17. *U.S. Governors, Chicago Tribune* (Nov. 6, 1986): 5.

18. *U.S. Governors, Chicago Tribune* (Nov. 6, 1986): 5.

19. "State by State Reports of the Key Races and Issues," *Los Angeles Times* (Nov. 7, 1990): A20.

20. "Review: How Abortion Played Out Nationwide," *Abortion Rep.* (Nov. 9, 1990). ("Hafer tried to make her abortion rights support the whole issue.")

21. Brad Bumsted, "Casey for President in 1992?" *Gannett News Service* (Nov. 8, 1990). ("Casey's candidacy was hatched shortly after the *Webster* decision in July 1989. Pro-choice groups believed the decision would awaken a 'sleeping giant' for abortion rights.")

22. "1990 Elections: State by State; Northeast," *New York Times* (Nov. 8, 1990): B8.

23. "Pennsylvania: Hafer Running New TV Abortion Ad," *Abortion Rep.* (Oct. 25, 1990). ("On the small screen, a lone woman stands on a deserted street, a junk-yard dog barking in the background. Menacing music. A man lurches up behind the woman, grabs her, shoves her against a wall, and a shrill scream pierces the night. With an inset picture of Casey appearing, a 'bass voice' says, 'Many women in Pennsylvania are scared, and with good reason. Because Gov. Casey is committed to outlawing abortions—even for victims of rape and incest.'")

24. Brad Bumsted, "Casey Faces Tough Second Term," *Gannett News Service* (Nov. 7, 1990).

25. *Marbury* v. *Madison*, 5 U.S. 137 (1803); *McCullough* v. *Maryland*, 17 U.S. 316 (1819).

26. *Planned Parenthood of Central Missouri* v. *Danforth*, 96 S. Ct. 2831 (1972).

27. Lois Fecteau, "Casey Looks Back at First Year in Office," *United Press International* (Dec. 21, 1987).

28. 18 Pa. C.S.A. §§ 3205 and 3206 (1989).

29. 18 Pa. C.S.A. §§ 3205 and 3206 (1989).

30. 112 S. Ct. 2791, 2828-2832 (1992).

31. 112 S. Ct. 2791, 2831 (1992).

32. *Dred Scott* v. *Sandford*, 60 U.S. 393 (1856).

33. 93 S. Ct. 705 (1973).

34. *The Collected Works of Abraham Lincoln*, eds., Roy P. Basler et al. (New Brunswick, NJ: Rutgers University Press, 1953), 401.

35. *The Collected Works of Abraham Lincoln*, 400-3.

36. Don Ferhenbacher, *The Dred Scott Case* (New York: Oxford University Press, 1978), 575.

37. Don Ferhenbacher, *The Dred Scott Case*, 575.

38. Andrew Delbanco, ed., *The Portable Abraham Lincoln* (New York: Viking Press, 1992), 201.

39. Andrew Delbanco, ed., *The Portable Abraham Lincoln*, 201.

40. Andrew Delbanco, ed., *The Portable Abraham Lincoln*, 201.

41. See Lynn D. Wardle, "'Time Enough': Webster v. Reproductive Health Services and the Prudent Pace of Justice," *Florida Law Review* 41 (1989): 881.

42. *Roe*, 93 S. Ct. at 726. ("The Constitution does not explicitly mention any right of privacy.")

43. John F. Kennedy, *Profiles in Courage* (New York: Harper & Row, 1964).

44. *The Declaration of Independence*, par. 32 (U.S. 1776), reprinted in *The Documentary History of the Ratification of the Constitution*, vol. 1, Merrill Jensen, ed., (Madison, WI: State Historical Society of Wisconsin, 1976), 75.

45. *The Collected Works of Abraham Lincoln*, 435-36.

46. *The Collected Works of Abraham Lincoln*, 435-36.

47. Richard Marius, *Thomas More: A Biography* (New York: Alfred A. Knopf, 1984), 514.

48. Matthew 22:21 ("Render therefore unto Caesar the things which are Caesar's; and unto God the things that are God's.")

49. Daughters of St. Paul, *Pro-Life Catechism* (Boston, MA: St. Paul Editions, 1984), 40.

50. Catherine and William Odell, *The First Human Right: A Pro-Life Primer* (Huntington, IN: Our Sunday Visitor Press, 1983), 56.

51. President Clinton, remarks during a "Chillicothe Economic Discussion with Bill Clinton," Feb. 19, 1993, transcript available in *The Reuter Transcript Report* (Feb. 19, 1993).

52. *Roe*, 93 S. Ct. at 729. (The Court states, "The word 'person,' as used in the Fourteenth Amendment, does not include the unborn.")

53. Anthony T. Kronman, "Alexander Bickel's Philosophy of Prudence," *Yale Law Journal* 94 (1985): 1567, 1568-70.

54. John T. Noonan, Jr., "An Almost Absolute Value in History," in John T. Noonan, Jr., ed., *The Morality of Abortion: Legal and Historical Perspectives*, (Cambridge, MA: Harvard University Press, 1970).

55. Benjamin F. Wright, *American Interpretations of Natural Law: A Study in the History of Political Thought* (New York: Russell & Russell, 1962) 90-91.

56. Thomas Jefferson, *Notes on the State of Virginia*, ed. William Peden (New York: Norton, 1982), 163.

57. *Dred Scott*, 60 U.S. at 393.

58. *Roe* v. *Wade*, 93 S. Ct. 705 (1973).

59. *Roe* v. *Wade*, at 728.

60. *Roe* v. *Wade*, at 762-63 (White, J., dissenting).

61. *Roe* v. *Wade*, at 762.

62. 347 U.S. 483 (1952).

63. *Roe* v. *Wade*, at 762 (White, J., dissenting).

64. Exodus 21:13, ("Thou shalt not Kill.")

65. See, *Planned Parenthood of Southeastern Pennsylvania* v. *Casey*, 112 S. Ct. 2791 (1992).

66. Benjamin F. Wright, *American Interpretations of Natural Law*, 90-91.

67. Malcolm Muggeridge, "The Humane Holocaust," Afterword in, Ronald Reagen, *Abortion and the Conscience of the Nation* (Nashville, TN: Thomas Nelson Publishers, 1984), 84, 87-89.

68. Gerald N. Rosenberg, *The Hollow Hope: Can Courts Bring About Social Change?* (Chicago, IL: University of Chicago Press, 1991), 178-79.

69. H.R. 25, 102d Cong., 1st Sess. (1991).

70. See, e.g., "Basic Abortion Issue Settled," *The Atlanta Journal & Constitution* (Dec. 2, 1992): §A at 12.

When Does Human Life Begin?
Does Science Provide the Answer?

William S. Sly

When does human life begin? Eleven hundred physicians recently sponsored a pro-life newspaper ad which said that science gives the answer. Quoting Andrew Puzder's brief from the Webster case, it stated:

> The authorities in support of the medical/scientific fact that human life begins at conception are virtually endless.[1]

Yet only a week before, two hundred and fifty members of a group called the Religious Coalition for Abortion Rights argued that it is not a scientific issue. Their ad read:

> The question of when human life begins and at what point that life becomes a person is ultimately a matter for the religious conscience. Neither science nor the state can make this theological determination.[2]

What do the scientists themselves say? The answer depends on which scientist you ask! One of the most eloquent scientists to address this question in the Catholic tradition is Dr. Jérôme Lejeune. In his book entitled *The Concentration Can*,[3] Dr. Lejeune recounts the testimony he gave at a court trial in Maryville, Tennessee in the summer of 1989.[4] The setting was somewhat sensational. The court case involved two divorced spouses who argued over the rights and the humanity of seven frozen embryos. "Concentration Can" was the term Dr. Lejeune used to describe the liquid nitrogen tank in which they were stored frozen. How did they get there? The embryos had been produced in the test tube by a fertility clinic and frozen at the 4-8 cell stage in an effort to help the couple have a baby. That was before their divorce. The mother still wanted to try to give birth to the embryos or to provide them to other infertile couples. Her former husband wanted them destroyed. He argued that he had a constitutional right not to become a father against his will. The judge had to decide, for the first time in U.S. judicial history, whether such frozen embryos were human. Were they human beings to be protected, or common property to be liquidated?

Dr. Lejeune was the expert witness for the mother. He presented the scientific findings on the first stages of human life and testified that human life begins at conception. The trial court found his testimony convincing. Accepting Dr. Lejeune's testimony over that of others who testified against this position, the judge decided in favor of the humanity of the frozen embryos and awarded custody to the mother. However, that decision was later reversed by the Tennessee Court of Appeals.[5]

Dr. Lejeune is a widely known medical geneticist. He won world renown for his discovery of the extra chromosome 21 in Down syndrome over 30 years ago. He's been a staunch defender of the unborn ever since. His voice has often been a lonely one as he protested the application of his discovery to prenatal diagnosis, at least when it was aimed at fingering defective fetuses for abortion. His book deals directly with the issue of when human life begins. In it, he reviews the scientific evidence supporting his conviction that an individual human life begins at fertilization. Charles Rice of Notre Dame University described this book as "a powerful weapon in the fight to restore that conviction."[6] I recommend it for its clarity and consistency.

How did Dr. Lejeune describe for the trial court the normal process by which human life begins? He started from the beginning—with an egg and a sperm. Normally an egg (the ovum) ripens about once a month—roughly fifteen days after the menses. The follicle surrounding the egg ruptures, releasing the egg, which is taken up by the fallopian tubes. Lining the fallopian tube are undulating hair-like cilia which move the ovum in the direction of the uterine cavity. If the ovum is to be fertilized, it must encounter a sperm coming from the opposite direction. Unlike the ovum which is moved along passively, the sperm are powerful swimmers. They swim vigorously from the time they are deposited at the mouth of the womb. Some of them successfully navigate up through the cervix, through the uterine cavity, and enter the fallopian tube. In the tube, the ovum can encounter thousands to hundreds of thousands of sperm. Only one succeeds in fertilizing the ovum.

For Dr. Lejeune this is where human life begins. The youngest form of human being is the fertilized egg, also called the zygote. Before the sperm and egg were united, egg and sperm were both living cells, but neither was an individual human being. In fact, the sperm was only one of many thousands. Every one of them carried a different combination of the father's chromosomal information. Any one of them might have succeeded in fertilizing the ovum. However, once the ovum is fertilized by the successful sperm, we have a unique combination of maternal and paternal DNA that will be reproduced in all descendants of that first cell. To quote Dr. Lejeune:

> When the information carried by the sperm and ovum have encountered each other, then a new human being is defined, . . . its own personal and human constitution is entirely spelled out.[7]

The genetic information from each parent is encoded in DNA. You might visualize the DNA from each parent as a long thread—a meter or so in length—which is cut into 23 different size pieces. Each piece is coiled on itself very tightly and condensed further into a rod-like structure which we can actually see under the microscope. We call each of these rods a chromosome. The normal human zygote contains 46 of these chromosomes, of which 23 came from the male (packaged in the sperm) and 23 came from the female (packaged in the nucleus of the ovum). Lejeune likens these chromosomes to tiny mini-cassettes on which are written various parts of the human symphony:

> As soon as all the information necessary and sufficient to spell out the whole symphony is there, the symphony plays itself. That is, a new man is beginning his career.[8]

How is the information contained in these chromosomes decoded and expressed? Most of the information encodes cellular proteins. Cells rely on proteins to give them structure. They also depend on chemical reactions which are driven by other proteins called enzymes. Each different protein is assembled from different combinations of building blocks called amino acids. To build a protein, we select from the twenty different types of amino acids and add them one at a time to a growing chain. The blueprint for making these proteins is present in the DNA of the 46 chromosomes. What the DNA specifies is the sequence in which the different amino acids are added. Once assembled, each newly made protein folds into a unique, complex, three-dimensional structure to assume its functional role in the cell.

To specify these proteins, the DNA relies on a simple code that is found in the sequential arrangements of its four component bases. These bases—abbreviated A, T, G, and C—are arranged along both strands of the double-stranded DNA structure. Each base on one strand pairs with a specific base on the opposite strand—e.g., all As pair with Ts and all Gs with Cs. Each A-T and G-C base pair can be thought of as one rung on a long ladder. The vertical elements of the ladder are formed by alternating sugar-phosphate bonds, from which each base projects to meet the other member of a base-pair projecting from the opposite strand.

A genetic messenger molecule called messenger RNA is produced by reading sequentially from one strand of the DNA molecule (one side of the ladder). The messenger RNA molecule carries the information from the chromosome in the cell nucleus to the protein synthesis machinery. Through this messenger, a specific sequence in the DNA, like TTG GAC GCG AAG CTA, etc., tells the cell which protein to make. Each three letter code word dictates which amino acid building block is to be added next to the growing protein. Although it is a slight oversimplification, one may think of a gene for a protein 100 amino acids long as a segment of DNA which corresponds to 300 bases (100 triplet code words in the messenger molecule).

The genetic code for human proteins is not unique to humans. Human proteins are made from the same amino acid building blocks as proteins from pigs or pumpkins. In fact, the genetic code is identical for nearly all living organisms. What makes guppies different from groundhogs, and both different from humans, is not that each has a different genetic code. The hereditary differences between different organisms are explained by differences between the sequences of the bases in their DNA and by differences in the number and arrangement of their genes.

This universality of the genetic code implies that we humans are related to every other organism on the planet. Yet each individual human zygote is unique. No two individuals have exactly the same DNA sequences. Recent advances in DNA typing make it relatively easy to prove the uniqueness of each individual's DNA from conception onward.

The only exceptions are identical twins, in which case one individual zygote gives rise at a later stage to two individuals who share the same DNA.

Although the sperm and egg each contribute 23 chromosomes to the zygote, the male and female contributions are not identical or equivalent. Some information is read only from the father's chromosomes—other information, only from the mother's chromosomes.[9] Experiments with mice have shown that if all the chromosomes come from the male (e.g., from two sperm nuclei), the "zygote" fails to grow. The converse is also true. If all 46 chromosomes come from the female (e.g., from two ova), the zygote also fails. The female genes can provide information for mouse body parts, but they don't express the information necessary for forming a placenta. In the mouse, information from the male chromosomes is necessary to make the placenta and supporting structures. The same is true for humans. For that reason, we need both a mother and a father to produce a normal baby.

Let's resume our developmental journey. Lejeune describes how, very soon after fertilization,

> the very young human being splits into two cells, then three, then four. It continues by multiples of two to produce a ball of cells called the blastula.[10]

By the fourth day, cell division and differentiation have produced the blastocyst. This is a thick-walled, hollow sphere which resembles a tennis ball thickened at one pole. In cross section, it looks something like a class ring with a heavy stone. The heavy stone part will become the embryo. The cells of the remainder of the sphere will become the placenta.

The embryo grows initially inside a thick protective layer. At six to seven days, it begins to hatch and produces a layer of cells called trophoblasts. These cells can destroy tissue in their path. They allow the embryo to attach to the uterine walls, to form capillaries, and draw nourishment from maternal capillaries. By the end of the first week, we have an embryo of dozens of cells, attached to the wall of the uterus.

Over the second week, a complex set of cell divisions and differentiation steps take place. These events turn the embryo into a flat, disk-like structure about 1/16th inch in diameter. By the end of the second week, an indentation forms down the middle of the disk. This is called the primitive streak. During the third week, the streak extends and deepens to form a groove. Cells along this groove will eventually house the nerves of the spine. This is the beginning of the central nervous system. By three weeks, the cardiac tube begins to beat.

During the second month, most of the major organs of the body start to form. The embryo grows from a fraction of an inch to several inches. By the end of the second month, Lejeune calls the embryo "Tom Thumb." It has grown limbs with fingers and toes, and has a four-chambered heart. It's easy at this point to tell the human embryo from that of a chicken or a calf. From this point on, we will no longer refer to it as an embryo, but will refer to it as a fetus. This means that its full form is already present. However, Lejeune argues that this distinction is artificial, because it was distinctively human (chromosomally) from the outset. This is as much of embryology and fetal development as Lejeune thought was relevant to the humanity of the frozen embryos.

Lejeune's testimony did not go unchallenged. Three expert witnesses disagreed.[11] A biologist argued that the frozen embryos were really only "pre-embryos." He considers pre-embryos (from the zygote to 11-14 days) a stage of development where they simply possess the potential for life. In fact, during this period he considers the pre-embryo to be only a mass of undifferentiated cells. He argued that only after attachment to the uterine wall does the primitive streak appear, cells become different, and organs form. Professor John Robertson, a lawyer who had researched the issue for the Ethics Committee of the American Fertility Society, concurred with the biologist and argued that it is "not clear" that a human pre-embryo is a unique individual. Dr. Irving Ray King, a practicing physician, also defended the distinction between the pre-embryo (before 14 days) and the embryo after 14 days when cell differentiation has occurred. Nonetheless, the trial judge accepted Lejeune's argument that human life begins at conception. He considered the seven frozen embryos that had been produced in vitro to be human beings, and he awarded custody to the mother for the purpose of implantation.[12]

The judgment in this case was soon reversed by the court of appeals. The court held that the trial court's conclusion that the frozen embryos were human beings had ignored the public policy implicit in the Tennessee statutes, the case holdings of the Tennessee Supreme Court and the teachings of the United States Supreme Court.[13]

Moreover, the Court of Appeals believed that

> it would be repugnant and offensive to constitutional principles to order Mary Sue (Davis) to implant these fertilized ova against her will . . . (and) equally repugnant to order Junior (Davis) to bear the psychological, if not the legal, consequences of paternity against his will.[14]

Consequently, the court remanded the case to the trial court with instructions "to enter a judgment vesting Mary Sue and Junior with joint control of the fertilized ova and with equal voice over their disposition."[15]

In June of 1992, the Tennessee Supreme Court agreed with that view of the constitutional status of the frozen embryo in an opinion that authorized the clinic to discard the embryos if the two parents could not reach agreement on using them for research.[16] The mother, since remarried, appealed to the United States Supreme Court. She argued that the embryos were human beings and deserved protection. As legal authority for that assertion, she cited a 1988 White House statement in which Ronald Reagan proclaimed the "unalienable personhood of every American from the moment of conception." In February 22, 1993, the United States Supreme Court turned down her appeal without comment.[17]

Thus, Dr. Lejeune's articulate and convincing arguments that human life begins at conception persuaded the lower court, but did not influence the ultimate disposition of the seven frozen embryos. Nor has Dr. Lejeune's eloquent analysis greatly influenced other scientists in the wider abortion debate. In fact, very few scientists concur with Lejeune and with the Catholic position that human life begins at conception, and that the fertilized ovum and pre-implantation embryo is a human being, that is, a human person having the moral and legal status of human beings outside of the womb.

Other scientists have suggested alternate approaches to define when the fetus becomes a human person. For example, Professors Harold Morowitz and James Trefil of George Mason University[18] conclude in their recent book *The Facts of Life*[19] that "humanness" is attained when the cerebral cortex is recognizably human and "wired for thinking." Using a combination of evolutionary arguments and embryological evidence, they assert that the evolution of the human brain about three million years ago distinguished man from other creatures. They then draw a parallel in fetal brain development, arguing that the fetus becomes significantly different from an animal fetus when it "acquires humanness" near twenty four weeks of gestation. These two scientists defend the *Roe v. Wade* distinction of the third trimester fetus from the fetus that preceded it. They argue that by the third trimester it acquires the neuronal connections required for human thought, and "acquires humanness."

For those interested in a thorough description of the scientific facts of fertilization, fetal development, and neonatology, *The Facts of Life* has much to recommend it. However, many may find their argument either unpersuasive or morally offensive. I found particularly weak the argument that we will soon be able to develop individuals from the egg alone without the sperm. The importance they place on this argument greatly detracts from their otherwise scholarly effort.

Scientific advances are raising new moral issues in this debate. For example, advances in genetic technology have made it possible not only to produce human embryos in the test tube, as was done in the seven frozen embryos Dr. Lejeune tried to defend. It is even possible now to remove one or two cells from an eight cell embryo to study them for genetic defects.[20] The intent is to select only those embryos without genetic defects for implantation to produce a normal baby. Following screening for cystic fibrosis and several other inherited defects, a number of successful pregnancies have been produced with these techniques. But this technology has not escaped criticism. A recent *Ethics and Medics* issue from the Pope John Center examined the ethical issues surrounding pre-implantation genetic diagnosis.[21]

The Pope John Center article points out that, increasingly, without fanfare, pregnancy in certain circles is not considered to have begun until implantation. To this trend, the Pope John Center vigorously objects.

Even the four cell embryo is considered already a human being—indeed, already a human person. As such, it has a basic right to life which no human power can rightfully destroy. If permitted to develop, the embryo will become a born human child, and eventually a human adult.[22]

This is as clear a statement of the Catholic position as one could find. Yet, the number of scientists like Lejeune who share this position are outnumbered by those like Morowitz and Trefil who hold contrary opinions. Accordingly, the conclusion that "even the four cell embryo . . . has a basic right to life that no human power can rightfully destroy" is not obvious to many scientists who come from other traditions. However, the scientists who disagree on this issue would not do so on the basis of the biochemical and genetic individuality of the zygote or embryo. Ruth Hubbard, a developmental biologist from Harvard, pointed out in her review of the book by Morowitz and Trefil that the differences among scientists are not really scientific differences.[23] Few scientists would quarrel with Lejeune on the molecular basis of heredity and development. However, many would argue over the point when the developing individual acquires a "basic right to life" that takes precedence over all other considerations. That is an ethical issue rather than a scientific issue.

Framing a public policy in the face of such diverse opinions is indeed a challenge. This conference provides a wonderful opportunity for its many talented participants to discuss approaches to meet this challenge.

NOTES

1. Newspaper advertisement in the *St. Louis Post-Dispatch*, January 31, 1993 (advertising supplement).
2. Newspaper advertisement in the *St. Louis Post-Dispatch*, paid for by the Religious Coalition for Abortion Rights, January 22, 1993.
3. Jérôme Lejeune, *The Concentration Can* (San Francisco, CA: Ignatius Press, 1992).
4. *Davis* v. *Davis*, 1989 Westlaw 140495 (Tenn. Cir. Sept. 21, 1989).
5. *Davis* v. *Davis*, 1990 Westlaw 130807 (Tenn. App., Sept. 13, 1990), *affirmed*, 842 S.W. 2d 588 (Tenn. S. Ct., June 1, 1992).
6. Jérôme Lejeune, *The Concentration Can*, 204.
7. Jérôme Lejeune, *The Concentration Can*, 31.
8. Jérôme Lejeune, *The Concentration Can*, 35.
9. Jérôme Lejeune, *The Concentration Can*, 44.
10. Jérôme Lejeune, *The Concentration Can*, 55.
11. Jérôme Lejeune, *The Concentration Can*, 149-55.

12. *Davis* v. *Davis*, 1989 Westlaw 140495 at p.1 (Tenn. Cir., Sept. 21, 1989).

13. *Davis* v. *Davis*, 1990 Westlaw 130807 at p. 3 (Tenn. App., Sept. 13, 1990).

14. *Davis* v. *Davis*, 1990 Westlaw 130807 at p. 3 (Tenn. App., Sept. 13, 1990).

15. *Davis* v. *Davis*, 1990 Westlaw 130807 at p. 3 (Tenn. App., Sept. 13, 1990).

16. *Davis* v. *Davis*, 842 S.W. 2d 588 (Tenn. S. Ct. 1992).

17. *Stowe* v. *Davis*, 113 S. Ct. 1259 (1993).

18. Harold Morowitz is a professor of biology and natural philosophy; James Trefil is a professor of physics.

19. Harold J. Morowitz and James S. Trefil, *The Facts of Life: Science and the Abortion Controversy* (New York: Oxford University Press, 1992). Also see, Harold J. Morowitz and James S. Trefil, editorial in *The New York Times*, November 25, 1992.

20. A. H. Handyside, J. G. Lesko, J. J. Tarin, R. M. K. Winston, and M. R. Hughes, "Birth of a normal girl after *in vitro* fertilization and pre-implantation diagnostic testing for cystic fibrosis,"*New England Journal of Medicine*, 327 (1992): 905-9. A. H. Handyside, E. H. Kontogianni, K. Hardy, and R. M. L. Winston, "regnancies from biopsied human pre-implantation human embryos sexed by Y-specific DNA amplifications," *Nature*, 334 (1990): 768-70.

21. Albert S. Moraczewski, "Genes and Pandora's Box," *Ethics and Medics* 18, no. 3, (March 1993): 1-2.

22. Albert S. Moraczewski, "Gene's and Pandora's Box," 1-2.

23. Ruth Hubbard, "Which Facts, Whose Life?," *Nature* 360 (1992): 379-80.

Resolving Conflicting Normative Claims in Public Policy

Russell Hittinger

I

Conflicting normative claims about human conduct not only set the outer boundaries for debate over issues of public policy; they can also frustrate and ruin policy discussions. Normative conflicts are of different sorts, and perhaps we would do well to at least briefly consider four kinds of conflict.

1. Conflict can arise from diametrically opposed judgments about the moral properties of human acts, in which case disagreement arises whether an act is morally good, wicked, or indifferent. Historically, public debate over such issues as slavery, distilled spirits, divorce, and abortion either began, or quickly became, a debate over the moral species of actions. This animated the debate whether certain acts ought to be proscribed or tolerated at law.

2. Conflict can also arise from disputes about the method or authority by which the moral properties of human acts are to be judged. For example, a biblical fundamentalist and a secularized, professional ethicist are liable to disagree not merely over issues of prudence, but over the principles and offices of authority.

3. Normative conflicts can stem from very different conceptions of the societal roles and symbols of culture. Today, discussion of gender and sexual roles quickly becomes a contest over first principles rather than a deliberation over the details and applications of public policy. For example, the political rhetoric about

"family values" often hides fundamental disagreements over what a family is or ought to be in the first place.

4. Finally, normative conflicts can spring from different ideas about the ends and powers of government, especially where these ideas evince real differences over political morality. In our polity, this level of conflict usually involves debate over rights, especially insofar as rights are understood to be immunities of individuals from ordinary politics, in which majorities enact statutes and policies.

The abortion debate actuates all of these normative conflicts. In this respect, it resembles the problem of slavery. In his study of the *Dred Scott* case, Don Fehrenbacher reports that prior to the adoption of the Thirteenth Amendment in 1865, there were over five thousand appellate cases (mostly at the state level) concerning American slavery.[1] This quantity of appellate decisions indicates the extent to which statutory codification failed to bring the desired result. Slavery was the kind of issue that generated so many conflicts that neither legislatures nor courts were successful in ironing out the contradictions which cropped up in virtually every sector of the law. Each one of the areas of conflict outlined above became a site first of skirmishes, and finally of full scaled sectional conflict. Despite their best efforts, nineteenth-century Americans ultimately failed to keep the slavery issue within the domain of public deliberation and prudence. In short, they failed to maintain a policy discussion.

Although (as I shall point out later) there are many ways that abortion parallels the slavery problem, the comparison breaks down when we stop to consider the fact that whereas slaves were brought ashore in Virginia in 1619, giving Americans nearly a quarter of a millennium to take a moral and political measure of the problem, abortion came upon our polity suddenly, by a judicial fiat that abrogated the settled laws of all but three of the states. Legal abortion in the United States is not the result of a policy discussion. Even the proponents of legal abortion understood that the abortion right represented not an evolution, but a revolution in the principles traditionally animating American institutions, both public and private. Whereas nineteenth-century Americans had the opportunity to test their legislative arts and political prudence on the issue of slavery, we had no such opportunity in the matter of abortion. We never had the chance to sort out where we agree or disagree, much less to carefully distinguish between conflicts over principle and conflicts over policy.

My aim in this paper is to sort out questions of principle from questions of policy in the matter of legal abortion. Since I cannot treat each of the areas of normative conflict outlined above, it will be necessary to focus upon the latter one: namely, conflicts over the ends and powers of government, particularly in the area of rights. Accordingly, I shall not try to resolve the issue of whether abortion is morally wrong. For the purposes of this paper I take it for granted that the direct and deliberate killing of the unborn is morally unjustified. Those who believe that, at the level of personal morality, the issue is more complicated than what is allowed by my assumption might nevertheless find something of value in the way I address the public and political level of the problem. I do not tackle the problem of what ought to count as the proper method or authority in making moral judgments. Nor do I intend to address the cultural and social issues concerning the status of women and the meaning of the family. Scholars such as Kristin Luker and Mary Ann Glendon have helped us to see that the conflicts over abortion are not just driven by abstract questions of political and legal theory. I readily grant that any complete estimation of normative conflict over abortion must engage the kind of cultural analysis undertaken by Luker and Glendon.[2]

I prescind from these levels of the problem in order to focus directly upon the political nature of the conflict. My reasons are twofold. Whatever evil there is in the fact that an innocent child is killed, this evil can be distinguished from the harm done to the common good when the fundamental law of a polity not only recognizes an individual's right to kill the innocent, but also when the right is defined in such a way as to put it out of the bounds of policy and political deliberation. Hence, it is at this public and juridical level that we make judgments not merely about the moral goodness or badness of a personal act, and not merely about the moral estate of the culture, but about the moral goodness or badness of the law. Only at this level can judgment go so far as to reach the issue of the very legitimacy or illegitimacy of the polity itself.

Second, there is no point to discussions about policy unless there is some ground on which prudence can authentically deliberate about the means (e. g. laws or policies) to be chosen for a public end. The Supreme

Court has made the issue of abortion a matter of principle rather than of prudence. The legal and political status quo created by the Court in *Roe*, and reaffirmed in *Casey*, has taken the matter out of the domain of legislative prudence, toleration, and public policy. Once we pay attention to the problem at this level, we can see that the assertion that one is personally opposed to abortion, but obedient in the public domain to a contrary principle—the so-called "Cuomo position"—completely misidentifies the nature of the debate.[3] One must now reckon with the fact that the "public" principle is that the issue is publicly put out of bounds. One therefore does not choose whether to comply with a particular legislative enactment or judgment of policy; one must choose whether to comply with the principle that the issue of abortion is not a public matter—that it must be removed from the domain of deliberative politics.

When we say that someone is the bearer of a fundamental right, we are saying that something is owed him.[4] As scholastic philosophers would say, a certain *debitum* is at stake in the order of justice. The question, therefore, is whether the entire polity is obligated to recognize this *debitum* which, in the case of abortion, is the right of an individual to kill the unborn. The Supreme Court has declared that this is a fundamental right, not a mere legislative grace, nor a mere result of a prudential policy. Thus, one who says that he or she is personally opposed, but publicly obedient, to the right is either saying (i) that the polity ought to respect the rights claim, because it is indeed something owed to the rights claimant, or (ii) that the legal status quo permits one to act as though the alleged right is simply the creature of positive law, tolerated for the sake of the common good. I intend to show why the first is not supported by any sound moral logic, and why the second is not supported by the legal facts of the current regime of abortion rights.

My procedure will be as follows. First, I will outline a menu of options for how government can stand toward abortion. There is more than one way that government can recognize a "right" to abortion. Second, I will discuss the option adopted by the Supreme Court. Third, I will delineate its ramifications for political morality. Fourth, I will discuss where this leaves the public official who wants to bring the issue into the sphere of public policy without violating principles of moral conscience.

II

We live in a political culture in which many people want abortions, if not for themselves, then for others, and if not for others then at least for public peace on the controversy. Leaving to one side the problem of what Americans believe about the medical and moral facets of abortion, let us turn to the menu of options with respect to what they can have government do about the matter.

First, government can legislate on the issue. For our present purposes it is immaterial whether the problem of abortion is legislatively addressed in terms of criminal or (in the fashion of most Western European codes) the civil law. Whether the legislature deals stringently or tolerantly with the matter, the guiding principle would be the requirements of the common good. We can imagine a situation in which an abortifacient pill is so readily available and easily hidden that a legislature prudentially declines to criminalize its possession. We can imagine the legislature reasoning that criminalization of the matter would require a dangerous augmentation of the surveillance powers of government; or, perhaps, that from such criminalization would ensure a myriad of legal problems deleterious to an effective and fair administration of the law.

In any case, a legislature can create a kind of right in which citizens are immune from prosecution for committing what the legislators regard as morally wicked acts. But the "right" is a creature of positive law, and as a creature of positive law it can be modified or even abolished without violating the moral order of justice. For the "right" was never grounded in what was due to the person in any absolute sense, but rather in what a legislature judged to be in the needs and exigencies of the common good.[5]

The legislative option not only allows for an authentic debate about matters of public policy, it also provides an intelligible context for the "Cuomo position"—that one is personally opposed to an action, but that in the public sphere another principle must be considered. Unfortunately, this option does not represent the legal status quo. The Supreme Court has forbidden Americans to legislate or to conduct any serious public business on the subject of abortion. It has insisted that the right to abortion is a right to the action itself—as the *Casey* Court asserted, legislation must not impose an "undue burden" on the woman's exercise of the right.

Another option is for government, or some sector or department of it, to do nothing about abortion for the reason that it lacks power over the matter. In his debates with Stephen A. Douglas, Abraham Lincoln conceded that it was permissible to view the problem of slavery very narrowly, as "a mere negative declaration of a want of power in Congress to do anything in relation to this matter in the territories."[6] In contrast to the states, which are governments of general jurisdiction (having police powers), the United States government is a government of delegated powers. In order to give lawful commands, the civil contract requires the officer of *this* government to have the requisite delegated power. So, for example, if by some strange oversight the United States government had never been delegated power to prosecute its own officers for treason, we could say that the government has no power. The moral merit or demerit of the treasonous action. is immaterial and irrelevant. Rather, what is relevant are the precise powers delegated to the various offices of the government to do or not do something about the action.

But notice that, according to this option, the citizen does not have a right to perform the action (treason, abortion, or whatever). Rather, the citizen has a right that government not exceed its delegated powers. The "right" to commit the morally wicked act is actually a liberty exercised in the absence of a governmental power.[7] What is important for our purposes is that the want of a governmental power can provide an intelligible context for the proposition that one is personally opposed to abortion, but publicly forbidden to deal with it.

Yet, as Lincoln pointed out in connection with Stephen Douglas's position on the *Dred Scott* decision, the rationale of the decision went beyond the declaration of a want of power.

> I know the opinion of the Judges states that there is a total absence of power; but that is, unfortunately, not all it states; for the Judges [of the Supreme Court] add that the right of property in a slave is distinctly and expressly affirmed in the constitution. It does not stop at saying that the right of property in a slave is recognized in the constitution, is declared to exist somewhere in the constitution, but says it is *affirmed* in the constitution. Its language is equivalent to saying that it is embodied and so woven into that instrument that it cannot be detached without breaking the constitution itself.[8]

The same point needs to be made with respect to the judicially imposed right to abortion. The *Roe/Casey* Court did not argue that abortion is a liberty exercised in the absence of a governmental power. Rather, it argued that one has an inherent right to procure an abortion, and that the limits of governmental power follow as an implication of the individual's right. As Lincoln said in connection with the Court's declaration of a constitutional right to hold slaves, it makes a considerable difference whether the right follows as an implication of a limit on governmental power, or whether the limit on the government's power follows as an implication of the right.

While this option is a subtle, even elegant, way to conceptualize how public officials can be bound not to legislate on a matter of conscience, it is not analytically useful for our purposes. The Court has not used it as a justification for the regime of abortion rights since *Roe*. Moreover, the Court did not adopt this option for the good reason that there is not a shred of constitutional warrant for it. Until 1973, it was a settled matter of constitutional law that the states, being governments of general jurisdiction, had no want of police power over this issue.[9]

This leaves us, then, with a third option: the government recognizes that the citizen is a bearer of a fundamental right to procure an abortion. This option presents a clear, if misguided, position on the relationship between government and the practice of abortion. Considered as a fundamental right, the abortion right represents an immunity (a Dworkinian "trump") against the ordinary political process.[10] Government is duty bound not to recognize something about itself, but rather to recognize something that belongs to individuals. As George Washington maintained in his famous Address from the Hebrew Congregation of Newport, Rhode Island: "It is now no more that tolerance is spoken of, as if it was by the indulgence of one class of people, that another enjoyed the exercise of their inherent natural rights."[11] President Washington was no philosopher, but he certainly understood the logic of a fundamental right.

If there is a morally intelligible compromise on the terms presented by this option, I must confess that I don't know what it might be. Suppose, for example, that a kidnapper were to hold three children hostage. We can imagine the various ways that the problem would fall under prudence. For instance, we might deliberate about how to negotiate the release of some or all of the hostages; we might deliberate about what kind of force, if any, ought to be used; we might even deliberate about who has authority, if indeed anyone has it by positive law, to resolve the issue. But it surely would make no sense to negotiate whether or not the kidnapper has a right to do what he does. If he has such a "right" there is nothing to negotiate.

Lincoln had it right when he said that "whoever desires the prevention of the spread of slavery and the nationalization of that institution, yields all when he yields to any policy that either recognizes slavery as being right, or as being an indifferent thing."[12] As he observed in his famous Cooper Institute speech:

> Holding, as they do, that slavery is morally right, and socially elevating, they cannot cease to demand a full national recognition of it, as a legal right, and a social blessing. Nor can we justifiably withhold this on any ground save our conviction that slavery is wrong. If slavery is right, all words, acts, laws, and constitutions against it, are themselves wrong, and should be silenced, and swept away.[13]

In the same vein, James Madison, a slave holder, argued at the Constitutional Convention that it would be "wrong to admit in the Constitution the idea that there could be property in men."[14] With consummate clarity, Madison understood that to recognize such a right in the fundamental law would forever take the matter of slavery out of the sphere of governmental prudence, and would bind the entire polity to the protection of a wrong. Madison and his southern colleagues wanted to take something like a "Cuomo position" on slavery, but at least Madison understood what had to be done to create a plausible context for effecting a public compromise. The compromise was to make the slave owner's "right" a mixture of the first two kinds of rights I have outlined: namely, a right created by positive law in the states, and a liberty exercised in the absence of a power in the United States government.

Despite persistent constitutional questions about "error(s)" in the *Roe* holding;[15] despite "philosophic questions" about abortion;[16] despite their dubiety about the so-called "substantive due process" analysis;[17] despite their admission that some among them "find abortion offensive to our most basic principles of morality";[18] despite the fact that they concede that most abortions are efforts at birth control;[19] despite the fact that they themselves continually refer to fetal life as "the child"[20]—the authors of the joint opinion in *Casey* nonetheless argue that "central holding" of *Roe v. Wade* must be upheld. Although the Court adopted a mode of reasoning that mimicked an enquiry into public policy,[21] the principle governing the "central holding" was deemed a matter of right rather than policy.

What in their estimation was to be purchased by this judicial sentence on abortion? The authors of the joint opinion speak of the woman's right of "autonomy" and "liberty" to make "intimate" decisions.[22] With respect to the word "liberty" in the due process clause of the Fourteenth Amendment, the authors of the joint opinion explain that:

> At the heart of liberty is the right to define one's own concept of existence, of meaning, of the universe, and of the mystery of human life. Beliefs about these matters could not define the attributes of Personhood were they formed under compulsion of the State.[23]

We are given to understand that governmental interference in the matter of abortion constitutes nothing less than personicide. When the state outlaws abortion, or places undue burdens in the path of a woman seeking one, the state deprives the woman of a crucial self-defining decision, and robs her of those attributes of selfhood constituted by free choice. The "legitimacy" of the judiciary and the rule of law, they contend, requires the recognition of this right.[24]

I submit that the joint opinion represents a kind of end-game on the issue of judge-made abortion law. In the first place, the Court has imposed a right of liberty that, by logic of analogy, and by consistency of application, would guarantee that a government of positive laws is morally impossible. Such a comprehensive right as the one announced in *Casey* implies that ordered liberty effected by the "compulsion of the state" necessarily violates the most solemn natural right of citizens to maintain the integrity, if not the very existence, of their persons. Read literally, and applied consistently, this right would give citizens an immunity from virtually all positive laws.[25]

No previous deliverance of a legislature or court, including the infamous *Dred Scott* decision, has played such an end-game with the logic of rights. In the second place, the Court explicitly argues that the legitimacy of the Constitution, the judicial office, and indeed the common good itself are at stake. The Court does not merely assert that the social, political, and economic equality of women depend upon the judge-made law concerning abortion. The Court is not merely effecting matters of policy (though, as I will point out later, the Court also included a policy argument along with the rights analysis). It also declares that the "covenant" between government and the people, as well as the bond linking one generation of citizens with another, stands or falls on this issue.[26]

III

Citizens and public officials who understand in conscience the moral wrong of abortion are put in a position where the first obligation and virtue must be to tell the truth about where things stand. The truth of the matter is that abortion has been taken off the plate of political prudence and policy. I suggest that it is especially important for Catholics—who have come rather late to this game of fundamental rights—to take careful stock of what it means to bind the polity to the principle of inherent individual rights.

What does the logic of rights entail? If someone has a right, it means that others are duty-bound to do or not do something with respect to the claimant. It is important to understand that so long as we are not speaking in some loose or metaphorical sense about rights, a right does not bind its holder, but rather makes others duty-bound. For this reason, rights language can never be a merely private thing. Catholics who want to find some way out of the crisis of conscience on the abortion issue need to appreciate the fact that the rights solution guarantees that the issue cannot be demoted to the sphere of a mere private conscience. As I will now explain, a right binds other people, and, as such, leaves no room for retreat from the public sphere.

In the matter of abortion who is bound? We are. "We," that is, insofar as we are citizens who deliberate and act through democratic assemblies.[27] The alleged right to abortion, therefore, does not bind some anonymous government, but rather renders the citizens themselves duty-bound to recognize the right of those who elect to kill the unborn. Thus, it is both false and useless to pretend that the moral issue is transacted in a merely private sphere, because the principle of the right binds all of the citizens as to what they may legitimately do *qua citizens* (e.g. in making and enforcing laws, in formulating policies, and in conducting any public business that touches upon the alleged right). To paraphrase the language of *Casey*, citizens may not act through democratic assemblies to impose "undue burden(s)" upon the choice to have an abortion. We need to keep clearly in view not just what the woman does, but also what we may not do. To leave out of the picture the constraints placed upon the citizenry is to miss the central moral implication of what it means to have a right of this sort.

Moral conscience cannot be relieved by the legal fact that citizens also have a right not to kill their unborn children. Whether we elect to kill them or not, the principle stands undiminished and unqualified. For the law recognizes a civil right of individuals to commit wrongful acts of homicide, and prohibits the citizens, working through democratic assemblies, from proscribing such acts. The unborn children of women who elect not to kill them remain in the same position vis-a-vis the law as those unborn children who are killed. All children in the womb have been excluded by legal fiat from the protection of criminal laws that prohibit homicide. Put bluntly, but accurately, mothers who choose not to kill their unborn children are exercising the very same "right to choose" as those who decide to kill.

Therefore, when the judicial branch of the United States government upholds the abortion right, and prohibits citizens from legally protecting the unborn, the government is requiring the citizens to treat some human persons as subhuman. What any of us do in a merely private capacity is irrelevant to the issue at hand. Had *Dred Scott* been maintained, it would have been irrelevant to a Vermont farmer that he chose not to use slave labor, so long as the law required him to cease and desist from legislating or conducting any public business touching upon slavery.[28]

The political harm of the abortion right, however, goes beyond the issue compelling citizens to treat persons as subhuman. We must not lose sight of the moral fact that the harm done in abortion is not merely the harm to the unborn, nor the harm done to the conscience of citizens who are wrongfully limited in their actions *qua* citizens. Looking at the problem from the standpoint of the common good, abortion rights undermine the first end, if not the first act, of civil government.

By transferring the power over life and death to private choice, the state threatens, if it does not violate, the civil contract. In effect, the power originally invested in civil government is relinquished. For John Locke, of course, this would be tantamount to returning to a pre-civil condition, in which each individual is a judge and executor of the law of nature. When a woman asserts a right to abortion, she is asserting a private franchise to kill her unborn child. Under current law, she may do so on the basis of her own estimation of the human status or worthiness of those she kills. But given this substantive breach of the social contract, what would prevent anyone else from broadening that breach by claiming a private franchise to kill *any* person who, in their estimation, commits an unjustifiable homicide of abortion?"

I am certainly not suggesting that the moral wrong of abortion consists only in the fact that it is done by private parties rather than by public officers. Rather, I am calling attention to the specifically political wrong of abortion rights. No government has rightful power to kill those who are in no dereliction of any moral duty or civil or criminal law. Because government does not have such power, it cannot transfer it to private parties. Government does indeed have the power to use lethal force for the sake of justice in the commonwealth. But here the power is exercised legitimately only in the light of a public end, and even then only according to public procedures and the most exacting standards of accountability. The power of lethal force does not belong to the individual citizen, except as it is recognized at common law in the case of self-defense. Neither the *Roe* nor *Casey* Courts made any pretense that this is what is at stake in the right to abortion. Rather, the woman is alleged to have a right to kill the unborn for private ends, without any public accountability or justification.

In fact, the abortion cases make it clear beyond any doubt that the reason and ground of the right consist in the woman's estimation of her private good. Of course, the Court could have argued that the right consists in the woman's liberty to effectuate some public good—such as population control. Then, the abortion right would be analogous to the liberties and rights claimed by parents to educate their children, or perhaps the liberties and rights of workers to engage in collective bargaining. On this view, we might invoke a principle of subsidiarity, according to which the government recognizes certain competencies and rights of individuals to bring about public goods. But, with respect to the abortion right, the "good" in question is essentially private; indeed, the Court has repeatedly insisted not only that the right stands in sharp contrast to the public good represented by the pro-natalist policies of the state, but that it trumps the state's interests during the first two trimesters. Therefore, the abortion right is nothing less than a purported right of individual citizens to use lethal force without being deputized to do so, and without any of the constraints that the government ordinarily imposes upon itself when it kills persons.

A state that cedes to private parties its authority to determine who is and who is not a person worthy of moral respect, and that goes further to recognize a private franchise to execute said judgment in the way of lethal force, is a state that has moved to the precipice of relinquishing formal authority over the common good in the matter of life, including its authority to make the rest of us obey the constraints it would place upon our efforts to protect the innocent.

It is difficult to see what other authority a government retains once it privatizes lethal force. Locke argued that when government arbitrarily confiscates property it subverts the interest that citizens have to remain in the civil sphere.[29] But this argument can be made just as forcefully in terms of arbitrary power over life and death. A citizen who takes this power is no longer a citizen, but rather someone who declares himself either to stand outside the civil order or to proceed as though no civil order exists. If those who elect to kill the innocent can proceed under these assumptions, on what grounds can the rest of us continue to be bound to civil authority—except, perchance, by our own private choice?

Bringing my two arguments together, we can see that the abortion right denies to the governed any political capacity to secure, in Locke's words, the "mutual preservation of their lives." This is not hyperbole. The judge-made law absolutely prohibits a father from employing any public means of stopping, and from seeking any public remedy for, the killing of his innocent child. Under the most solemn edict of the Supreme Court, in which all other branches and departments of government have acquiesced, the citizens are prohibited from including within the blessings of government the "mutual preservation" of father and unborn child, grandmother and grandchild, neighbor and child, etc.

IV

The Catholic Church came rather late to the political language of fundamental rights. Sometimes the Church has spoken of rights as so many legislative desiderata, and at other times as so-called trumping rights.[30] That is to say, some rights seem to require the prudential insights and policy discussion of legislatures, while other rights resist the compromises typical of policy decisions. The latter kind of right dictates where lines drawn by policy are either acceptable or unacceptable.

The Church argues that the direct and deliberate killing of the unborn is forbidden as a fundamental term of justice. The new *Catechism of the Catholic Church* puts the issue bluntly, yet fairly and accurately:

The moment a positive law deprives a category of human beings of the protection which civil legislation ought to accord them, the state is denying the equality of all before the law. When the state does not place its power at the service of the rights of each citizen, and in particular of the more vulnerable, the very foundations of a state based on law are undermined.[31]

It is important to note that equal protection provides no ground for proportional reasoning. When we say that every person deserves equal protection of the laws, we are not affirming a proposition amenable to prudential weighing and balancing. There is not such a thing as a little bit of equal protection. In this respect, it is not like governmental toleration of some morally wicked acts, where the toleration is justified by appeals to the common good. Where there is no equal protection, there is no juridical common good. Equal protection of the laws is not a matter vouchsafed to the order of prudence. Rather, equal protection is a principle that either is or is not satisfied. To say that one is privately opposed, but publicly obedient to the abortion right means that one is for the removal of one class of human beings from equal protection of the laws. This is not a derogation from the ideal of the law. It is a negation of the principle itself.

I conclude by returning to the analogy between slavery and abortion. In 1859, Lincoln contended that this slavery element is a durable element of discord among us, and that we shall probably not have perfect peace in this country with it until it either masters the free principle in our government, or is so far mastered by the free principle as for the public mind to rest in the belief that it is going to its end.[32]

During the early years of the Republic, there was a fragile political peace on the issue of slavery because, as Lincoln observed, the laws reflected the policy that slavery was a restricted right en route to gradual abolition.[33] It was the Court's holding in *Dred Scott* that changed the nature of the game.

The Supreme Court has done with abortion what the Court did with slavery in *Dred Scott*. We are left in a dilemma very similar to the one faced by the two parties on the eve of the Civil War. The path in the road is clearly marked. Either we acquiesce in the principle that the polity is bound by the judicially imposed "right," or we repudiate that principle in the hope of moving the problem back into the domain of deliberative prudence. If, in the hope of short term peace, we acquiesce in the first path, we will not only suffer a protracted conflict over abortion, but will find that the stakes inexorably will come to include questions about the legitimacy of regime. If we take the latter path, we will not know in advance how things will turn out. For all we know, once the issue is moved back into the area of policy and prudence, there will be compromises which continue to allow the premeditated killing of the unborn. But at least we will have relieved conscience at one level. At least we will have taken the steps necessary to allow human intelligence to work on the problem.

It is necessary to abandon the rhetoric of "personally opposed, but..." Whatever subjective hopes and aspirations are represented by this rhetoric, it is not a true description of the situation. It misrepresents both the moral and legal terms of the controversy. The American people can do without public officials preaching on matters of personal morality. But they can rightly expect the public terms of the issue to be formulated truthfully. Truthfully said, the judge-made right to abortion is not the result of a (properly) legislative act whereby the people, after deliberating about the needs of the common good, have enacted statutes tolerating abortion.

No doubt, some citizens and public officials would like to believe that the abortion "right" merely reflects a policy of toleration, and that toleration provides an undesirable, but defensible, context for distinguishing between private and public responsibilities. Others would like to believe that the Court has left more than a few crumbs of the issue on the plate of public policy. The truth, however, is that the abortion right prohibits significant policy making in this area and cancels out any defensible notion of toleration. If Catholics wish to tolerate abortion and to live in civil peace in this society, they will have to will the means necessary to do so. That is to say, they will have to will to abrogate the alleged "right" to abortion as it has been defined and imposed by the Supreme Court. So long as the status quo remains, conscientious Catholics will be forced into a situation in which they do not merely dissent over abortion, but over the moral nature of the American regime itself. *How* the abrogation of the judge-made law is to be accomplished is a complicated question that stands beyond the confines of this article. *That* it must be abrogated is the conclusion that follows proximately from the arguments given in these pages.

NOTES

1. Don E. Fehrenbacher, *The Dred Scott Case: Its Significance in American Law and Politics* (New York: Oxford University Press, 1978), 33.

2. Kristin Luker, *Abortion and the Politics of Motherhood* (Berkeley, CA: University of California Press, 1984); Mary Ann Glendon, *Abortion and Divorce in Western Law* (Cambridge, MA: Harvard University Press, 1987).

3. I refer here to the position of Governor Cuomo described in a 1984 speech at Notre Dame. In this paper I do not analyze the speech itself, but rather use the rubric "Cuomo position" to represent the generic position that one can condemn abortion as a private rule of conduct, but support it publicly in terms of toleration.

4. A fundamental right, in the sense of W. N. Hofeld's understanding of a "claim right." A has a *claim* right that B should do X, if and only if B has a *duty* to A to X. This is a "right stricto sensu." Hofeld also spoke of juridical meanings of rights as powers and immunities. A has *power* (relative to B) to X, if and only if B has a *liability* to have his legal position changed by A's X-doing. B has *immunity* (relative to A's X-doing), if and only if A has no power (i.e. a *disability*) to change B's legal position by X-doing. A. N. Hofeld, *Fundamental Legal Conceptions* (New Haven, CT: Yale University Press, 1919). For a

discussion of the difference between claim rights and rights as powers and immunities, see John Finnis, *Natural Law and Natural Rights* (Oxford: Clarendon Press, 1980), 199-205. It will become clear in the course of this paper that the judge-made abortion right is a claim right in the strict sense of the term. Rights as powers and immunities are irrelevant in the relationship between mother and unborn child, since the Court has held that the unborn child has no legal abilities or disabilities to be changed by the mother's claim.

5. This does not mean that a "human" right, due to the person by nature or by the moral order, cannot be qualified in light of the common good. I leave this issue to one side in order to focus upon a "right" that is simply the creature of positive law.

6. "Speech at Columbus, Ohio (September 16, 1859)," in *Lincoln: Speeches and Writings 1859-1865* (New York: The Library of America, 1989), 53.

7. Here, I rely upon an especially clear analysis of this matter by Robert P. George, in *Making Men Moral: Civil Liberties and Public Morality* (Oxford: Clarendon Press, 1993), ch. 4: "Rights and Wrongs."

8. "Speech at Columbus," 53.

9. A point that has been carefully surveyed and documented by John T. Noonan, Jr., *A Private Choice* (New York: The Free Press, 1979).

10. Ronald Dworkin, *Taking Rights Seriously*, rev. ed. (Cambridge, MA: Harvard University Press, 1978), ch. 4.

11. "Address to the Hebrew Congregation of Newport, Rhode Island (August 17, 1790)," in John C. Fitzpatrick, ed., *The Writings of George Washington from the Original Manuscript Sources, 1745-1799* (Washington, D.C.: Government Printing Office, 1909), vol. 1, 566. I am indebted to Walter Berns for bringing this passage to my attention. See Walter Berns, *Taking the Constitution Seriously* (New York: Simon and Schuster), 166.

12. "Speech at Cincinnati, Ohio (September 17, 1859)," in *Lincoln: Speeches and Writings 1859-1865*, 86.

13. "Address at Cooper Union" (Feb. 27, 1860)," in *Lincoln: Speeches and Writings 1859-1865*, 129.

14. Max Farrand, ed., *The Records of the Federal Convention of 1787*, rev. ed., 4 vols. (New Haven, CT: Yale University Press, 1937), II, 417.

15. *Planned Parenthood of Southeastern Pennsylvania* v. *Casey* (hereafter, *Planned Parenthood* v. *Casey*), 112 S. Ct. 2791, 2816 (1992).

16. *Planned Parenthood* v. *Casey*, 2806.

17. *Planned Parenthood* v. *Casey*, 2804.

18. *Planned Parenthood* v. *Casey*, 2806

19. *Planned Parenthood* v. *Casey*, 2806, 2808, 2809.

20. *Planned Parenthood* v. *Casey*, 2811, 2830, 2831, 2832. Except when the interests of the state are involved, in which case they use the semantical device of "fetal life" (2811).

21. "Where, in the performance of its judicial duties, the Court decides a case in such a way as to resolve the sort of intensely divisive controversy reflected in *Roe* and those rare, comparable cases, its decision has a dimension that the resolution of the normal case does not carry. It is the dimension present whenever the Court's interpretation of the Constitution calls the contending sides of a national controversy to end their national division by accepting a common mandate rooted in the Constitution." *Planned Parenthood* v. *Casey*, 2815.

22. *Planned Parenthood* v. *Casey*, 2806, 2816.

23. *Planned Parenthood* v. *Casey*, 2807.

24. *Planned Parenthood* v. *Casey*, 2814.

25. Of course, the Court has no intention of applying this very general and potent right across the board. Indeed, they take pains to point out that the liberty of the woman is "unique to the human condition and so unique to the law" (*Planned Parenthood* v. *Casey*, 2807). The joint opinion's remarks about the "unique" nature of the right provides some check upon an analogical expansion of the right. Despite what some anti-abortion pundits have suggested, the right asserted in *Casey* is not a mere liberty interest. Rather, it is a fundamental, if not a natural, right. The fact that the authors of the joint opinion also say that the right is not "absolute" is neither here nor there (*Planned Parenthood* v. *Casey*, 2819). By the terms "not absolute," they very clearly mean that the state has interests which can bear incidentally upon how the right is exercised. Thus, the Court upheld the informed consent and parental consent parts of the Pennsylvania bill on the basis that no right is absolute. Yet governmental regulation of rights that are not absolute are not therefore subject to a lower standard of judicial scrutiny. In this respect, the Court explicitly draws a parallel with some governmental regulations on the exercise of the right to vote (*Planned Parenthood* v. *Casey*, 2818-19). In either case, government may regulate the right so long as it does not place an "undue burden" on its exercise. On strict scrutiny applied to impairment of the right to vote, see *Kramer* v. *Union School District*, 395 U. S. 621 (1969); *Harper* v. *Virginia Board of Elections*, 383 U. S. 663, 666 (1966).

26. *Planned Parenthood* v. *Casey*, 2833.

27. "We," also, in the sense that the Court is only authorized to impose judgment in the light of what "we the people" established as the constitutional rules of the polity.

28. Suppose, for example, that this Vermonter also were to learn that the United States government planned to exact taxes to build slave pens not just in Alabama but in Vermont; that public monies were being used to educate future farmers of their options to use slave labor; and that these monies were also to be used to conduct experiments with the bodily parts of slaves. If this Vermonter and his fellow citizens had not lost their moral sensitivities altogether, they

would have been morally justified in taking whatever actions that prudence might dictate are necessary to the end of separating themselves from that government.

29. John Locke, *Second Treatise of Government*, XI, #138. Locke makes it very clear that when he says that the protection of property is the first end of government, he also means "mutual preservation of their lives" (Ibid., IX, #123).

30. For an overview, see my article "The Problem of the State in *Centesimus Annus*," *Fordham International Law Journal* 15:4 (August 1992): 952-96.

31. *Le Catechisme de l'Eglise Catholique*, #2273, citing the document *Donum Vitae* III from the Congregation for the Doctrine of the Faith.

32. "Speech at Columbus," 37.

33. "Speech at Columbus," 38.

Theological Parameters: Catholic Doctrine on Abortion in a Pluralist Society

James J. Walter

INTRODUCTION

No issue since the Vietnam conflict, or maybe since Prohibition,[1] has so plagued the American moral conscience as has abortion. The 1973 Supreme Court ruling on *Roe* v. *Wade* has plunged this country into what seems to be such an endless—and nearly hopeless—polarization of extreme positions that the American public has begun to lose confidence that any moral middle ground can be found. Many in society are numbed by the frequent revision of abortion laws at the federal and state levels, congressional proposals to prevent legal constraints on abortion,[2] Republican executive attempts to establish "gag rules" and the latter's recent reversal by President Clinton. We are told in nearly every survey that a majority of the American people believe that the Supreme Court went too far when it granted a fourteenth-amendment right to an abortion. The abortion of 1.6 million fetuses each year becomes even more complex and debatable when public funds are used to finance these medical procedures.

Politicians have hardly been immune to the machinations of this debate. Not only have they been forced to state publicly their personal views, but in many cases their positions on abortion have become the litmus test for election. Possibly no group in society dreams more of the day when this controversy will go away than those running for public office. The situation is further complicated for those politicians who are Catholic. The legacy of the 1984 presidential election campaign still lingers. The intramural debate between John Cardinal O'Connor, the archbishop of New York, and Governor Mario Cuomo and Congresswoman Geraldine Ferraro, the democratic candidate for vice-president, poignantly illustrates the additional pressures that Catholic politicians face.[3]

In an address at Georgetown University, William Byron, S.J., the outgoing president of The Catholic University of America, claimed that academics concerned with the protection of human life have much work to do. He argued that it is the academic's responsibility to clarify the philosophical foundations of the abortion issue and to provide those in public office with the reasoned arguments necessary to move this debate to higher ground.[4] To meet Fr. Byron's challenge, I offer my own reflections as a Catholic ethicist on the theological parameters that determine the Catholic church's position on abortion.

The purposes of my paper are both theological and practical. They are theological because I will discuss the theological beliefs and value judgments that underlie the official church's moral position on abortion. I will concentrate primarily on the official teachings of the Catholic church, i.e., the teachings from the authoritative magisterium. Consequently, I will not focus much attention on the theological perspectives and critiques offered by many contemporary Catholic theologians. In addition, my intent is not to discuss directly the *morality* of abortion; others have done this elsewhere.[5] Though the Church's moral position on abortion is not solely based on religious views, an argument that I will develop later, nonetheless, theological beliefs about who God is and how God acts in the world lie behind and influence the Catholic moral position.

My purpose is also practical in that I seek to help all politicians, but in particular those who are Catholic, to understand better the Catholic position on abortion and, in light of this understanding, to help them better negotiate the abortion controversy in a pluralist society. To this end, I will highlight and briefly analyze some background issues related to abortion, e.g., views of the human person and community, that become neuralgic points between the Church's position and those positions embraced by our contemporary pluralist society.

Before I proceed, though, a few definitions of the terms in the title of this paper are necessary. "Theology" is a discipline that reflects on religious experience and religious texts in order to understand. Theology is not faith itself, nor is it doctrine. Theological reflection proceeds from faith, and its object is an interpretation of the meaning of faith in a culture. As St. Anselm of Canterbury defined theology after the turn of

92

the first millennium, it is *fides quaerens intellectum*, faith seeking understanding. "Doctrine" or teaching, on the other hand, is one moment in faith's attempt to say what is the case about reality, and thus doctrine establishes the common beliefs of a church about what is true, real, and valuable.[6] However, only a few doctrines are considered irreformable or infallible (dogmas) in the Catholic tradition, while most others possess various levels of authoritative but noninfallible weight.

Similar to its root meaning in mathematics, I will use the word *parameter* to signify a constant or a variable that determines the Catholic church's moral position on abortion. Actually, there are several theological parameters that come together in a complex form to make up the Church's teaching. I will show that there are several theological and moral beliefs that constitute the *substance* of the Catholic position on abortion. These basic affirmations and value judgments about God, humans and the world go to the very core of the tradition, and they are what have been explicitly taught or implied in various doctrines. They are the constants; they neither can nor should change if the Church is to remain faithful to its own tradition.

On the other hand, basic beliefs are always further interpreted and applied in detail to concrete situations and circumstances of human life. Though these further interpretations and applications may take regular form, appear over a long period of time, and even find themselves somehow articulated in doctrines, they do not have the same status in the tradition as the basic beliefs and value judgments.[7] As important and necessary as they may be, interpretations-applications are "variables," i.e., by nature they are open to change or reformulation.[8] Such a claim should not be construed to imply that every further interpretation must necessarily be changed; rather, the claim simply implies that a development of doctrine on concrete moral issues within the Catholic church is indeed possible.

I am aware that what I have called basic beliefs and value judgments (constants) are themselves interpretations. However, I would argue that they differ from interpretations-applications (variables). The latter are either second-level interpretations or applications of basic beliefs about God, humans and the world. For example, I may hold to the basic theological belief that God's presence and power are not only transcendent to but also immanent in the world. Thus, I may believe that God is related to or acts immanently in the world (constant), but then I may interpret *how* God acts in the world by holding the further belief that God possesses certain rights to act in areas of human life analogous to how human agents possess rights to act in the world (variable). On the basis of this second-level interpretation—God is another actor in the world with certain rights to act—I might infer or somehow derive a moral principle, which itself is a further interpretation, that embodies my understanding about how God acts immanently in the world. For example, I might infer the moral principle that human agents may never directly kill an innocent person from my theological belief that only divine activity possesses legitimate power, dominion, and rights over the life and death of innocent persons. Finally, I may apply the moral principle to a concrete instance of human behavior, e.g., abortion, and prohibit the action on the basis of my theological interpretations. As I will argue later, the second-level interpretation that God acts in the world with certain rights, i.e., in a way similar to how human agents act, is open to change or reinterpretation. It should be obvious that any strict application of a second-level interpretation to a moral issue would also be variable in the sense that I am using the term here.

I will show later that there are four theological parameters that function in the magisterium's position on abortion: anthropological, ethical, value, and legal. In each parameter there are both constants and variables, as difficult as it may be to distinguish these two in practice. If true dialogue is to go forward between the Catholic and other positions on abortion in society, then anyone thoughtfully engaged in this dialogue must take notice of what is the substance and what is an interpretation-application of the tradition.

Finally, there is the term *pluralist*. By pluralist I mean that there are multiple and competing views and convictions about the nature of persons, society, morality, etc., that function at the public level in society. *A priori*, none of these views is considered true, and *de facto* none commands universal public acceptance. In fact, each view must compete in the public arena for attention, and persuasion is the vehicle by which any one of these views is accepted. Not only is secular society pluralist in this country, but there is a certain plurality of positions within and between the various Christian churches on concrete issues like abortion.[9] Consequently, one of my practical purposes will be to concentrate on those points of convergence and divergence—points of agreement and disagreement—between the Catholic tradition and society's pluralist position on abortion. Throughout the paper, I hope to offer politicians some horizons and perspectives on the interaction of the Catholic position within a pluralist society.

BRIEF SUMMARY OF THE CATHOLIC CHURCH'S MORAL TEACHING ON ABORTION

My intention in this section is to present a concise summary of the Catholic magisterium's moral position on abortion. I am interested neither in debating this moral position nor in establishing its validity; rather, I am interested only in stating what this position is, in assessing the status and authoritative weight of the teachings that proclaim the position, and in analyzing the various sources that the magisterium draws on in formulating its position.

MORAL POSITION

Historically, the Christian tradition in general has approached the abortion issue with great respect for all human life. Though there is very little explicit evidence from the Hebrew and Christian scriptures that would warrant an absolute prohibition of abortion,[10] it is clear from many texts that every life is valued because of its relation to God's creative activity (e.g., Gen. 4:1; Job 31:15; Isa. 44:24; Jer. 1:5). Very early in the Christian era, however, we begin to find many writers condemning abortion, e.g., the author of the *Didache*, Tertullian, Jerome and Augustine. Surely, these early Christian authors not only wanted to distance the Christian community from the pagan practices of abortion and infanticide but also to call the members of this community to imitate the love that God has for all human life, especially for innocent human life. Despite the centuries-long debate over when the human soul is infused into the body (animation), and thus exactly when the fetus becomes a *person*, the Catholic tradition has consistently condemned abortion from the time of conception as a grave sin, even though the penalties for aborting an animated fetus were greater than those for aborting an unanimated one.[11]

The deep respect for and the protection of all human life have come down through the centuries to be formulated into a moral norm that has been proclaimed often by the modern magisterium. The moral norm as we find it formulated in many recent documents can be succinctly stated as: all direct killing of innocent human life either as a means or as an end is morally wrong. I will leave to another section the discussion of what precisely constitutes *direct* killing as a means or as an end and why these acts are absolutely prohibited on theological and ethical grounds. What is important here is the tradition's evaluation of both the moral status (value) of all unborn life and the claims that this life makes on us. At the outset, it is important to note that the Catholic tradition has never taught any definite philosophical position on when the human soul is infused, and thus when the fetus becomes a *person*.[12] Nonetheless, it is the case that the tradition has viewed all unborn life as "innocent," and it has stated in the recent *Instruction on Respect for Human Life* that from the moment of conception the life that is present at all stages of development must be treated *as a person*.[13] In other words, although the tradition has not definitively defined when nascent life becomes a person, all human life from the moment of conception must be treated and respected as the *moral equivalent* of a person. No matter at which stage of development, the unborn life is granted an identical ethical value,[14] and it must "be respected in an absolute way."[15] Consequently, all unborn life makes a moral claim on us to respect its fundamental right to life.[16]

STATUS AND AUTHORITATIVE WEIGHT OF THE TEACHINGS

Teachings on the respect for human life at all its stages and on the corresponding presumption against taking human life are long-standing, authoritatively proclaimed by the Church, and consistently expressed in both papal and conciliar texts. This set of doctrines is certainly central to the core of the Catholic Christian tradition. They state not only that life itself is truly a fundamental value but also what moral attitudes and dispositions we should have toward life.

On the other hand, a question arises about the status and authoritative weight of a second set of teachings. These doctrinal claims are concerned with the probability of the human soul (animation) being present from the time of conception, the teaching in the *Instruction* that

96

all unborn life is the moral equivalent of a person, and the teaching that all direct abortions are morally wrong. Concerning the last of these doctrines at least, some of the recent documents that I have briefly surveyed claim that this teaching has not changed and is unchangeable.[17] It would take me too far afield to discuss all the ramifications of a claim such as this,[18] but I would state succinctly that none of these teachings has the same status as the first set mentioned above. Nor does any of them constitute the core of the Catholic tradition. They are either second-level interpretations or applications—and thus variable parameters—that attempt to make concrete the more general and central attitudes and value judgments taught in the first set of doctrines, i.e., constant parameters. Consequently, the weight of the second set of teachings is not as substantial as those in the first set.[19]

SOURCES OF THE MORAL POSITION: REASON AND REVELATION

One of the distinguishing characteristics of the Roman Catholic tradition is the way that it utilizes the resources of both reason and revelation in approaching moral issues. Its basic conviction is that in the moral order it is neither reason alone nor faith alone that discovers the truth. Rather, it is reason *and* faith; better stated, it is reason informed by faith. Because the basic values of the moral life are available to all people of goodwill and knowable through rational insight and reflection, the conclusions reached on specific issues as abortion are not *logically* dependent on Christian religious beliefs.[20] Consequently, one of the more common misperceptions in the public debate over abortion is that the Catholic church has sought to impose a specifically religious morality on society. Though the Catholic position is nourished and supported by religious resources, the condemnation of all direct abortions is not established exclusively on the basis of these resources.

Historically, the Catholic tradition has relied on Thomas Aquinas' theory of natural law as a way of formulating its position on the ability of reason to discern objective morality. Though Aquinas' synthesis is a second-level interpretation, and therefore variable, what is central to the Catholic tradition are its claims that humans are intelligent, that reality is intelligible, and that reality, when grasped by intelligence, imposes on the person an objective moral obligation. The commitment of the tradition to the position that morality is both objective and available to reason is one basis for why all recent magisterial documents on morality, even those specifically devoted to abortion, include a separate section on rational, i.e., natural law, arguments against certain actions.[21]

The claims that objective morality is available to human insight, however, do not make the resources of faith irrelevant to moral decision making. As the *Pastoral Constitution on the Church in the Modern World* (*Gaudium et Spes*) asserted, "For faith throws a new light on everything, manifests God's design for man's total vocation, and thus directs the mind to solutions which are fully human" (§11). The resources of explicit faith and revelation enable us to know more clearly and fully the nature of human persons and their worth, but they do not bypass what reason has arrived at, nor do they add new content in terms of general values and obligations to the moral life.[22] Because the Catholic tradition does not hold to an exclusively religious position on abortion, any charge that the Church is merely imposing a religious morality on others in society is false. Consequently, Catholics, whether they are speaking as citizens or as politicians, should not cast the tradition's position in purely religious terms. Dialogue between the magisterium's position on abortion and other positions in society is possible based on rational reflection and moral argument.

THEOLOGICAL PARAMETERS

I would like to turn now to the four theological parameters that lie behind and determine to a great extent the official church's moral position on abortion. The parameters are theological in the sense that they all imply basic beliefs and value judgments about God, humanity and the world. These beliefs and value judgments are also interrelated. For example, the sacredness of human life, which is a basic judgment about the value of human life, is an implication of Christian convictions about who God is. The theological interpretation of how God is related to and acts in human history, i.e., a theology of divine providence, underlies the Church's view of human authority over the taking of human life, especially innocent life. Some elements within each of these parameters are constants because they constitute the substance of the tradition, and some elements in each are variables because they are second-level interpretations or applications of more fundamental and basic perspectives. While analyzing each parameter I will briefly compare its contents with what I understand to be the dominant "societal views" on the respective issues. By societal views I mean the beliefs and positions that appear to operate at the public or social level, albeit these positions may not necessarily operate at or even inform the more personal or private level of people's lives. My purpose here will be to locate points of agreement and disagreement between the two perspectives so that an informed discussion of the morality of abortion might proceed toward a more intelligent and comprehensive public policy.

ANTHROPOLOGICAL PARAMETER

This parameter is concerned with the tradition's basic beliefs about who the human person is, the general condition or situation of humanity as a whole, and the value accorded to human life. These beliefs are related intimately to and rely on theological beliefs and convictions about who God is and how the divine relates to the created order.

There are several theological doctrines that come to bear on this parameter. The doctrine of creation is a coherent combination of basic affirmations about the created nature of all that is, that there is a divine creator whose presence is both transcendent to but also immanent in this creation, that humankind is created in the image and likeness of the divine other, and that humans are essentially free creatures who share responsibility in the unfolding nature of God's creative act. This doctrine also affirms the fundamental unity of the human body and spirit, and it professes that true humanity is found only in human community.

The doctrines of the fall, of the covenantal relationship between humanity and God, of the incarnation of Jesus Christ, of redemption, and of God's call to an ultimate future (eschatology) also contribute to and fill out the tradition's theological anthropology. Though all humanity is fallen due to human fault and continues to be prone to sin, the imperfection and sin that now infect our personal and social lives are neither all-pervasive nor ultimately victorious. All humanity is called again into a covenantal relation with God, and this covenant reaches its fulfillment in the incarnation of Jesus the Christ. This man, who is both fully human and fully divine, took upon himself all human malice by

99

freely accepting the cross. The redemption of all humanity, which was wrought through the death and resurrection of Jesus, not only heals us but it becomes the primary symbol of God's call for all to participate in the fullness of the divine future. God's eschatological future, which contains the fullness of all the created order and human history, is already partially present here and now in the preaching of the good news and in the personal and social relations that we create with one another.[23]

The theological convictions about the nature, situation and future of humanity both entail and generate basic value judgments about human life in general and about innocent human life in particular. Though these value judgments are deeply informed and supported by the scriptures and a doctrinal tradition, the Catholic church has consistently argued that the values themselves are available to rational human insight and reflection. Based on the privileged insight into the nature of true humanity, the resources of faith do enable Christians to articulate human values more clearly. However, religious resources themselves are not the origin of these values, that is, human values are neither divinely revealed nor in principle discoverable only by believers.

The most fundamental value judgment that applies to the discussion of abortion is concerned with the dignity and sanctity of each human life. The Catholic tradition has consistently affirmed this value judgment, as has the Christian tradition in general. The inherent and equal value of each human life is inferred from the beliefs that we are created in the image of God, redeemed by Jesus and called to a future destiny with God. What is noteworthy here is that the value judgment itself is based not on one Christian doctrine alone but on a series of doctrines, viz., creation, incarnation-redemption, and eschatology.[24] What is also noteworthy is that the theological or doctrinal grounding of this value judgment has not precluded the Catholic tradition from arguing that the value of human life can also be founded on humanist or rational grounds.[25]

Historically, a further specification of this general value judgment has been made to apply to *innocent* human life. In this case, all innocent life is valued as absolutely inviolable.[26] Because all nascent life is classified in this category, the fetus's life possesses this inviolable status. Now, two further interpretations have been added to this value judgment that fill out the Catholic position on abortion. The first interpretation, which I have already noted above, is that human life from the moment of conception must be respected and treated *as a person*.[27] This means that the fetus, like every other person, must be treated as possessing the fundamental right to life. The second interpretation, which is formulated as a moral principle, is that fetal life may never be directly taken, just as no other *innocent person's life* may be directly taken either as a means or as an end. As I will show later, the latter interpretation-principle is most often justified by reference to the theological affirmation that God alone is the lord of life and death.[28] What is both interesting and important here, however, is that this theological justification is used only when innocent life is at stake. I am not aware of any other instance of killing in which this theological affirmation is used to prohibit a deadly deed, e.g., in cases of capital punishment, self-defense and just war.

One further set of issues must be examined briefly before proceeding to a description and analysis of the anthropology that appears to predominate in U.S. secular society. These issues are concerned with the tradition's evaluations of the role of human freedom and choice, on the one hand, and of the responsible use of modern technology, on the other. These two evaluations are interconnected in the abortion debate, and both are determined to a large extent by the Church's theological anthropology and by a specific, but revisable, interpretation of divine providence.

First, the level of freedom that I am addressing is the capacity to choose. In the Catholic tradition freedom is only the presupposition or the *conditio sine qua non* for an action to enter into the moral order; the fact that a person has freely chosen to do something does not in itself make an action moral or immoral. As I will show below, this is important because some people in society hold to the view that the freedom to choose is not only an absolute value but that it alone is what makes actions right or wrong.

Second, a more problematic issue arises when one places human freedom in the context of modern technology and its application to issues of life and death. To rephrase the problem in terms of a question, one might ask—as the Catholic tradition has repeatedly done since the beginning of this century—should issues concerned with the beginnings of human life and with death be subjected to human choice and the application of technology?[29] In other words, do humans have the right to use technology over the origin and destiny of the human person? This is an important question because, as David Thomasma has rightly noted,[30] the responsible use of technology is the nub of the ethical problem with abortion.

In general, the Catholic church has evaluated the development and application of technology as at least ambiguous. Particularly in this century, one of the central concerns of the Church has been to protect the dignity and sanctity of the human person against the onslaught of burgeoning technology. Science and technology must be constantly evaluated in light of the fundamental criteria of the moral law, that is according to whether they are in the service of the human person.[31]

Has God shared divine power with humanity to intervene into the very processes of the generation of human life or to take life? This is a complex question, and it would require a more detailed analysis than I can provide here. However, the tradition's answer to the question is in the negative, at least as far as *innocent* human life is concerned. In the abortion debate, when humans use their freedom to employ technology in such a way as to directly take innocent life, they act from the lack of a legitimate right (*ex defectu juris in agente*), and their actions are judged to be intrinsically immoral. The theological position on divine providence adopted by the Church has been that God, as the lord of life and death, has decided to withhold from humanity the power over, and thus the right to kill, innocent human life. However, God has delegated to certain members of the human community, e.g., government officials or soldiers, the right to kill non-innocent human life. Thus, within the Catholic church there is more at stake in the abortion debate than merely the *moral* issue of directly killing innocent life. It also involves the *theological* issue of the life and death of the innocent being subject to human choice and technology within the context of a specific second-level interpretation of divine providence.[32] The obvious theological question that must be raised here is whether God has really reserved divine power over the life and death of the innocent, or whether, similar to all other areas of human choice, God has shared even this power with humanity so that the fate of the unborn is truly subject to *free* but *responsible* human choice.[33]

If we turn now to an analysis of the dominant anthropological views of U.S. society, what we find is a different interpretation of the nature of the human person and of human freedom and technology than that found in the Catholic tradition. The value judgments that will flow from this secular anthropology will sometimes be at variance with the Church's judgments on several key issues.

Robert Bellah and his colleagues have appropriately described the dominant anthropology in the U.S. as individualism. They borrow a quotation from Alexis de Tocqueville to define individualism as "a calm and considered feeling which disposes each citizen to isolate himself from the mass of his fellows and withdraw into the circle of family and friends; with this little society formed to his taste, he gladly leaves the greater society to look after itself."[34] Further refined, individualism becomes ontological in that citizens believe "that the individual has a primary reality whereas society is a second-order, derived or artificial construct."[35] Lying at the very core of modern American culture, individualism has increasingly pursued individual rights and personal autonomy in contrast to the biblical view of the essential sociality and inter-relatedness of the human family.[36] The liberal secular view does exalt the value of human dignity, and in this regard it would agree with the Catholic tradition. However, this liberal ethos interprets human dignity and its sacredness in an individualist and rights-oriented way. Consequently, the emphasis on protecting the individual's right to privacy generates the normative value judgment that, "Anything that would violate our right to think for ourselves, judge for ourselves, make our own decisions, live our lives as we see fit, is not only morally wrong, it is sacrilegious."[37] In assessing this perspective, Richard McCormick has stated accurately that, "The good life—and eventually the morally right and wrong—is irreducibly pluralistic, because it is tied to individual preferences, which are precisely individual."[38] The result is that genuine public discussion of complex moral issues such as abortion is thwarted, and so each person retreats into his or her own moral world where individual preferences hold sway. In this private world, morality becomes a matter of personal taste about which there can be little or no rational, public argument.

Joseph Tamney and his coauthors have argued that the defense of legalized abortion is rooted in individualism.[39] In attempting to increase the zone of privacy, American society has pursued the libertarian desire to limit the role of government.[40] In this sense, liberal society cherishes the Enlightenment stress on freedom *from* external constraint and authority.[41] Whereas the Catholic perspective has sought to place limits on the exercise of human freedom in its interpretation of divine providence, individualism has steadily fought to extend the role of freedom to include control over one's body and the fate of unborn life. In this sense, liberal society cherishes the modern technological emphasis on the freedom *to* control and to have dominion over the self and world. Freedom to choose is not merely the necessary condition for an action to be assessed morally, as it is in the Catholic tradition; freedom to choose alone is both necessary and sufficient in itself to make an action morally right.[42] The result is that individual freedom, understood now as autonomy and enshrined legally in the constitutional doctrine on privacy, not only is viewed by many as the central value at stake in the debate over abortion, but, as we shall see later, it trumps every other value in situations of conflict between maternal and fetal lives.[43]

As inveterate pragmatists, U.S. citizens place a high value on technology and its application to solve human problems. Their imaginations and feelings are so shaped by technology that they view the world through what Daniel Callahan has called the "power plasticity" model of reality.[44] The world and we are malleable, and the answer to both personal and social problems is to intervene with increasing technology. It is not difficult to conclude from this view of reality that technology creates its own morality based on human control and the imposition of free human choice. The development and use of technology in modern medicine, especially in the emergence of neonatal medicine, embryology and genetics, now control the very way that the whole abortion debate is framed.[45] Even the establishment of the time of viability by the Supreme Court in 1973 was itself controlled both by the general inability of medicine to care for fetuses whose gestational age was less than twenty-eight weeks and by the techniques available to determine genetic defects.

This brief review of the two different anthropologies and the value judgments that flow immediately from each of them was constructed to highlight some of the neuralgic points between the Catholic tradition and society's position on abortion. Failure to attend to the radical differences that endure at this level of the debate will inevitably continue the gridlock that we experience today. Though it is important to focus analyses at the *moral* level of this debate where questions of rightness and wrongness of abortion must be discussed, I have attempted to show that these analyses rely on deeper and more profound *anthropological* and *theological* analyses and basic value judgments that undergird and inform the moral life.

The second theological parameter that informs the Catholic position on abortion is ethical. The magisterial condemnation of all direct abortions is a complex normative judgment, and it is based on two distinct sources: one is an ethics that connects sex and procreation, and the other is an ethics of killing the innocent.[46] The tradition has argued that the conclusions of both ethics are grounded in a natural-law theory of morality, and so it is assumed by the magisterium that these normative judgments are in principle open to the ethical insight of all people of goodwill. Despite this assumption, however, many in society intensely disagree with the Catholic position on these two ethics. It is possible that only a minority of people in the U.S. believe that there is a necessary or essential link between sexual relations and procreation. Furthermore, one of the most disputed issues in the abortion debate among feminists and others who support a pro-choice stance concerns the value or innocence of the fetus. Consequently, the official Catholic position on the value of nascent life has been rejected repeatedly in favor of the value of the woman's right to choose.

(1) The Ethics of Sex and Procreation

The substance of the Catholic position on sex is that human sexuality is created by God and therefore constitutes a basic human good. It is a great gift from God by which humans share in the creative activity of the divine. Sexuality is neither divine nor is it demonic, but it can be turned to the service of God's kingdom.[47] The fact that Jesus took on all of human nature, including sexuality, testifies to the essential goodness of human sexuality. When this view of sexuality was made more concrete in the fourth and fifth centuries to counteract negative evaluations of the body and of procreation espoused by various factions, St. Augustine formulated second-level interpretations to protect the biblical and Christian view. These interpretations described human sexuality as created by God solely for the sake of procreation.

In the thirteenth century, Thomas Aquinas undertook the task of constructing a systematic and theological theory of natural law in which he argued that God had placed the sexual inclination in humans, just as God had done in the animal kingdom, for the sake of reproducing the species.[48] Noteworthy here is how Thomas interpreted God's creative intentions vis-à-vis human sexuality. He believed that some divine purposes for humanity are embodied in the nature of biological acts, e.g., sexual intercourse. Since God is the author of nature, to act against the divine purposes in nature was a direct affront against God. Aquinas defined the natural law as a participation of God's eternal law in a rational creature. At the level of the natural law that pertains to procreation, he argued that all humans absolutely know what the creator had intended when they engage in sexual intercourse.[49] The Thomistic positions on the natural law and on the ethics of sexuality were frequently adopted by subsequent theologians and popes.[50] Later, another second-level interpretation developed concerning the inseparable link between the unitive and procreative aspects of sexual intercourse. The application of this interpretation, which was formulated into a moral principle, prescribed that *each and every act* of marital sexual intercourse must be both an expression of love (unitive significance) *and* open to procreation.[51]

The import of this ethic of sex for our purposes is that all direct abortions sever what was willed by God as an inseparable link between sexual activity and procreation. Consequently, on the basis of this ethic the magisterium would condemn any action that intentionally terminates a pregnancy. Though the ethic is based on a theological understanding of natural law and thus God's purposes for humanity, again the tradition has consistently argued that the moral judgments that flow from this theory are available to all people.

(2) The Ethics of Killing the Innocent

The second ethic that applies to abortion in the Catholic tradition is the ethics of killing the innocent. Here we enter into the very heart of the magisterium's moral and theological position on abortion. It is also here that we encounter the absolute or exceptionless rule prohibiting all direct killing of the innocent either as a means or as an end. Theologically, the magisterium's interpretations of divine providence, the divine-human relation, the nature and scope of God's dominion and authority over life

106

and death, and the significance of redemptive suffering are the background to this ethic.

The Catholic Christian position has consistently understood human life to be a great and fundamental good, and consequently it has constantly taught the presumption against the taking of all human life. It seems to me that both this value judgment and the presumption against taking life make up the substance of the tradition.[52] On the other hand, the tradition has developed second-level interpretations to deal with conflict situations. Thus, the Church has morally permitted the taking of human life, e.g., in self-defense, just war, and capital punishment. The theological defense of this position is that God has delegated to humans the authority and responsibility in some circumstances to take non-innocent life, and the ethical rationale of the position can be traced back to a moral judgment about what would occur if all killing were forbidden. Theologically and ethically, the problematic issue in general is the killing of any innocent human life, but more specifically it is the *direct* killing of innocent life. Because the tradition morally permits the *indirect* killing of the innocent, it is erroneous to say that the Catholic church absolutely prohibits *all* abortions. In approaching this complex and problematic area in the Catholic tradition, it might be best first to define what "innocent" means and then to indicate briefly how the magisterium determines the directness or indirectness of killing through a discussion of the principle of double effect.

Though historically the term is not absolutely clear,[53] "innocent" has been used to place a limit on the prohibition against killing to instances where no material injustice was involved.[54] When Aquinas discussed the case of killing the innocent, he prohibited such taking of life because the righteous person does nothing to harm the community or the common good of society.[55] Thus, the innocence of a person seems to be determined morally on the basis of the absence of injustice being perpetrated on another person or on the community. Because the tradition has argued that the fetus in no way perpetrates any kind of injustice on either society or on the mother, even if it threatens maternal life by developing in an extrauterine site, the Catholic church judges all fetal life to be innocent life and thus inviolable from direct attack.

Notwithstanding its inviolability from direct assault, the fetus's life can be taken in certain circumstances of conflict. To understand how and why exceptions are made to the taking of innocent life, we must turn to a discussion of the principle of double effect.[56] This moral principle, which itself is a second-level interpretation of the conditions under which the presumption against killing can be limited, was established to deal with actions that produce more than one effect in conflict situations. It presumes that one effect of the action is good and that the other is evil, and then it seeks to determine if the *action* can be performed in such a way that the evil effect, e.g., death of the innocent, is not traced back to the will or intention of the agent. The principle is not applicable to just any action that produces two effects, one good and the other evil; it applies only to a certain class of actions whose evil *effect* is judged already to be *morally* evil.[57] In the issue of abortion, the actions that produce a morally evil effect are those performed from a lack of a legitimate right on the part of the human agent (*ex defectu juris in agente*). For these actions to be performed morally, and thus for the evil effect to be tolerated or permitted, all four conditions of the principle of double effect must be fulfilled. If the conditions are fulfilled, then the deadly act against the innocent is considered an indirect act of killing. On the contrary, a violation of any of the four conditions presumes that the agent intended the death of the innocent either as a means or as an end, and thus the action is prohibited absolutely. The four conditions of the principle of double effect follow:

1) The action, considered by itself and independently of its effects, must not be morally evil;
2) The evil effect must not be the means of producing the good effect;
3) The evil effect is sincerely not intended, but merely tolerated; and,
4) There must be a proportionate reason for performing the action, in spite of its evil consequences.[58]

In the twentieth century, the tradition has applied this principle to the potentially fatal cases of ectopic pregnancy and of a pregnant but cancerous uterus. Recently, the principle has been applied to instances of maternal hemorrhage during pregnancy and of all extrauterine pregnancies.[59] Surgical measures to save the mother's life are permitted in these situations even when fetal death is certain because the physician's action is aimed at curing a life-threatening condition of the woman. The mother's life is preserved by such actions without procuring the death of the fetus as the means to this end. If the medical procedure has only one effect, viz., the death of the fetus, or if it produces the good effect through or by means of the fetus's death, then the tradition assumes that the physician intended or wanted to kill innocent life. In the latter cases, the action is judged to be a direct abortion, and it is absolutely prohibited in every situation of conflict.

The ethics of killing the innocent, as interpreted and applied through the principle of double effect, is in fact a moral construct that is derived or inferred from a specifically theological interpretation of God's providence. The recent *Instruction on Respect for Human Life* has convinced me increasingly that the magisterium has adopted a rather anthropomorphic image of God in its theological interpretation of God's dominion and lordship over the life and death of the innocent.[60] This image construes God anthropomorphically by implying that the divine acts in the world in ways that are similar to how human agents act.[61] In other words, when God providentially acts in the world, the divine possesses certain rights and has a specific "place" in which to act. For example, one of the central reasons why the *Instruction* condemns the voluntary destruction of human embryos in cases of *in vitro* fertilization is because,

By acting in this way the researcher usurps the *place of God*; and, even though he may be unaware of this, he sets himself up as the master of the destiny of others inasmuch as he arbitrarily chooses whom he will allow to live and whom he will send to death and kills defenseless human beings.[62]

Not only does this image portray God as having a place to act, but it depicts the divine as possessing specific rights that belong exclusively to the divinity. The *Instruction* states,

Human life is sacred because from its beginning it involves "the creative action of God," and it remains forever in a special relationship with the Creator, who is its sole end. God alone is the Lord of life from its beginning until its end: No one can in any circumstances claim for himself the right to destroy directly an innocent human being.[63]

What is implied in this quotation is the narrowing of the prohibition against direct killing to innocent life. In other situations of conflict, the tradition permits the killing of human life, and this is justified on the basis that God has delegated to certain members of the human community the right to kill. As Jan Jans has argued, "If to speak of delegation, therefore, is to have any sense, it can only mean that God possesses certain categorical rights, which normally belong to Him exclusively, but which under circumstances can be delegated to humans."[64] On the other hand, God has not delegated to any member of the human community the divine right to directly kill innocent life, and thus God remains the sovereign over the life and death of the innocent. Consequently, it seems that the wrongfulness of directly killing a fetus is not derived from the intention of causing death; it is morally wrong on the theological grounds that God has not authorized such killing.[65] To act without divine authorization is to act from the lack of a legitimate right, and such actions are judged to be intrinsically morally wrong.[66] Because the indirect killing of the innocent does not violate God's sovereignty,[67] it can be performed licitly to save the life of another, e.g., a pregnant woman.[68]

One final issue remains to be discussed briefly at this point. The theological interpretation of God's dominion entails a theological corollary in the Catholic tradition. This corollary is concerned with an interpretation of the meaning and relevance of redemptive suffering. The tradition has taught that suffering is part of the human condition, but it is multiplied and made worse by sin. In most cases suffering ought to be relieved by human efforts, but in some situations it can and must be accepted redemptively. It seems that this is the substance of the Catholic tradition. However, when suffering can and should be alleviated, and when it must be endured redemptively, are determined not on theological grounds but on the basis of moral criteria. How the tradition determines when suffering is to be tolerated is dependent on a second-level interpretation that is itself open to reformulation.

When their actions conform to the moral law, human agents are considered to be co-creators with God. As co-creators they have the moral obligation and responsibility to relieve human suffering. On the other hand, when an action is judged to be immoral, e.g., on the basis of the principle of double effect, one's moral obligation is both to acknowledge God's sovereignty and to accept the suffering that results from obeying the moral law.[69] In the latter situation, humans are not considered to be co-creators with God in the relief of suffering; rather, they are creatures who must submit themselves to God's sovereign will and join their suffering to Christ's cross. The suffering that results from avoiding an immoral act such as the direct abortion of innocent life is not meaningless, and it is not without redemption. Thus, this interpretation of suffering is used as the theological justification for actions already judged to be right on moral grounds, and it is the theological warrant for prohibiting actions previously judged to be morally wrong.[70]

VALUE PARAMETER:
SCALE OF VALUES AND REASONS TO JUSTIFY ABORTION

The third theological parameter is concerned with a number of issues related to the concrete values at stake in the abortion question. The primary issue in the abortion debate revolves around the value that is or should be accorded to the fetus. In other words, the core issue is the evaluation or moral status of nascent life. However, there are always other important values involved in any decision to abort fetal life, e.g., the welfare of pregnant women, the freedom of women to determine their reproductive futures, and the interests of others—such as the father, family and community.[71] When two or more of these values conflict, which one takes precedence over the others? This question, then, asks whether there is a scale or hierarchy of values that comes into play in conflict situations such that values higher in the scale must be preserved at the expense of values lower in the hierarchy. Because values are used as reasons to justify or not to justify abortion, this issue is obviously concerned with the reasons considered morally sufficient to defend one's choice about abortion. Since all these issues rely on some explicit or implied moral theory about the nature and epistemological status of values, I will begin by briefly describing the moral theory adopted by the Catholic tradition.

The substance of the Catholic position on the moral theory of values and of the rightness and wrongness of actions can be described as moral realism. Values are objectively real, and they are capable of being grasped through human reason and experience. Rightness and wrongness of actions are objective judgments, and some views of what constitutes the good life are plainly superior to others.[72] This theory has historically been conveyed through a second-level interpretation called natural-law morality. One rendition of this natural-law morality—a rendition that appears to be adopted by the modern magisterium—purports that there exists a hierarchical order of values and goods such that there can be no true conflict of rights and obligations. As Josef Fuchs, S.J., once claimed about the abortion issue:

> There exists indeed *an order* of goods and values, of commands and demands through the very nature of things, so that there can be no true conflict of rights but at most an apparent conflict. The two obligations concerning a pathological birth, to preserve the life of the mother and not to kill the child, only seem to contradict one another. There is in fact no commandment to save the mother at all costs. There is only an obligation to save her in a morally permissible way and such a way is not envisaged in stating this given situation. Consequently only one obligation remains: to save the mother without attempting to kill the child.[73]

This interpretation of the objective and fixed order of values and obligations is clearly the backdrop for the Catholic position on abortion.

The Catholic tradition holds that all nascent life from the moment of conception is to be considered objectively valuable. The fetus possesses the objective right to life, which society must respect, and it must be treated as a person. As innocent, the fetus's life may never be taken as a means to a further value or as an end in itself. Though recent statements from the magisterium do recognize that there are difficulties when the value of innocent life comes into apparent conflict with other values in the situation, nonetheless the magisterium denies that these values can ever justify the direct killing of the fetus. As the *Declaration on Abortion* states:

> Divine law and natural reason, therefore, exclude all right to the direct killing of an innocent man. However, if the reasons given to justify an abortion were always manifestly evil and valueless the problem would not be so dramatic. The gravity of the problem comes from the fact that in certain cases, perhaps in quite a considerable number of cases, by denying abortion one

endangers important values to which it is normal to attach great value, and which may sometimes even seem to have priority. We do not deny these very great difficulties. It may be a serious question of health, sometimes of life or death, for the mother; it may be the burden represented by an additional child, especially if there are good reasons to fear that the child will be abnormal or retarded; it may be the importance attributed in different classes of society to considerations of honor or dishonor, of loss of social standing, and so forth. We proclaim only that none of these reasons can ever objectively confer the right to dispose of another's life, even when that life is only beginning.[74]

As this quotation makes clear, the magisterium denies that any value, as serious as it may be, can justify a direct abortion. Though one might offer genuinely important reasons for directly killing the fetus, these reasons can only make the abortion in some circumstances a lesser evil; the reasons themselves can never justify the act.[75]

It is frequently claimed by many in the abortion debate that, in arguing its position, the Catholic tradition denies the freedom of the woman. Several recent documents have addressed this claim,[76] even if the reply may appear less than satisfactory to many. The position espoused in these documents is that personal freedom must always begin by recognizing and respecting human relationships and justice.[77] Because a direct attack on nascent life violates its right to life, a woman's freedom to choose another value at the expense of the fetus's life would violate justice and her natural relationship to the fetus. Thus, the woman's right to self-determination is not denied; rather her right is placed within a hierarchy of rights that is both objective and fixed. Even in an indirect abortion, which is considered morally permissible under the principle of double effect, only the necessity to save the life of the mother can be used as a moral reason for indirectly aborting the fetus.[78]

When the Catholic position on this parameter is compared with the pro-choice position in secular society, several areas of disagreement become poignantly apparent. Pollsters continue to tell us that many U.S. citizens would personally permit direct abortions only in situations of rape, incest, or where the mother's life is endangered. However, less than two percent of the twenty-seven million abortions in this country have been performed for one or other of the above reasons; the vast majority of the fetuses were aborted as a form of birth control. At a public level, then, the right of the woman to autonomy continues to hold sway in the public mind. Perhaps Robert Bellah and his associates are correct that freedom "is the most resonant, deeply held American value,"[79] and so Americans appear to be publicly resistant to limitations on this value.

Though many U.S. citizens are not pro-choice at a personal level of morality, a certain moral agnosticism appears to pervade public life and morality. Pro-choice advocates in particular seem to hold to moral agnosticism as a moral theory, and this position is opposed to the Catholic position on value. In moral agnosticism one does not believe that there is any objectivity to values, or at least one has little confidence that values can be known. As David Carlin, Jr., describes this position:

> Thus there can be no agreement as to what constitutes the good life for human beings. Every person's individual view of the good life is just as valid as every other person's. If you and I differ in our moral views, there is no way either of us can prove the other wrong; all we can do is tolerate our mutual differences. But if there is no science of the good life and no inner light to reveal it to me, how do I find my values and my moral code? I choose; I simply choose; there is no alternative. In the world of the moral agnostic, choice is the essential action and tolerance the supreme virtue.[80]

There is also in the U.S. a popular morality or structure of moral thinking that is utilitarian.[81] Rightness and wrongness are determined solely on the basis of the results of actions. Because utilitarianism denies the intrinsic rightness or wrongness of actions and because it tends to view the person functionally, it too will clash with the Catholic position on the objective moral assessment of acts and on the intrinsic value placed on persons.

The evaluation of fetal life in the above perspectives will differ substantially from the Catholic tradition. Some view the fetus as living, but disposable tissue; others evaluate the fetus as making some moral claims on us, but these claims are overridden by either maternal or familial concerns.[82] In the first view, the fetus makes no moral claims on us whatsoever, at least not until the legally-established point of viability, and some forms of this position maintain that the value of the fetus is really contingent on the pregnant woman's bestowal of humanhood.[83] In the second view, there is some recognition of the value of fetal life, but the scale of values does not necessarily favor the fetus. In a 1987 survey, the following reasons and percentages were given by abortion patients. Three quarters of the respondents said that a baby would interfere with work, school or other responsibilities; two thirds said that they could not afford a child; and one half replied that they did not want to be a single parent or that they had problems in their relationship with husband or partner.[84] The clear implication of this survey is that a variety of personal, familial or economic values can and do override the value of fetal life, but the most important singular value seems to be the freedom of women to choose. There is little doubt, then, why the Supreme Court legally enshrined this value in its extension of the fourteenth-amendment liberty to include the freedom of women to choose an abortion.

Richard McCormick has proposed two different sets of rules to guide the public discussion of this debate and to help mediate the differences between the Catholic and societal positions.[85] Unfortunately, his efforts to find a mediating position have not been met with much success. In one way, given the opposing philosophical theories of value that are at work on each side, it is quite understandable, albeit distressing, that there is a lack of public support for discussion that attempts to appreciate the worth in each position.

LEGAL PARAMETER:
RELATIONSHIP BETWEEN CIVIL LAW AND MORALITY

The final parameter is concerned with the Catholic church's theological position on the relationship between civil law and morality. Broader issues lie behind this discussion, e.g., the general relation between religion and society and the relationship between church and state, but I will restrict my analysis to the narrower topic. We need to pursue briefly why the Church is involved in the public debate over abortion and how the tradition views the function of law in society. Historically, the Catholic tradition has focused on the legal and public implications of issues of conscience, although other Christian denominations have focused more on the moral limits of law and public policy.[86] In addition, the Catholic tradition has generally feared that the use of law primarily to protect the freedom of individuals could lead to moral anarchy, and such anarchy would hardly be conducive to making abortion unnecessary.[87]

Let me begin with what I take to be the substance of the Catholic tradition. If procured abortion is categorized as a religious issue and not as a moral one, then the controversy is immediately transposed into a debate about religious freedom. The consequence of this categorization is that pro-choice constituents will and do claim that one group cannot impose its religious beliefs and morality on others in a pluralist society.[88] However, the Catholic tradition does not consider abortion to be solely a religious issue. Abortion is essentially a moral issue, and the natural-law arguments designed to arrive at the Church's conclusion are considered to be intelligible to others on rational grounds. Thus in the Church's view, its doctrinal position on abortion does not result in the imposition of a specifically religious morality on society but rather represents a reasoned argument that can be accepted by many.[89] In addition, the substance of the tradition has contended that civil law and morality are objectively related to one another, and therefore human laws cannot be decided by mere judicial positivism, by simple expediency, or irrespective of moral criteria. There are both theological and moral reasons why the Church is involved in the public debate over abortion. The theological reasons are related to the tradition's various ways of relating civil law and morality,[90] and the moral reasons are concerned with both the rights of nascent life and justice in society.

The tradition has employed two distinct theological approaches to the relation between civil law and Christian morality.[91] Before Vatican II, the standard interpretation of this relationship was that civil law applied the natural law to the changing and particular cultural circumstances of different societies by promulgating the conclusions of the natural law directly or by specifying what the natural law had left undetermined. Though civil law was not identified with the natural moral law, nevertheless a very close relation was fashioned between the two. In this view, civil law is concerned with what is necessary for the common good, and it may tolerate moral evil to avoid greater evil in society or to protect a greater good. Just laws never violate the true freedom of citizens, but anything that is contrary to the natural law will ultimately produce bad consequences.[92] Thus in this first interpretation, the moral reason why the Church is involved in the abortion debate is because procured abortions violate the natural law by directing killing the innocent. As a result, this view frequently imposed obligations on civil authorities, especially on those who were Catholic, to pass various laws against procured abortions to protect the life of the innocent.

An alternative interpretation was adopted at Vatican II.[93] This approach makes a distinction between the secular and sacred orders of human life, and also between society and the state. In the latter distinction the state is viewed as playing a limited role in society because the purposes of the state are neither the same as nor coextensive with society's purposes. The state has the responsibility for the public order, i.e., the orders of peace, justice and public morality, which is only one aspect of the common good of society. The primary role and function of civil law in issues of *private* morality—actions that have little effect on others—was formulated by Vatican II as, "For the rest, the usages of society are to be the usages of freedom in their full range. These require that the freedom of man be respected as far as possible, and curtailed only when and insofar as necessary."[94] However, in matters of *public* morality—actions that have a greater impact on others in society—the state has the responsibility to protect the rights of individuals by serving the order of justice. The state can intervene through the passing of civil laws to limit the freedom of individuals when the rights of innocent people are being violated.[95] However, many would argue that even the intervention of the state through law can be limited by the criterion of feasibility. Within a pluralist society where people disagree on moral issues, the state must prudentially consider the practicality and feasibility of a law before enacting it to restrict people's freedom. Clearly, the ethos of a pluralist society would concur much more with this interpretation than with the one adopted before Vatican II.

Because the Church maintains that the fetus must be respected and treated as a person who possesses the right to life, it argues that the state must intervene to protect the fetus's right by limiting a woman's freedom to choose a direct abortion. In fact, this value judgment about the status of the fetus forms one of the bases for the moral reason why the Church is involved in the public debate over abortion. More specifically, because the moral rights of the innocent are violated in direct abortions, and thus the order of justice is thereby transgressed, not only the state but also the Church must be involved to find ways to prevent these actions.[96] The unanswered question raised by many in society about this second perspective, though, is whether any law that restricts a woman's freedom to a procured abortion can meet the test of the criteria of practicality and feasibility in a pluralist society. Many people of goodwill do not share the tradition's value judgment that fetal life is the moral equivalent of a person with legal rights, and this fact is a source of tremendous divergence between the ecclesial and societal positions. It is certainly possible that one could accept the Church's second approach to the relation between civil law and public morality but deny that the fetus has any moral status at conception. Consequently, if the fetus has little or no moral status at conception or somewhere else along the gestational continuum, then killing the fetus for the sake of other values would neither violate anyone's rights nor vitiate the orders of justice and public morality. I do think that most in society would accept the second formulation of the civil law-public morality relation, so the divergence between the two views continues to revolve around the moral status of fetal life.

Though the Catholic tradition has officially adopted the second theological approach to the relation between civil law and morality, several recent official documents on sexual and medical ethics have continued to use the first approach. For example, in the *Declaration on Abortion*, the Congregation for the Doctrine of the Faith states that, "It is true that civil law cannot expect to cover the whole field of morality or to punish all faults. No one expects it to do so. It must often tolerate what is in fact a lesser evil, in order to avoid a greater one."[97] This is the basic assumption of the first approach in that it assumes that the function of civil law is to apply the natural law.[98] Later in the document it is stated that

> The law is not obliged to sanction everything, but it cannot act contrary to a law which is deeper and more majestic than any human law: the natural law engraved in men's hearts by the Creator as a norm which reason clarifies and strives to formulate properly, and which one must always struggle to understand better, but which it is always wrong to contradict.[99]

It is obvious here that the Congregation holds to the first approach in which civil law must respect the natural law, and thus these human laws should not be contrary to God's moral law.

In conclusion, as long as one accepts the tradition's value judgment on the fetus's moral status, one *could* argue in either interpretation of the relation between civil law and public morality for a legal restraint on a woman's freedom to choose a procured abortion. However, the fact that official documents vacillate between two distinct theological interpretations has compromised the Church's efforts in its public arguments against direct abortion. This is especially true in a pluralist society that values individual freedom and restrains legal intervention as much as U.S. society does. It is equally true in a legal environment in which the country's highest court has subscribed to a constitutional doctrine that appears at face value to be a form of judicial positivism. As the Supreme Court has recently stated, this doctrine holds that "where reasonable people disagree the government can adopt one position or the other."[100]

CONCLUSION

My intention in this paper has been to locate and analyze some of the theological parameters that underlie the Catholic tradition's moral position on abortion. The Catholic position is rather complex, and so any reductionist or simplistic view of its moral position should be resisted in public debate. There are indeed several points of serious disagreement between the Catholic tradition and that of our secular society. Much of this disagreement revolves around the issues of anthropology, the moral status of the fetus, the meaning of sex and its relation to procreation, moral theory and how one resolves conflicts between values. To deal with these differences, though, it is most important not to focus simply on the conclusions that a tradition or a society can reasonably articulate and passionately support. My purpose here is not to underrate the significance of conclusions to moral issues; conclusions are significant, and they can result in immense political and moral consequences. However, behind people's moral conclusions to very complex questions there always exist fundamental beliefs about and basic value judgments on a host of issues. It is one's positions on these more essential issues, e.g., anthropology, and the nature and hierarchy of values, that determine conclusions. Informed discussion will not proceed to a more reasonable and just public policy on abortion until greater efforts are focused at these deeper and more enduring levels of the abortion debate. William Byron was correct indeed to remark that intellectuals *and* politicians have much work to do to accomplish this task.

When politicians engage the Catholic position on abortion within our pluralist society, it is helpful to recall that not everything found in this moral position is part of the substance of the tradition. Second-level interpretations and applications have been articulated historically in the tradition to specify and to make concrete what is held to be true and valuable at a more fundamental level. To call these parameters "variable" does not *necessarily* imply that they must change. However, I have used this language to indicate where perspectives and horizons for future discussion and possible change might exist on the Catholic side of the debate. I would assume likewise that there are "variable" parameters in society's position that provide the opportunities for future discussion and change.

To a great extent, the Church's position is controlled theologically by a certain "variable" interpretation of how God relates to humanity and to the created order. In turn, this rather anthropomorphic interpretation of divine providence influences a number of other important interpretations and value judgments, e.g., the immorality of directly killing the innocent, and the relationship between civil law and morality. If we were to understand that God operates most appropriately in the world through the exercise of free human activity, then we would realize that in fact we are the ones who are truly responsible for the decisions over life and death.

Despite potential abuse, such an interpretation would not make morality less objective, nor would it make us into gods. At the least, this view morally and politically would require us to create social and economic conditions that would make decisions for procured abortions far less likely.[101] In addition, it would require all of us to cooperate responsibly in fashioning a more reasonable and just public policy on abortion. To be sure, such a policy must meet the criteria of practicality and feasibility in a pluralist society, and it must accept the fact that people of goodwill can and will disagree. However, the policy can no longer be based on either moral agnosticism or on legal positivism. To reject both of these positions does not leave us with only one other option as the basis for public policy, viz., the existence of a concrete moral order that is already-out-there-to-be-looked-at-and-respected. We do have another option, and this realist position holds that values are indeed objective and

120

that we must create both moral and legal orders based on these values. Values will conflict in a finite and less-than-perfect world, and so we must responsibly choose which values we can and will preserve. Reasonable and objective criteria should guide our choices, and our attitudes should be to preserve as many values as possible in conflict situations. This implies that the resolution of value conflicts at the level of public policy cannot be decided by always preferring one of the values *regardless of the circumstances*, e.g., freedom of the woman to choose or the value of fetal life, or by denying the very existence of one of the values at stake. To settle this complex issue in either of those two ways is to abdicate the moral and political responsibilities that are truly ours to take up as God's gift and challenge.

NOTES

1. David R. Carlin, Jr., argues that the debate over abortion promises to be the deepest and most intense moral controversy since Prohibition or slavery. See his "The New/Old Abortion Battle: Taking Up Where We Left Off," *Commonweal* 118 (September 13, 1991): 505.

2. Congress currently is debating H. R. 25, the so-called Freedom of Choice Act, that would prohibit states from legislating abortion restrictions. For a response to this bill from the director of planning and information in the National Conference of Catholic Bishops, see Helen Alvare, "Testimony Opposing 'Freedom of Choice Act,'" *Origins* 21 (April 2, 1992): 692-96.

3. For a brief history and analysis of this intramural debate during the 1984 presidential campaign, see Richard P. McBrien, *Caesar's Coin: Religion and Politics in America* (New York: Macmillan Publishing Company, 1987), 135-68. For Mario Cuomo's lecture that he delivered at the University of Notre Dame on September 13, 1984, see his "Religious Belief and Public Morality: A Catholic Governor's Perspective," in Patricia Beattie Jung and Thomas A. Shannon, eds., *Abortion and Catholicism: The American Debate* (New York: Crossroad Publishing Company, 1988), 202-16.

4. William Byron, S.J., "Abortion Debate: How Intellectuals and Moral Leaders Can Help Politicians," *Origins* 22 (June 18, 1992): 81 and 83-87.

5. The literature discussing the morality of abortion is voluminous. For a brief sample of the literature dealing with the Catholic moral position, see Jung and Shannon, *Abortion and Catholicism*; Susan T. Nicholson, *Abortion and the Roman Catholic Church* (Knoxville, TN: Religious Ethics, Inc., 1978); Germain Grisez, *Abortion: the Myths, the Realities, and the Arguments* (New York: Corpus

Books, 1970); Edward Batchelor, Jr., ed., *Abortion: The Moral Issues* (New York: Pilgrim Press, 1982); and John Connery, S.J., *Abortion: The Development of the Roman Catholic Perspective* (Chicago, IL: Loyola University Press, 1977).

6. Stephen Happel and James J. Walter, *Conversion and Discipleship: A Christian Foundation for Ethics and Doctrine* (Philadelphia, PA: Fortress Press, 1986), 125-26.

7. There is a hierarchy of truths or doctrines in the Catholic tradition. As the Second Vatican Council maintained in its *Decree on Ecumenism* (*Unitatis Redintegratio*), "When comparing doctrines, they [Catholic theologians] should remember that in Catholic teaching there exists an order or 'hierarchy' of truths, since they vary in their relationship to the foundation of the Christian faith" (§11). See Walter M. Abbott, S.J., ed., *The Documents of Vatican II* (New York: America Press, 1966), 354.

8. The distinction that I am making between substance (constant) and inter-pretation-application (variable) is similar to the one that Richard McCormick has made between a principle and a formulation-application. See Richard A. McCormick, S. J., *The Critical Calling: Reflections on Moral Dilemmas Since Vatican II* (Washington, D.C.: Georgetown University Press, 1989), 147-53.

9. For a concise summary of the many positions on abortion among Christian denominations and non-Christian religions, see The Park Ridge Center Report, *Abortion, Religion, and the State Legislator after "Webster": A Guide for the 1990s* (Chicago, IL: The Park Ridge Center, 1990), 12-16. In addition, for a concise description of the various moral positions on abortion within the American Jewish communities, see Scott Aaron, "The Choice in 'Choose Life': American Judaism & Abortion," *Commonweal* 119 (February 28, 1992): 15-18.

10. There is only one reference in the Hebrew scriptures that deals explicitly with the issue of abortion (Exodus 21: 22-23), and it seems that this text is concerned primarily with meting out a penalty for a man who strikes a pregnant woman and causes her to miscarry her fetus.

11. See Connery, *Abortion*, 105-224; and the Sacred Congregation for the Doctrine of the Faith, *Declaration on Abortion* (Washington, D.C.: USCC, 1974), §7.

12. *Declaration on Abortion*, n. 19; the Sacred Congregation for the Doctrine of the Faith, "Instruction on Respect for Human Life in Its Origin and on the Dignity of Procreation," I, 1, in *Origins* 16 (March 19, 1987): 701; and Connery, *Abortion*, 212. Over the past several decades several contemporary Catholic theologians and physicians have argued that hominization is not possible until after developmental, and not merely biological, individualization has occurred around the fourteenth day after fertilization. For a sample of the literature arguing this position, see Andre E. Hellegers, M.D., "Fetal Development," *Theological Studies* 31 (1970): 3-9; Charles E. Curran, "Abortion: Law and Morality in Contemporary Catholic Theology," *The Jurist* 33 (Spring 1973): 162-

83; Gabriel Pastrana, O.P., "Personhood and the Beginning of Human Life," *The Thomist* 41 (April 1977): 247-94; Norman Ford, S.D.B., "When Does Human Life Begin?: Science, Government, Church," *Pacifica* 1 (1988): 298-327; Thomas A. Shannon and Allan B. Wolter, O.F.M., "Reflections on the Moral Status of the Pre-Embryo," *Theological Studies* 51 (December 1990): 603-26; and Richard A. McCormick, S.J., "Who or What is the Preembryo?," *Kennedy Institute of Ethics Journal* 1 (March 1991): 1-15. For a recent article that strongly opposes this position, see William E. May, "The Moral Status of the Embryo," *Linacre Quarterly* 59 (November, 1992): 76-83.

13. The phrases "respected as a person" or "treated as a person" occur several times in the *Instruction*. For example, see Part I, 1 (pp. 701-2 in the *Origins* edition).

14. *Instruction*, Foreword (p. 699 in *Origins* edition).

15. *Instruction*, Introduction, 5. (p. 701 in the *Origins* edition).

16. *Declaration on Abortion*, §11.

17. *Declaration on Abortion*, §7; and *Instruction*, I, 1 (p. 701 of the *Origins* edition). Both documents are either quoting or paraphrasing a remark made by Paul VI in one of his speeches entitled *Salutiamo con paterna effusione*, which was delivered on December 9, 1972.

18. In the *Dogmatic Constitution on the Church* (*Lumen Gentium*) at the Vatican II it is stated that even non-infallible teachings impose on Catholics an obligation of "religious submission (*obsequium religiosum*) of will and of mind" (§25). See Abbott, *The Documents of Vatican II*, 48. To say the least, the precise meaning of "religious submission" has been debated by contemporary theologians and canonists.

19. There is a hierarchy of authority in official Catholic documents. The fact that all the documents on abortion reviewed thus far have come from a Roman congregation indicates that these teachings do not possess the same weight and authority as those from a pope or a council. The intent of most of these documents is to recall or to clarify teachings, not to proclaim new teaching.

20. As the *Declaration on Abortion* states, "Respect for human life is not just a Christian obligation. Human reason is sufficient to impose it on the basis of the analysis of what a human person is and should be" (§8). This position has been regularly stated by Cardinal Bernardin in his various speeches on the "consistent ethic of life." For a collection of his speeches, see Thomas G. Feuchtmann, ed., *Consistent Ethic of Life* (Kansas City, MO: Sheed & Ward, 1988). For a more detailed discussion of reason's ability to reach conclusions on abortion, see the commentary in *Ethics and the Search for Christian Unity: Two Statements by the Roman Catholic/Presbyterian-Reformed Consultation* (Washington, D.C.: USCC, 1981), 8, 17-18.

21. For example, Paul VI devoted several paragraphs of his encyclical on birth control *(Humanae Vitae,* §§10-12) to natural-law arguments against all

artificial means of regulating births. The CDF also devoted the entire third part of its document on abortion (*Declaration on Abortion*, §§8-13) to a consideration of the immorality of procured abortion *in the light of reason*. Similar claims and arguments are made in the CDF's document on sexual morality. See the *Declaration on Certain Questions Concerning Sexual Ethics* (Washington, D.C.: USCC, 1976), §3.

22. Though I would argue that this claim is central to the Catholic position, nonetheless it a claim that has been debated among contemporary theologians. For a collection of recent essays on the issue of whether Christian faith adds new content to the moral life, see Charles E. Curran and Richard A. McCormick, S. J., eds., *Readings in Moral Theology No. 2: The Distinctiveness of Christian Ethics* (New York: Paulist Press, 1980).

23. For a more comprehensive account of the tradition's theological anthropology, see "The Pastoral Constitution on the Church in the Modern World (*Gaudium et Spes*)," Part I, in Abbott, *The Documents of Vatican II*, 209-48.

24. For example, see *Gaudium et Spes*, §29; and the *Instruction on Respect for Human Life*, Introduction, 5. (p. 701 of the *Origins* edition).

25. See the *Declaration on Abortion*, §8; and the NCCB's *Documentation on Abortion and the Right to Life II* (Washington, D.C.: USCC, 1976), 24. David Thomasma has argued recently that the inherent and equal value of all human beings can be grounded on philosophical and political views of the human person. See David C. Thomasma, *Human Life in the Balance* (Louisville, KY: Westminster/John Knox Press, 1990), ch. 6 and 7.

26. For example, see the *Instruction on the Respect for Human Life*, Introduction, 5 (p. 701 of the *Origins* edition).

27. Paul VI did not formulate the status of the fetus in exactly these terms, but he did describe nascent life as *une personne en devenir* (a person in the process of becoming). See Pope Paul VI, "Pourquoi l'église ne peut accepter l'avortement," *Documentation Catholique* 70 (1973): 4-5.

28. For example, see the *Instruction on the Respect for Human Life*, Introduction, 5 (p. 701 of the *Origins* edition).

29. This question has been asked consistently whenever a new technology has been developed and then applied to life and death issues. For example, Paul VI raised this question in his encyclical on artificial birth control (*Humanae Vitae*, §§2-3), and the CDF raised the same query with regard to modern reproductive technologies in its *Instruction on Respect for Human Life*, Introduction, 1 and II, B, 5 (pp. 699 and 707 respectively in the *Origins* edition).

30. Thomasma, *Human Life in the Balance*, 147.

31. For example, see the *Instruction on Respect for Human Life*, Introduction, 2 (p. 699 in the *Origins* edition).

32. Denis O'Callaghan has pointed out that traditional Catholic morality made exceptions to moral principles, e.g., no killing of the innocent, "where

these depended on chance occurrence of circumstances rather than on free human choice." Thus, the tradition made exceptions precisely because "the occurrence of the exception was determined by factors of chance outside human control." When O'Callaghan applied his point to the issue of abortion, he argued that in cases of tubal pregnancies the tradition "accepted what is in principle an abortion because it posed no threat to the general position." In other words, the "tubal pregnancy is a rare chance occurrence, an occurrence which is independent of human choice and so does not lay the way open to abuse." See Denis O'Callaghan, "Moral Principle and Exception," *The Furrow* 22 (November 1971): 686-96, especially at 694. In my opinion, as long as the tradition was assured that the deadly deed against innocent life was not subject to human choice but was due only to factors outside human control, the right of God to be the lord over life and death was protected against human striving to usurp God's providential power.

33. For a more extensive discussion of how different views of human freedom and technology play an important role in the religious debate on abortion, see John Badertscher, "Religious Dimensions of the Abortion Debate," *Studies in Religion* 6 (1976-77): 177-83. Charles E. Curran has argued recently that "the Catholic tradition in moral theology in the past and also today does not and should not appeal to divine providence in any way to change, alter, or attenuate human responsibility and actions in this world." See his *The Living Tradition of Catholic Moral Theology* (Notre Dame, IN: University of Notre Dame Press, 1992), 213. I agree with the general substance of Curran's argument, but I think that there is one exception where his assessment of the tradition does not apply, viz., when the tradition attempts to resolve conflict situations in which the death of an innocent person is a foreseen consequence.

34. Robert N. Bellah et al., *Habits of the Heart: Individualism and Commitment in American Life* (San Francisco: Harper & Row, 1986), 37.

35. Bellah, *Habits of the Heart*, 334.

36. For an excellent contrast between liberalism and communitarianism as ways of interpreting the human condition, see David Hollenbach, S.J., "Liberalism, Communitarianism, and the Bishop's Pastoral Letter on the Economy," in D. M. Yeager, ed., *The Annual of the Society of Christian Ethics* (Washington, D.C.: Georgetown University Press, 1987), 19-40.

37. Bellah, *Habits of the Heart*, 142.

38. McCormick, *The Critical Calling*, 220. In a section below (C. Value Parameter) I will argue that in many cases the moral theory of rightness and wrongness that lies behind this individualist perspective is moral agnosticism.

39. Joseph B. Tamney, Stephen D. Johnson, and Ronald Burton, "The Abortion Controversy: Conflicting Beliefs and Values in Society," *Journal for the Scientific Study of Religion* 31 (March 1992): 32-46.

40. Tamney, Johnson, and Burton, "The Abortion Controversy," 33.

41. Bellah and his coauthors also note that Americans place a high value on being free *from* any type of external limitation. See Bellah, *Habits of the Heart*, 25.

42. For a critique of this view of morality as exclusively a matter of human agency and freedom, see Sidney Callahan, "Abortion and the Sexual Agenda: A Case for Prolife Feminism," in Jung and Shannon, *Abortion & Catholicism*, 133-34.

43. For an interesting analysis of the anthropology adopted by the Supreme Court in the *Roe* v. *Wade* decision, see Edward McGlynn Gaffney, "Law and Theology: A Dialogue on the Abortion Decisions," *The Jurist* 33 (1973): 134-52, especially 142-50.

44. Daniel Callahan, "Living with the New Biology," *Center Magazine* 5 (1972): 4-12.

45. Daniel Callahan, "How Technology is Reframing the Abortion Debate," *Hastings Center Report* 16 (February 1986): 33-42.

46. This is the thesis of Susan Teft Nicholson's monograph on the ethics of abortion within the Catholic tradition. See her *Abortion and the Roman Catholic Church*.

47. James P. Hanigan, *What Are They Saying About Sexual Morality?* (Ramsey, NJ: Paulist Press, 1982), 12.

48. Thomas Aquinas, *Summa Theologiae*, I-II, q. 94, a. 2.

49. For a more comprehensive study of both St. Augustine's and St. Thomas' positions on the nature of human sexuality and its relation to procreation, see Louis Janssens, *Mariage et Fécondité: De "Casti Connubii" à "Gaudium et Spes"* (Paris: Editions J. Duculot, S.A., Gembloux, 1967), especially 13-61.

50. Both Pius XI in his encyclical *Casti Connubii* (1930) and Paul VI in his encyclical *Humanae Vitae* (1968) accepted Thomas' natural-law position on the link between sexuality and procreation.

51. For example, see Paul VI, *Humanae Vitae*, §12; and CDF, *Instruction on Respect for Human Life*, II, B, 4 (p. 705 in the *Origins* edition).

52. Richard McCormick also holds this conclusion. See his *The Critical Calling*, 150.

53. See Lisa Cahill, "A 'Natural Law' Reconsideration of Euthanasia," *Linacre Quarterly* 44 (1977): 47-63.

54. McCormick, *The Critical Calling*, 226.

55. Thomas Aquinas, *Summa Theologiae*, II-II, q. 64, a. 6.

56. Despite the fact that the premises of this principle can be found in Aquinas' *Summa Theologiae*, II-II, q. 64, a. 7, the conditions of the principle date from the sixteenth and seventeenth centuries. The precise formulation that is used today dates from the mid-nineteenth-century manual *Compendium Theologiae Moralis* by Jean Pierre Gury. For an historical study of the principle,

see Joseph T. Mangan, S.J., "An Historical Analysis of the Principle of Double Effect," *Theological Studies* 10 (1949): 41-61. Over the past several decades the validity of the principle of double effect has been contested. For a collection of essays that assess this principle, see Charles E. Curran and Richard A. McCormick, S.J., eds., *Readings in Moral Theology No. 1: Moral Norms and Catholic Tradition* (New York: Paulist Press, 1979).

57. The Catholic tradition has recognized that there are different kinds of evil. Some evils are natural, e.g., tornadoes, some are physical evils, e.g., amputation of a limb, but other evils enter into the moral order and thus are assessed as moral evil. The crucial issue is on which grounds does the effect of an action enter into the moral order and thus become subject to a negative moral evaluation. I will argue below that the grounds are principally, though not only, theological in nature.

58. Gerald Kelly, S. J., *Medico-Moral Problems* (St. Louis, MO: The Catholic Hospital Association, 1958), 13-14.

59. See the *Ethical and Religious Directives for Catholic Health Facilities* (Washington, D.C.: USCC, 1971), §§13-17.

60. Jan Jans also draws this same conclusion in his assessment of the 1987 *Instruction.* See his "God or Man?: Normative Theology in the Instruction *Donum Vitae*," *Louvain Studies* 17 (Spring 1992): 48-64.

61. See Josef Fuchs, S.J., *Christian Morality: The Word Becomes Flesh* (Washington, D.C.: Georgetown University Press, 1987), 40-44 and 71-73.

62. *Instruction on Respect for Human Life* I, 5 (p. 703 in the *Origins* edition). Emphasis mine.

63. *Instruction on Respect for Human Life*, Introduction, 5 (p. 699 in the *Origins* edition).

64. Jans, "God or Man?," 58.

65. See Bruno Schüller, S.J., "The Double Effect in Catholic Thought: A Reevaluation," in Richard A. McCormick, S.J., and Paul Ramsey, eds., *Doing Evil to Achieve Good: Moral Choice in Conflict Situations* (Chicago, IL: Loyola University Press, 1978), 189.

66. See Josef Fuchs, S. J., *Christian Ethics in a Secular Arena* (Washington, D.C.: Georgetown University Press, 1984), 78-80 and 102-4.

67. David F. Kelly, *The Emergence of Roman Catholic Medical Ethics in North America: An Historical-Methodological-Bibliographical Study* (New York: The Edwin Mellen Press, 1979), 275.

68. An alternative to this anthropomorphic interpretation of how God relates to humanity and to the world is to construe God as the transcendent other who immanently acts through free human activity. In this image, God is neither another actor in the world alongside human agents, nor does God possess certain categorical rights, some of which are delegated and some of which are exclusively reserved to the divine. For a further discussion of this image of God,

see Happel and Walter, *Conversion and Discipleship*, 89.

69. See David F. Kelly, *The Emergence of Roman Catholic Medical Ethics in North America*, 276. A clear example of this reasoning is found in the *Instruction on Respect for Human Life*, II, 8. (p. 708 in the *Origins* edition). Also, see the *Declaration on Abortion*, §24, where heroism is called for to remain faithful to the requirements of the moral law, and §27 where redemptive suffering is the theological consequence of remaining faithful.

70. For an analysis of how the liberal ethos in society views sacrifice and suffering, see Lisa Sowle Cahill, "Abortion, Autonomy, and Community," in Jung and Shannon, *Abortion & Catholicism*, 91-92.

71. For a brief discussion of some of these values, see Lisa Sowle Cahill, "Abortion," in James F. Childress and John Macquarrie, eds., *The Westminster Dictionary of Christian Ethics* (Philadelphia, PA: The Westminster Press, 1986), 1-5.

72. For a further discussion of moral realism in relation to the abortion issue, see Carlin, "The New/Old Abortion Battle," 505.

73. Josef Fuchs, S. J., *Natural Law: A Theological Investigation* (New York: Sheed and Ward, 1965), 131. Emphasis in the original. It is doubtful that Fuchs himself any longer holds to such a position.

74. *Declaration on Abortion*, §14.

75. See the commentary in the document containing the joint statement on abortion by the Roman Catholic/Presbyterian-Reformed consultation, *Ethics and the Search for Christian Unity*, 18.

76. For example, see the *Declaration on Abortion*, §15.

77. See the NCCB's *Documentation on Abortion and the Right to Life II*, 11. Also, see the *Declaration on Abortion*, §20, where the CDF clearly states that, "One cannot invoke freedom of thought to destroy this life" (fetal life).

78. See the commentary in the joint statement by the Roman Catholic/Presbyterian-Reformed consultation, *Ethics and the Search for Christian Unity*, 19.

79. Bellah, *Habits of the Heart*, 23.

80. Carlin, "The New/Old Abortion Battle," 505.

81. Richard A. McCormick, S. J., *How Brave a New World?: Dilemmas in Bioethics* (Washington, D.C.: Georgetown University Press, 1981), 204.

82. McCormick, *How Brave a New World?*, 191.

83. For an analysis and critique of this perspective, see S. Callahan, "Abortion and the Sexual Agenda," 134.

84. *Chicago Tribune* (Sunday, July 5, 1992): 4, 1.

85. Richard A. McCormick, S. J., "Rules for Abortion Debate," *America* 139 (1978): 26-30; and "Abortion: The Unexplored Middle Ground," *Second Opinion* 10 (March 1989): 41-50.

86. See the commentary in the joint statement by the Roman Catholic/Presbyterian-Reformed consultation, *Ethics and the Search for Christian*

Unity, 3-4.

87. Roman Catholic/Presbyterian-Reformed consultation, *Ethics and the Search for Christian Unity*, 21-22.

88. McBrien, *Caesar's Coin*, 167.

89. This is the constant claim by Cardinal Joseph Bernardin in his many speeches on the "consistent ethic of life." See Fuechtmann, *Consistent Ethic of Life*.

90. To pursue adequately all the theological reasons, it would be necessary to discuss in some depth what the Church understands its general mission to the world to be. This ecclesiological parameter is beyond the immediate scope of the paper. For a recent article that describes how ecclesiology shapes Catholic public policy on abortion, see J. Bryan Hehir, "Policy Arguments in a Public Church: Catholic Social Ethics and Bioethics," *The Journal of Medicine and Philosophy* 17 (June 1992): 347-64.

91. Charles E. Curran has succinctly summarized these two approaches in his *Ongoing Revision: Studies in Moral Theology* (Notre Dame, IN: Fides Publishers, 1975), 107-43. The standard and most formative scholarship done in this area remains the work written by John Courtney Murray. For example, see Murray's *We Hold These Truths: Catholic Reflections on the American Proposition* (New York: Sheed and Ward, 1960) and *The Problem of Religious Freedom* (Westminster, MD: The Newman Press, 1965).

92. Curran, *Ongoing Revision*, 121-22.

93. See the "Declaration on Religious Freedom" (*Dignitatis Humanae*), in Abbott, *The Documents of Vatican II*, 675-700.

94. *Dignitatis Humanae*, §7.

95. *Dignitatis Humanae*, § 7, footnote # 20

96. This moral argument was used by Archbishop John R. Roach and Cardinal Terence Cooke in their testimony before Congress. See their "Testimony in Support of the Hatch Amendment," in Jung and Shannon, *Abortion and Catholicism*, 29-30. Also, see Cardinal Joseph Bernardin's statement on abortion in the NCCB's *Documentation on Abortion and the Right to Life II*, 38.

97. *Declaration on Abortion*, §20. For a similar argument, see the *Instruction on Respect for Human Life*, III (p. 709 in the *Origins* edition).

98. Curran, *Ongoing Revision*, 137. Also, see Richard M. Gula, S.S., *Reason Informed by Faith: Foundations of Catholic Morality* (Mahwah, NJ: Paulist Press, 1989), 254-55.

99. *Declaration on Abortion*, §21. For a similar argument, see Paul VI's encyclical on birth control, *Humanae Vitae*, §23. This kind of reasoning also appears to be the rationale used in the revised version of the document on discrimination against homosexuals by the Congregation for the Doctrine of the Faith. See "Responding to Legislative Proposals on Discrimination Against

Homosexuals," *Origins* 22 (August 6, 1992): 173-77.

100. See the Supreme Court's ruling on the Pennsylvania Abortion Control Act, Part I, in *Origins* 22 (July 9, 1992): 116.

101. Bishop Untener's pastoral letter to Catholics in Saginaw, Michigan who are contemplating an abortion decision is one of the most compassionate and far-reaching proposals for change of social conditions that I have read. See Bishop Untener, "Those Struggling with Abortion Decision," *Origins* 21 (January 16, 1992): 516.

Catholic Commitment and Public Responsibility

Lisa Sowle Cahill

INTRODUCTION OF THE PROBLEM

The Roman Catholic Church teaches that direct abortion is always wrong—but U.S. culture, with its political traditions of individual liberty, accepts that a woman's "right to choose" is part of her reproductive self-determination. The Catholic politician often experiences a clash of duties: to be faithful to his or her religious community, and to serve the public within the parameters established by American law and judicial precedent. How can these duties be brought together in forming abortion policy?

It is important at the outset to note three points about the public character of the Church's engagement on abortion: 1) The Catholic Church does not base its abortion teaching on magisterial authority primarily, but on natural law. In other words, the position is not advanced as a matter of faith or religious belief as such, but as a requirement of broadly shared values deriving from a reasonable recognition of the nature and value of human life: 2) Although Catholicism's "pro-life" advocacy is often criticized as dogmatic and authoritarian because it is advanced by a religious body, it is erroneous to think that any individuals or groups could instead assume some other secular or "neutral" posture which is tradition-free. Religious, philosophical, and moral commitments back all participants in the abortion debate, and none should be excluded for that reason: 3) The key question thus becomes how best to engage various communities in the public debate in a positive, constructive, mutually respectful way, in order to reduce abortions and improve the situations of the women who seek them. How can the Catholic politician further this goal?

Because of the network of problems of which abortion is the outcome and symptom, I believe that Catholic opposition to abortion-on-demand may not translate easily or practically into public advocacy for the recriminalization of abortion. Other alternatives may be both politically and morally preferable, as suggested by Supreme Court's Missouri (*Webster*) and Pennsylvania (*Casey*) decisions. Positively, these decisions tend to return moral debate about abortion to the local community. They hold out to Catholic politicians the possibility of creating greater social consensus about how to recognize the seriousness of the abortion "choice," and how to reconcile values such as care for the unborn, the welfare of families, roles of women in public and professional life, greater personal investment of men in the family, and the duty of all to work toward the benefit of those socially least well off. As such consensus grows, abortion may be limited, even as the freedom and welfare of women and families is enhanced.

Abortion has often been approached in an essentially individualist way by Roman Catholics; we need to draw on the social tradition of the Church to build a community of support around pregnant women. Too frequently, the morality of abortion is posed in terms of a conflict of individual rights (mother and unborn child), with social consequences of abortion policy construed primarily in terms of potential threat to additional individual lives. Yet Thomas Aquinas, whose thought is the foundation of Roman Catholic moral theology, does not even use the term "individual rights." Instead, the dignity and welfare of the individual is placed in the context of a rightly ordered community, in which each member participates by contributing to the common good and having a share in its benefits. This approach has been developed further in the Catholic social encyclicals.

What would a view of abortion look like that was anchored more firmly in Catholic social ethics? It would draw on the social justice tradition of Catholicism in order to develop a more positive and supportive approach to women, children, and families, especially in the event of a problem pregnancy. It would be more sensitive to the ways in which reproductive roles have an impact on women's equality, and would support the life of the unborn in ways which do not undermine the social progress of women. It would assist Catholic politicians at the practical level in developing policy which not only protects the unborn, but furthers the social roles of women by providing economic and educational support. It would recognize that "conscience" is not merely an inner moral compass, but a capacity for moral discernment which is formed in community and is responsible to enhance the community as ensuring the right of all persons to participate in the common good.

The politician is a public actor with public roles and responsibilities; indeed the complexity of these responsibilities no doubt is often the source of his or her experience of lack of "fit" between perceived church teaching on abortion and perceived public responsibilities. One initially attractive solution is to relegate the Roman Catholic tradition on abortion to a "private" or at least "religious" realm which can be segregated from one's formal political role. Yet, since abortion is a social and moral issue, as well as a personal and religious one, the "personal religious belief" vs. "public role" split is not an adequate solution to political responsibility on abortion. If abortion is about basic human welfare, then pluralism about its permissibility cannot be accepted simply under the aegis of "religious freedom" or "individual conscience."

This paper will explore these issues in four parts: I. The status of *Catholic teaching* about abortion, especially as a conflict of fetal and maternal needs; II. *Abortion and social justice*, including the nature and purpose of abortion-related laws; III. *"Conscience"* as a concept with which the Catholic politician might understand his or her responsibilities in relating the morality of abortion to its legality; IV. Present *policy opportunities*, especially to influence public consensus about the morality of abortion.

ROMAN CATHOLIC ABORTION TEACHING

There are three aspects of the tradition which I wish to address here: the immorality of abortion, the status of the embryo/fetus, and the status and social position of women. It has been noted frequently and truly that the Christian community has from its beginnings consistently taught the immorality of abortion—but it has not always done so in the same way and for the same reasons.[1] Several factors are interrelated in the moral approach to abortion. The first two are the value of procreation as an outcome of sexual activity and the value of unborn human life, considered in its own right. A third is the value of the pregnant woman, including not only the modern value of a right to self-determination, but, more traditionally, her protection from physical, mental, and social harm. Finally, the interests of others, such as the husband/father, the family, and the religious and civil communities can all be weighed into the moral significance of pregnancy and childbirth. The moral dilemma of abortion arises precisely because these values and interests cannot always be realized simultaneously, and because their relative priority in the conflict case may not be a matter of clear consensus.

Generally speaking, Christianity places abortion in the context of respect for the lives of all human persons, and of the prohibition of the killing of the innocent. However, the Church has not been univocal in determining the point in the process of conception, gestation, and birth, at which the unborn offspring of human parents deserve the full respect and protection due "innocent persons." In addition, there has been some pluralism on the circumstances which morally might justify resort to abortion, and on whether morally justifiable abortions must always be "indirect." Much less, of course, has the Church been consistent in recognizing for pregnant women a right to self-determination and a sphere of well-being distinct from that of the family and *paterfamilias*.

The bible itself makes scant reference to abortion. The New Testament rejects evil drugs or potions (*pharmakeia*), which may include abortifacients (Gal 5:20; see, Rev 9:21, 18:23, 21:8, 22:5). Explicit condemnations of abortion and infanticide occur in two contemporaneous catechetical writings (the *Didache*, or *Teaching of the Twelve Apostles*, and the *Epistle of Pseudo-Barnabas*). In the New Testament period and in the three centuries following, during which Christianity spread in the Greco-Roman world, the cultural milieu included dualistic philosophical and religious sects which contrasted the body with the soul, and disparaged sexual union as merely a vehicle for the entrapment of souls in matter. More widespread was a low valuation of life in the womb, as well as of infants, so that both abortion and infanticide were widely practiced. Moreover, abortion could be a means of disguising illicit sexual activity, and at the least was an interference in the natural sequence of the reproductive process.

In the early church, condemnation of abortion focuses particularly on the integrity of the reproductive process and its contribution to marriage, the immorality of fornication and adultery, the value of life in utero, and the duties of mothers to love their offspring (Clement of Alexandria, the *Pedagogue*; Tertullian of Carthage, *The Veiling of*

Virgins). Though they all disapprove of abortion, Tertullian, Jerome, and Augustine distinguish stages of fetal development which make a difference in defining the act of abortion. Before a certain stage, abortion was not homicide, but more equivalent to contraception, that is, a violation of the nature of sex and reproduction. They distinguish between the formed and unformed, ensouled and unensouled, or "animated" or unanimated fetus, indicating that the soul is not infused by God until the body has developed appropriately. For instance, Augustine says that the fetus is animated (ensouled) at forty-six days, even though both contraception and abortion are condemned, even in marriage (*On Marriage and Concupiscence*).

A contributing factor in the lack of distinction between contraception and abortion was the lack of knowledge in the ancient world about human reproductive biology. The common belief that the semen contained the miniature "man" (the *homunculus*) meant that wasting of seed would be considered the moral equivalent of abortion of at least an unformed fetus.

Thomas Aquinas likewise did not hold that ensoulment occurs at conception, but followed Aristotle's estimate that the male fetus is ensouled at forty days and the female at ninety (*Commentary on Book III of the Sentences of Peter Lombard*). Aquinas (following the Septuagint translation of Ex 21:22-23) says that one who causes an abortion by striking a pregnant woman commits homicide only if the fetus is formed (Summa Theologiae II-II., q. 64. a. 8).

The distinction between the ensouled and unensouled fetus was influential until the eighteenth century, while theologians debated whether some consideration might override the value of fetal life, especially before ensoulment. Most important was preservation of the life of the mother, though health and reputation are also considerations. In the eighteenth century, church teaching turned strongly toward treating the unborn with the care due any human person, and in the next century, limited even "life against life" abortions to those in which the procedure is aimed primarily at relieving a condition of the mother, so that the fetus is only "indirectly" destroyed. The two most frequently cited examples of indirect abortion are the removal of a cancerous uterus from a pregnant women, and the removal of a inflamed fallopian tube resulting from an ectopic pregnancy. In 1889 the Holy Office ruled that it was not morally safe to perform any operation directly destroying the fetus, even though without it, both mother and child would die. In 1869, the penalty of excommunication had been exacted against those who performed abortions, and the 1917 Code of Canon Law explicitly extended excommunication to "mothers" who procure abortion as well.

Condemnations of abortion in the present century appear in the 1930 encyclical on marriage, *Casti connubii*, which rejects the idea that the "innocent" unborn can in any way be considered an unjust aggressor; Vatican II's *Gaudium et Spes* (1965), which refers to abortion as an "unspeakable crime"; and the 1974 Vatican *Declaration on Abortion*, which calls abortion "a question of human life, a primordial value, which must be protected and promoted" (§1).[2] This last document denies the proposition that the right to life can vary by stages, and presents "modern genetic science" as confirming (though not proving) this fact. Cautioning that "it is not up to the biological sciences to make a definitive judgment on questions which are properly philosophical and moral, such as the moment when a human person is constituted or the legitimacy of abortion," the *Declaration* nonetheless concludes that even if doubts exists as to whether "the fruit of conception is already a human person," "it is objectively a grave sin to dare to risk murder" (§13).[3] The essential position that the status of the embryo and fetus is a philosophical point not definitively settled by science, and that, given the doubt, the embryo must be treated as if it were a person from conception, is reiterated in the 1987 *Instruction* on reproductive technologies (*Donum Vitae*).[4] "The human being is to be respected and treated as a person from the moment of conception; and therefore from that same moment his rights as a person must be recognized, among which in the first place is the inviolable right of every innocent human being to life" (I.1).

Partly because the latter document was issued to deal with widening use of reproductive therapies in the West, and also because of the development of new abortifacient methods of birth control, such as RU-486, the discussion of the status of the unborn has continued in recent months, revolving around the earliest stages, up to implantation at about fourteen days.[5] Norman Ford's *When Did I Begin?* is part of a proliferating literature taking up the question whether there may be any significant developmental stages in embryonic-fetal development which can be associated with developing "personhood." Although Ford, an Australian priest, maintains that he does not intend to challenge the magisterium's present decision to protect the zygote from its first

136

moments, he nonetheless subjects that teaching to scientific and philosophical scrutiny. Indeed, he even aims "to prove that the commonly accepted assumptions of the broader community and of the Church lack the necessary biological and philosophical support."[7] Ford argues that there is no "living ontological individual" as long as the cells of the zygote are in their totipotential state, since twinning is still possible. It is only at the primitive streak stage, when individuality is settled, that ensoulment can take place. Among those who support Ford is Richard McCormick, who contends in an article covering both public policy and magisterial statements on the subject, that "the moral status—and specifically the controversial issue of personhood—is related to the attainment of developmental individuality (being the source of one individual). This contrasts with the view that holds that personhood occurs earlier, at the point of genetic uniqueness."[8]

Why is this history of church positions on the embryo, fetus, and abortion relevant to our discussion here, and why is it important to note some of the directions of the ongoing debate? In order to respond adequately to current teaching it is crucial to realize three things. First, there has been and continues to be qualification and development in the Roman Catholic tradition on abortion. Second, the current magisterial position is not presented as definitive and absolute, particularly concerning the status of the embryo/fetus, which has bearing on the classification of early abortion as a moral action. Third, the teaching of the magisterium does not warrant appeal to scientific information about the genotype or development of the unborn human being as though it were philosophically or morally conclusive. Much of the current North American debate about abortion—its morality and legality—makes precisely the opposite assumptions about what it is that the Catholic Church in fact holds.

An important aspect of Roman Catholic abortion teaching is its approach to the role and status of women. Clarifying the evolution of this approach will be important in setting the abortion question in the context of a fully *social* ethics, and especially in relating Catholic commitment to the North American political scene. Although Thomas Aquinas wrote that woman was created by God solely to be a help to man in the work of reproduction,[9] Catholic theology and social teaching have moved gradually to expand women's roles, even while giving a certain precedence to the maternal one. It also recognizes that personal and social conditions may make maternity a difficult burden for many women, and that women's situation is frequently characterized by the marks of social injustice. Thus, to outlaw abortion as "an unspeakable crime" is not an adequate solution to the abortion problem.

Support for this conclusion may be drawn from Roman Catholic teaching documents. The 1974 *Declaration* recognizes this fact to an extent, but its clear and insistent subordination of the mother's welfare to that of the embryo's existence in even the earliest stages, while logically consistent with its position on the conceptus, still comes across as less than fully empathetic in regard to the plight of some women. For instance, even if it is "a serious question of health, sometimes of life or death, for the mother, "none of these reasons can ever objectively confer the right to dispose of another's life, even when that life is only beginning" (§14). At the same time, the Declaration does acknowledge that the "movement for the emancipation of women, in so far as it seeks essentially to free them from all unjust discrimination, is on perfectly sound ground" (§15), and that social help should be assured for unmarried mothers (§23).

Concern about the social rights of women is reiterated in writings of John Paul II, and has been applied in our own context by the National Conference of Catholic Bishops. In *Familiaris Consortio*,[10] the pope affirms the "equal dignity and responsibility of men and women," and concludes that it "fully justifies women's access to public functions." "On the other hand the true advancement of women requires that clear recognition be given to the value of their maternal and family role, by comparison with all other public roles and all other professions," although these various roles should be "harmoniously combined" (§23). The dignity of women claims male support both in society and in the family. Among the offenses against women's dignity, John Paul includes discrimination against "unmarried mothers" (§24). In his 1988 letter, *Mulieris Dignitatem*,[11] he elaborates on the maternal role in honor of the Marian Year, but also adopts recent feminist biblical interpretations to show that, according to Genesis, women and men were created in a state of equality, not subordination (§6), and that a woman, Mary Magdalene, was the first witness to the resurrection and "apostle to the apostles" (§16). Drawing on the episode in John (8: 3-11) of the woman caught in adultery, the pope notes that the "historical situation of women" is "weighed down by the inheritance of sin," expressed for instance in "habitual discrimination against women in favor of men." "Jesus seems to say to the accusers, Is not this woman, for all her sin, above all a confirmation of your own transgressions, of your 'male' injustice, your misdeeds?" (§14).

Referring to just those cases of pregnancy which often result in abortion, the pope continues. "A woman is left alone, exposed to public opinion with 'her sin,' while behind 'her' sin there lurks a man—a sinner, guilty 'of the other's sin,' indeed equally responsible for it." Yet all too often, "she alone pays and she pays all alone!" Social forces and lack of support too often lead women to the extreme solution of abortion.

> How often is she abandoned with her pregnancy, when the man, the child's father, is unwilling to accept the responsibility for it? And besides the many 'unwed mothers' in our society, we also must consider all those who, as a result of various pressures, even on the part of the guilty man, very often 'get rid of' the child before it is born (§14).

A female student at Columbia College once wrote a letter to the editor of the *New York Times* which confirmed many of the pontiff's perceptions of the situation of many young women. Living in "a society dominated by the male libido," she has the "power" to choose either the pill, with its potentially serious side effects; or to elect "less effective forms of birth control, which afford her monthly anxiety the likes of which young men have never experienced." If birth control fails,

> she has the power to 'choose' to become a mother or to deny herself motherhood. Either way, she must face another choice. If the baby is born, society lets her raise the child alone, or give it up for adoption and wonder all her life about the benevolence of the adoptive parents. If the baby is aborted, and society pats her reassuringly on the back, she can either succumb to consuming regret or stubbornly bury it each time it resurfaces.[12]

Insofar as this student speaks for a relatively privileged group, we are reminded that many women seeking abortions would face not only loneliness in parenting their children, but also serious financial and social deprivation. What about pregnant teenagers, poor women, women who are victims of domestic abuse, and women who suffer discrimination on the basis of race or ethnicity?

At the same time, this letter reminds us that economic factors are only a part of the problem of abortion. The typical abortion client is white, unmarried, middle-class, and between the ages of nineteen and twenty-one. The Columbia student indicates rightly that many of these young women do not have the confidence and self-esteem to act as autonomous and integral moral agents in the realm of sexuality. They are pressured by the demands that a patriarchal society encourages their partners to make, and they lack a sense of moral power adequate to enable them to choose their sexual relationships with full knowledge of and preparation for the consequences. Does Catholic teaching on sex and gender encourage or discourage a sense of moral self-determination for women? Catholicism has a valid and needed message on the importance of mutuality, fidelity and responsibility in sexual relationships, along with accountability for their procreative potential. However, this message is often undermined by the Church's still ambiguous message on the full familial and domestic equality of men and women.

The placement of abortion in a social context of economic discrimination against women, denial of equal male and female accountability for sex and procreation, and lack of real alternatives to the abortion decision for many set a social context for the moral evaluation of abortion which leads us to the next topic of abortion and law. The fundamental points which I will make are the following. The prevention of abortion is an appropriate public policy issue, to which Catholic legislators should be committed. However, the criminalization of the abortion act itself is an insufficient and perhaps even immoral response to abortion. This would be especially true if such a measure were adopted in disregard of the full teaching of the Church about pregnancy, children, and families; or without serious attention to the valid feminist claim that women's dignity requires equality in the family and in society.

ABORTION AND SOCIAL JUSTICE

Catholicism's approach to abortion, justice, and the law is rooted in its social justice tradition. A representative modern restatement of the heart of that tradition, drawing on Aquinas's notion of the common good as grounding the duties of individuals toward one another and toward the community, is contained in John XXIII's 1983 encyclical *Pacem in Terris* (*Peace on Earth*). First of all, "the common good of all embraces *the sum total of those conditions of social living whereby men are enabled to achieve their own integral perfection more fully and more easily*" (§58). Moreover, "since the whole reason for the existence of civil authorities is the realization of the common good," they must "respect its essential elements, and at the same time conform their laws to the needs of a given historical situation" (§54). In the modern papal social encyclicals, both rights and duties are connected with the common good. In U.S. episcopal teaching, the relation of individuals to the common good is envisioned in terms of *participation*. "*Social justice implies that persons have an obligation to be active and productive participants in the life of society and that society has a duty to enable them to participate in this way.*"[13] The center of Catholic tradition does not construe morality primarily in terms of rights, although rights language has become increasingly prominent in its twentieth century vocabulary. The basic premise, however, continues to be intrinsic sociality and hence the interdependence of persons. Rights exist as the necessary conditions of full social participation. Furthermore, they correlate with duties of social support, both civil and material. The basic right to life is a right of both the fetus and the mother; the right to the necessary social conditions of "participation" is a right of women, children, and families. "Participation" is a prominent theme in the U.S. bishops' economics pastoral as a way of relating individuals to the common good.[14] Catholic politicians, of course, must be sensitive not only to the right to life, but also to the right of social participation which fulfills life's promise. The social tradition of Roman Catholicism runs counter to the individualism of much of U.S. political and popular culture.

These affirmations about the common good, rights, duties, and participation are not derived primarily from any religious premises or dogmatic traditions of Catholicism. They are premised on a commitment to an objective moral order, the "natural law," which is in principle knowable by reason, and which can form the basis of a social consensus among persons and groups who may differ religiously and culturally. Religious themes, values, and symbols help highlight human values, but in the Catholic natural law tradition, moral knowledge is not dependent on religious authority. On this natural law basis, the Church itself claims to have a right and duty to participate in the political process in order to

141

ensure that common human values will be embodied in the institutions and practices of a society.

The contemporary rise of historical consciousness has clarified, however, why not all of the Church's moral teachings are readily accepted as reflecting common human insights about justice. In the first place, Catholic interpretations of the natural have been influenced in specifiable ways by the religious tradition in which they are undertaken. John T. Noonan, Jr., an important commentator on both the law and the morality of abortion, has noted that the Catholic tradition on abortion "is particularly rich in interaction between specifically supernatural themes—for example, the Nativity of the Lord and the Immaculate Conception of Mary—and principles of a general ethical applicability." Although its basic assumption of the equality of human lives is broadly accessible within Western humanism, the abortion teaching "in its totality cannot be detached from the religious tradition which has borne it." This is especially true of "its reliance on ecclesiastical authority to draw a line" around precisely which exceptions to the prohibition of abortion will be accepted and which rejected.[15] In the second place, there is no tradition-free ground on which to stand for "neutral" conversation with other actors in the public realm. Philosophers such as Alasdair MacIntyre[16] and theologians such as Jeffrey Stout,[17] George Lindbeck,[18] and Ronald Thiemann[19] have finally brought home the point that, in Stout's memorable phrase, there is no privileged "vantage point above the fray."[20] Or, as MacIntyre has it, "there is no standing ground, no place for inquiry, no way to engage in the practices of advancing, evaluating, accepting, and rejecting reasoned argument apart from that which is provided by some particular tradition or other."[21]

The language of neo-Thomist representations of Catholic social teaching does seem to suggest that natural law conversations among "all men of good will" can in fact proceed on such a universal, purely human and non-religious, non-cultural basis, and even that such an objective basis is a prerequisite to progress toward morally solid laws. It might, however, be better to see the language of "nature," "rights," and "reason" as a consensus-building language in our modern Western culture, one which is broadly enough shared because of our common membership in the Western political tradition, so that it can establish common ground among communities which may differ in other respects—philosophically, religiously, politically, ethnically.

142

The distinctive Catholic contribution to such a conversation could be the presumption that shared values will in fact reliably be discoverable, because—grounding the particularity of communities and encouraging their mutual understanding—there is a common human sense of values, however historically and partially expressed within the worldviews of the conversation partners. We can contrast the perspectives of Martin Marty (a Lutheran church historian) and of Bryan Hehir (a Catholic social ethicist) on this point. Both are highly supportive of church involvement in the public realm. But for Marty, religious thinkers can be successful because the "typical citizen" is dissatisfied with the spiritual shallowness of liberal culture, and is ready to use the religious community as a refuge for gathering strength to renew involvement; "the religious 'help' the liberal culture along because they return to it, having changed it somewhat and themselves more."[22]

According to Hehir, a key source of moral wisdom in the Catholic view is the "natural law ethic." "The dignity of the human person, protected by rights and duties rooted in human nature, is the standard in light of which every social system is judged."[23] In the first case, religious communities jostle in the public realm and make their distinctive contributions because they may find a sympathetic hearing among those who find the dominant discussion arid; but in Hehir's case, there is an assumption that the varied participating communities can *count on* values they have in common, and, moreover, have an obligation to clarify these as a part of public discourse toward the moral improvement of social systems. Although the objective moral order which traditionally has grounded the Catholic approach is now recognized not to be so easily or unambiguously accessible to well-intentioned reformers considering law in a rational mode, the commitment to an objective moral order is still alive in an epistemologically more modest guise. Religious groups may join other citizens in seeking a more just and more equitable continuation of the common life, and may make relevant contributions to reform of policy and law.

In defining the appropriate scope of law, and distinguishing law from morality as such, Catholic theologians and social ethicists often appeal to the work of John Courtney Murray. Murray makes a particularly central distinction between the common good and the public order, in light of which it becomes clear that legislation cannot secure the entirety of the common good, but has a delimited role within it. "The common good includes all the social goods, spiritual and moral as well as material, which man pursues here on earth in accord with the demands of his personal and social nature." The "public order," on the other hand, "is a narrower concept," and is the responsibility of the state. "It includes three goods which can and should be achieved by . . . the coercive discipline of public law."[24] These are the public peace, public morality (commonly accepted moral standards), and justice (what is due in light of the natural law, especially freedom and personal and social rights). Obviously, to argue that civil law properly restricts the right to choose abortion is to assume that abortion represents a conflict of the rights and freedoms of the mother and rights of the unborn offspring, and that it is incumbent upon the state to protect both. But it is also a legitimate and necessary function of law and policy to address another side of the conflict: enhanced social participation as a need of women and families.

Given Catholicism's protective attitude toward unborn life, it urges those responsible for civil law to extend that same protection, even from "the moment of conception." The *Declaration on Abortion* rejects as justifications for permissive laws, both the freedom to choose abortion as a lesser evil, and the harm that clandestine abortions might do to women. It also notes that lack of penal sanctions against abortion might be interpreted as a positive authorization. Support of such sanctions will indicate that the legislator "considers abortion a crime against human life" (§20). A law which would "admit in principle the licitness of abortion" is immoral, and the Christian can never comply with it, vote for it, or "collaborate in its application" (§21). The law should be an instrument to reform society, and to bring human behavior into closer conformity to "the natural law engraved in men's hearts by the Creator," which reason struggles to interpret.

Concurring in the outlines of this argument, *Donum Vitae* asserts that the "public authority" should be "inspired by rational principles," and that the "task of the civil law is to ensure the common good of people through the recognition of and the defense of fundamental rights and through the promotion of peace and of public morality." The "inalienable rights of the person" derive not from positive law alone, but "pertain to human nature and are inherent in the person" (III). However, the document also adds both that civil law cannot "take the place of conscience," and that law "must sometimes tolerate, for the sake of public order, things which it cannot forbid without a greater evil resulting" (III).

In these examples of teaching, the following points are prominent: 1) Civil law is based on rational principles and human nature, and the "Catholic" argument is a "human" moral argument which speaks to the moral principles grounding law; 2) Law protects the common good and fundamental rights deriving from human nature, especially the right to life; 3) Abortion is a violation of the right to life of the unborn, a claim advanced as a proposal of natural law (not religious authority); 4) Rejected arguments in favor of permissive abortion policy are that a restrictive law causes more harm in the form of illegal abortions, and that individuals must have the freedom to choose, in line with their own moral convictions. Both of these considerations are of less weight than the right to life of the fetus; 5) No one may vote for, collaborate with or implement an unjust law approving abortion "in principle"; 6) Legal reform should be undertaken as a path to social reform.

Granting the fundamental viability of the proposal that civil law can and should meet the test of common human values, and that the religious identity of the Catholic Church creates no obstacle to its participation in public discourse about law, points 3-6 above will still bear further scrutiny. Regarding point 3, the proposition that abortion is a violation of the right to life of the unborn, it must still be asked whether the scientific and philosophical evidence supports or undermines the full personal status of the embryo/fetus, about which the magisterium acknowledges doubt. In relation to point 4) about the overriding value of the embryo/fetus in comparison to considerations of harm or self-determination, one may question whether, if there is significant doubt about the full personal status of the embryo especially, then it follows that the doubt must always be resolved in favor of the embryo. What if immediate harm to the mother is grave and certain, whereas the violation of the "right to life" of an "innocent *person*" as a result of abortion is extremely uncertain? This is a question worth considering (and one which need not lead in the direction of a "pro-choice" position, even if more latitude is given to the mother than in current official teaching).

In response to point 5), it can be asked whether permission of abortion within certain parameters necessarily amounts to approval of abortion "in principle," or to what extent it does. To say that abortion is morally *neutral* is different from maintaining that it can be justified in some *exceptional* circumstances, and it is even further from holding that it is not always appropriately *punished*.[25] Further, does cooperation with

145

a law which does not perfectly reflect the moral realities necessarily denote approval? Standard criteria of a just law include the requirements that it be nondiscriminatory, not create greater evils than it avoids, and command enough respect to be enforceable. Absent these characteristics, a politician or legislator prudently might choose to defer enactment of a law which conforms to a moral ideal, but which in its practical consequences could contribute to injustice and hence to distrust of the law itself. A familiar objection to the "repeal" of *Roe* v. *Wade* is that it would contribute to the marginalization of poor women who would resort to incompetent and often unscrupulous practitioners in a desperate effort to end their pregnancies; who would lack the bare minimum of material welfare necessary to raise their children; who would have less access to birth control; and who might have fewer personal and cultural defenses against male expectations that women be sexually available and then assume both social and financial responsibility for resulting children. Respect for the law as a moral educator would have scant opportunity to flourish in the face of such results.

Abortion often is compared to slavery on the grounds that it violates the rights of a vulnerable minority, and that social change by means of coercive law is matter of justice, whether there is a social consensus supporting it or not, and whether or not some in the "oppressor class" might suffer immediate ill effects. While recognizing that slavery provides a compelling reason to regard the standard criteria of just law as non-absolute, one may still note that slavery and abortion are not parallel cases in every respect. First, the physiological, cognitive, and emotional resemblance of a black adult to a white one is certainly more firm than that of an embryo or an early fetus to a child; secondly, the master-slave relationship violated basic rights of the latter, while securing no similar rights of the former. In the case of abortion, it is acknowledged even in the magisterial teaching cited above that unavailability of abortion can place a woman at the ultimate risk.

Finally, with respect to point 6, which implies the educative and symbolic as well as the coercive functions of law, it can be noted that abortion laws carry symbolic meanings in more than one realm. A challenge for the Catholic position is to represent effectively the same symbolic endorsement of women's full equality, social participation, and rights as is now represented by the pro-choice position and policy. To many women, "pro-choice" is a flag which represents reproductive and

146

social justice. The symbolic power of abortion rights, much less the legitimacy of the agenda for equality which lies behind it, is simply not addressed by a single-issue focus on the right to life of the fetus. Neither can the status of the fetus be ignored—and it is a status which in my view is considerable, even if not the equivalent of full personhood from conception. But consistency with the full spectrum of Catholic teaching about abortion-related social issues demands attention to instruments of social reform in addition to and other than the recriminalization of abortion.

In a comparative study of abortion law,[26] Mary Ann Glendon notes that liberalization in most European countries occurred as a result of public debate contributing to a revised consensus. Even in highly pluralistic cultures, such as Great Britain, religious groups were not necessarily excluded from the political process. Only two of twenty countries studied (Ireland and Belgium) retained comprehensive prohibitions against abortion. Eleven countries, including the UK (England, Scotland, and Wales), allowed abortion "with cause" and contingent upon review. The actual accessibility of abortion continued to vary, however. The United States was among six countries which allowed elective abortion, at least in the first trimester. But, Glendon maintains, the 1973 Supreme Court decision in *Roe* v. *Wade* shortcircuited the process toward moderate change which was permitted to occur in Britain and elsewhere. *Roe* allowed the woman virtually absolute freedom to terminate her pregnancy in the first or second trimester, but at the same time isolated her as an individual decision-maker from the social and economic supports which might have provided access to realistic options other than abortion. Consequently, freedom of reproductive choice is illusory rather than real, and in fact provides a facade behind which the American public can appear supportive of women while denying them access to the socially more expensive choice of childbearing and parenthood. Daniel Callahan, an honest critic of his own finally pro-choice position, asks, "is it wholly an accident that our country combines the world's most liberal abortion laws with the poorest social support and systems for women, mothers, and children?"[27]

Although the compromise statute which might have emerged from the legislative process in the United States might have been permissive in the first trimester, it might also have employed moderate restraints on later abortions to affirm a moral ethos valuing children, women and the family, and providing alternatives other than abortion in the case of problem pregnancies. As Glendon suggests, "mores, not the law, are the best protection of the weak and dependent."[28] Even a law which permits abortion in some circumstances may have a more beneficial effect than either a law which holds fetal life to be of little value, or a law which is interpreted by many to signify disrespect for women and the integrity of their moral choices.

Among the most neglected words in the *Declaration on Abortion* are those which urge us to see that "it is above all necessary to combat (abortion's) causes," and "to do everything possible to help families, mothers, and children" (§26). Help for families and for unmarried mothers, assured grants for children, a statute for illegitimate children and reasonable arrangements for adoption—a whole positive policy must be put into force so that there will always be a concrete honorable and possible alternative to abortion (§23).

In summary, the moral obligation of Catholic legislators is to seek the support for women, children, and families which would decrease the number and degree of maternal/fetal conflicts and make the legal exclusion of abortion choice more credible. Legislative options may include the "discouragement" of abortion, along with "encouragement" of other solutions. Some of these options will be considered in the final section of this paper.

CONSCIENCE

The term "conscience" connotes to many an internal norm of decision-making—the sum total of one's inmost convictions and commitments. Conscience may be formed in interaction with Catholic tradition and other moral wisdom, but it is held together at bottom by a sort of innate, God-given, core knowledge of right and wrong. A definition current in Catholic thought of three decades past probably continues to describe pretty well the idea many people hold of conscience: "a judgment of the intellect, dictating what is to be done as morally good, or what is to be avoided as morally wrong, in the particular circumstances in which one is now placed."[29]

Conscience is both the ultimate guide to action, and a forum of immunity from external coercion. Vatican II reaffirmed the inviolability of conscience as the keystone of support for religious liberty: "man perceives and acknowledges the imperatives of the divine law through the mediation of conscience. In all his activity a man is bound to follow his conscience faithfully. . . . It follows that he is not to be forced to act in a manner contrary to his conscience."[30] And the Council also contributed to the view of conscience as an internal, God-given gauge: "in the depths of his conscience, man detects a law which he does not impose upon himself, but which holds him to obedience. . . . Conscience is the most secret core and sanctuary of a man. There he is alone with God, whose voice echoes in his depths."[31] In the realm of politics, conscience is often used either to separate personal morality from public responsibilities, or in a declaration of independence from received traditions, existing laws, or social pressure.

In the present discussion, "conscience" will likewise be used to mediate among the Roman Catholic official's multiple identities, as, for instance, church member, American citizen, and public representative. But this will be accomplished with a slightly different spin. In contrast to the usual understanding of conscience, its social and interactive dimensions will be developed. Conscience is not primarily a realm apart from external relationships, but the individual's mode of adapting and internalizing those relations, enabling him or her to respond to them uniquely through effective action. The tradition's way of handling the interactive aspect of conscience was via the idea that conscience must be "correctly formed." As Richard McCormick colorfully puts it,

> We are members of a community and we form our consciences in a community, a community of experience, memory, and reflection. People who think themselves autonomous in the formation of conscience are roughly analogous to patients who make their own diagnoses. Theirs is a path to the intensive care unit, and eventually to the morgue.[32]

St. Paul used a Greek work for conscience, which was common in the secular literature. He used it to indicate a law written on the heart, a moral guide even for pagans (Rom 2:15), which serves as a standard of individual moral rectitude (Acts 24:16; 1 Tim 1:19f).[33] But conscience is a social category also, as when Paul urges some of the Church members at Corinth to abstain from eating meat which had been offered to idols—not because it was intrinsically wrong, but because it might offend and lead away from the faith others who had "weak consciences" (1 Cor 8:10-12). Above all, Paul always defined the Christian life in terms of the "Body of Christ" and urged his followers to determine right and wrong in relation to what "builds up" the community, and what destroys it (1 Thess 5:11).

The major source for defining conscience in the Catholic tradition is Thomas Aquinas, who actually used several interrelated concepts. Most importantly, while Aquinas saw morality in terms of rational reflection on human tendencies and purposes, and on human fulfillment, he understood moral reflection to be carried out very much on the basis of human moral experience in community. There is a habitual knowledge in all persons of the most fundamental principles of the natural law (*synderesis*). However, the way basic principles (such as "preserve life") are specified for social life and for action requires that generalizations from experience be nuanced to the specific situation or social context. Objective ethical truth requires conditioning in light of all the morally relevant particularities of a situation.[34] Aquinas uses the word *conscientia* for the act of applying moral principles to particular actions.[35] Moreover, moral virtue requires the intellectual virtue of prudence, enhanced by experience, which permits the person to choose the right means to an end. Aquinas situated the intellect in a social and practical context. Moreover, in addition to the intellect, the emotions or passions are important elements in Thomas's ethics. To be virtuous is to educate the emotions properly so that they will support the will in inclining toward the true good for humanity, discerning the appropriate middle path between possible extremes.[36]

Owing to the complexity of the tradition, some contemporary authors thus distinguish at least three senses of "conscience," through which they attempt to confirm that conscience is not only an innate judging ability, but also a process of developing and internalizing a moral "sense" in relation to one's community, finally resulting in an informed judgment about appropriate action. Conscience can refer to a basic sense of value grounded in a knowledge of what it is to be human; to a process of grasping particular moral truths by making use of various sources of moral wisdom; or to a concrete judgment about a required action here and now.[37]

Recent work in community-oriented forms of "narrativist" ethics stresses the experiential and communal formation of moral identity.[38] What is "read" in the heart requires a process of interpretation within a framework provided by a critical reappropriation of one's context. Conscience is not just an ability to apply given norms, but "an organ of the interpretation, valuation and moral judging of human realities."[39] In her recent book, *In Good Conscience*, Sidney Callahan develops this theme in relation to moral development and moral education, highlighting the emotional component of moral perception and decision.

> Moral education can fail by slighting either the need for critical thinking or the need for personal motivations emerging from empathy, caring, and emotional attachments to a vision of the good. . . . Many factors operate in the moral enterprise: moral freedom, and human limits, active directed thinking and spontaneous preconscious operations, reason and emotion, the individual self and the constitutive community. . . . Moral communities partially shape self-conscious selves, who become free moral agents selecting and creating a moral world.[40]

The individualism of the standard, popular conception of conscience is corrected in this renewed appreciation of the sociality of the moral person. Conscience is not an internal, *a priori* law (Kant) or a small, insistent voice reminding us to do what we already know to be right (Jiminy Cricket?). Conscience must be formed and educated communally, even as the self is also formed in community. Three related points follow. First, it is not enough to see conscience as "presenting" to the self several distinct "sources" of information, which are then balanced and weighed in a process approximating an investment decision. The moral agent as a self develops a worldview only gradually and participatively, including a sense of personal identity, of the common good, and of the interdependence of one's own rights and duties with those of other persons. Thus the formation of the knowing and judging self, and the formation of conscience, are intertwined and in a sense "antecedent" to any particular moral decision. One contribution of "historical consciousness" is the recognition that persons themselves, and moral character as an aspect of personhood, take shape dialogically in relation to the traditions and practices in which they participate. We do not so much act morally

151

by accepting or rejecting moral information or possible conclusions, but by living integrally as the persons we are or are in the process of becoming. Conscience indicates the self-critical component of this process of identity formation, and denotes our ability to adjust our relationship to our moral environment, and to take effective action within it. (Our moral identity and values are not just "produced" by our environment, but also act and react in relation to it.) And it is part of the Roman Catholic affirmation of a fundamentally "objective" morality to maintain that self-criticism, as well as honest consideration and criticism of other moral views or proposals, can lead gradually to a more adequate and true moral understanding and to good moral actions.

Second, moral identity, self-criticism, decision and action, do not depend on an exclusively "rational" process, but involve all the dimensions of the person, including the passions and emotions, which both sensitize us to moral values and moral conflicts, and provide us with motives to act—whether through fear, empathy, anger, or love. Thirdly, both the formation and the exercise of conscience depend on the social *participation* which is crucial to many recent Thomistic interpretations of social justice. We recognize that the division between personal and social ethics is a false one, and the abortion debate is an excellent example. Individuals cannot become mature moral agents (have "properly formed consciences") unless they have the opportunity to be active members of the community in which the moral self (character) is formed within a participatory relationship to the common good. An agent under pressure, with little opportunity to share in the benefits of the common good, is an agent who is poorly educated to make a moral decision representing just relations within the community. Correlatively, genuine moral agency implies the ability to make decisions which express and deepen one's own social participation, while at the same time enhancing the opportunity for similar participation on the part of others. If we expect women and couples to act in ways which enhance the potential of their unborn children, then we must provide them with conditions of real moral agency and of adequate participation in their social world, as well as the prospect of sharing through their decisions in the responsibilities and opportunities which constitute the common good.

It is also the prospect of "shaping a moral world" (Callahan) that I wish primarily to stress in relation to the conscience of the Catholic politician. The "new" (but in a deep sense Thomistic) social model of ethics which we have been discussing yields a new social context for understanding conscience. Conscience is no isolated internal voice. It is an active capacity to listen, learn, judge, reinterpret, and act. It is a process of self-critical identity formation taking place in and through engagement with one's world. It also implies responsive action in the world, an active agenda to form or reform the world in the light of the moral wisdom which conscience integrates from experience. "My" conscience cannot be split off from "public" responsibilities.

POLICY OPPORTUNITIES

Recent polls indicate an American ambivalence about abortion which advises against attempts to eradicate it completely, but which opens a space in which current policies can be reconsidered. In a 1992 Wirthlin poll paid for largely by the USCC Secretariat for Pro-Life Activities, eighty-four percent of the respondents said they opposed using abortion as a method of birth control. Moreover, fifty-six percent said they either believed abortion should be prohibited completely or permitted only in extreme situations, such as threat to the mother's life, rape, or incest. Of the forty percent who said abortion should be legal for any reason, twenty-four percent wanted to limit it to the first three months. Only sixteen percent actually favored "abortion on demand" after the first trimester. Yet journalist Roger Rosenblatt, who seeks a way beyond our current abortion impasse, also notes that Americans are ambivalent about legally taking away the right to choose abortion. He interprets Harris and Gallup polls to mean that while seventy-seven percent of Americans polled in 1990 regarded abortion as a kind of killing, seventy-three percent thought abortion should remain legal. He concludes, "the key element for all is to create social conditions in which abortion will be increasingly unnecessary. It is right that we have the choice, but it would be better if we did not have to make it."[41]

An "incremental strategy" for abortion policy reform has recently been defended by Steven R. Hemler, who has served as president of a Tennessee affiliate of the National Right to Life Committee. Hemler believes that "ideal pro-life legislation" will be achieved and enforced only when there is a consensus among the American people that the unborn deserve legal protection.[42] In the meantime, "history shows us that wise political strategy involves an accurate understanding and assessment of political power and what is currently achievable; recognition of the imperfect world in which we live, and an understanding of our contemporary culture and a recognition of the present moral, political and social constraints on our actions."[43]

In moving toward some practical alternatives which Catholic politicians might endorse, I recommend and will rely upon here an article by Cathleen Kaveny, and published in *The Thomist* in the wake of *Webster* in the summer of 1991. Kaveny, a practicing attorney, has clerked for John T. Noonan, Jr., as well as completing a doctorate from Yale Divinity School.[44] The article combines a Thomistic analysis of the function of law with some practical suggestions for revision of the law toward a more rounded incorporation of the values of both maternal and fetal life.

Although Kaveny criticizes *Webster* (1989) for not providing a clear indication of the requirements state legislatures would need to meet in advancing new abortion laws, she acknowledges the significance of the fact that it (and now *Casey*, 1992) returns some of the responsibility to the local level. Lying within the purview of the pedagogical function of the law, she believes, is the teaching of a "virtuous response to abortion," a response imbued with proper sensitivity to its morality. Virtue, however, is not inculcated primarily through coercive measures. Correlatively, law is not limited to restraint, but also includes a totality of approaches across spheres such as health, education, and social welfare.[45] The educative function of the law can also extend to the facilitation of "each person's process of taking counsel" with an attitude of moral seriousness.[46] This might include dissemination of information about fetal development, methods of abortion, and alternatives to abortion. But attention to the pedagogy of the law also attunes us to the moral condition of those to whom it is directed. Law is "framed for the average person (and not the saint)," which means that "some abortions which we cannot consider just takings of human life nevertheless ought not to bring down upon those who obtain them the full weight of the criminal law. Elements of mercy, pardon, and excuse are characteristic of wise law."[47]

Moreover, Kaveny is attentive to the cultural ethos in which abortion decisions presently take place—some women may be wrong but existentially justified in perceiving abortion as the most reasonable solution of difficulties, since our culture associates it with self-determination, equality, and enhanced social opportunity. The pro-life legislative-educative policy which Kaveny in the end recommends entails the following points. Criminal sanctions should be reserved for those situations in which a social consensus already exists, and should be directed at physicians rather than women (who invariably act under duress). For instance, all third trimester abortions, except those necessary to safeguard maternal life, should be prohibited; fetuses should be delivered unharmed, as far as possible, and provided with life supports. Given the lack of social consensus about the protectability of life in the first trimesters of pregnancy, Kaveny concludes that any attempt to exercise penal sanctions here would be unstable and ineffective. Here the gradual achievement of a pro-life consensus is most important.

Educative legal ventures could include informed consent requirements, accompanied by a mandatory waiting and reconsideration period. Information would address not only fetal development and abortion procedures, but also alternatives to abortion, backed up by a "pro-life package." The latter would include a requirement of paternal responsibility for the child; the restructuring of adoption laws to permit the possibility of maternal choice of adoptive parents, and continuing contact with the child; high school and college assistance services which facilitate housing, medical care, and financial counseling; and, most generally and importantly, a nonviolent attitude toward the resolution of social problems across a spectrum of issues, and a generous and receptive attitude toward life in general. This last point, of course, reflects Cardinal Joseph Bernardin's "seamless garment" metaphor, which united abortion to other "life" issues, including the positive provision of social goods such as health care.[48]

In a commentary on the more recent *Casey* decision (which in Pennsylvania installs informed consent, a twenty-four hour waiting period, and parental consent for a minor) June O'Connor cites polls substantiating public support for the "permit but discourage" approach to abortion and sees *Casey* as embodying some of the values Kaveny recommends. Both time and consultation are important in making a wise abortion decision, and no truly deliberative choice can be accomplished without information and counseling. Even if some abortion decisions are justified, she contends, it is important that the larger community "communicate a cultural bias on behalf of life over death, presence over absence, support over isolation."[49] Returning abortion to the states presents the possibility of a "checkerboard" of discrepant policies on abortion. But it also represents an opportunity for local dialogue over this vexing problem, and an engagement of citizens in grass-roots discourse, which may contribute to the seriousness and the sensitivity of the atmosphere in which discussion is carried toward practical implementation. Catholic legislators need not position themselves toward the abortion policy dilemma so much as *individuals* confronting constraining church teaching, but as *community facilitators* who can introduce value questions into the debate at many levels, and keep attention focused on the forest of problems that lead to abortion, as well as on the trees of personal decision.

Another note of episcopal support for such a perspective comes from the U.S. bishops' *Putting Children and Families First,*[50] a statement which urges better social support for families, and calls it "a terrible sign of national failure" that many poor women feel "they must choose between life for their unborn child and a decent future for themselves and for their families" (A.1). As part of a comprehensive social agenda they mention jobs and employment, family-supporting welfare policy, childcare and flexible work time, ending discrimination by race and gender, education, food and hunger, health care, housing, and divorce and child support. Issues like these are contact points for a pro-life/pro-choice compromise.

Daniel Callahan, for instance, still willing to defend the pro-choice legal position, is aware that abortion "is often a cheap solution to deeply social problems."[51] In order to make abortion more serious morally and more exceptional socially, he advocates a plan with "two major ingredients" around which those with pro-life sympathies ought also to be able to rally.

> On the one hand, there would be a sharp restriction of late abortions, parental notification for teenagers, federally supported abortions only for medical or clear health reasons, mandatory counseling and waiting periods, and serious efforts to reduce the number of abortions, especially repeat abortions. There would be, on the other hand, a significant improvement in maternal and child benefits, improved counseling, and more effective family planning and contraceptive education and services.[52]

Some corresponding advice for the pro-life movement is offered by James Kelly. "If the Prolife movement is not to be painted into a corner by its opponents as mainly an antiwomen, anti-abortion movement . . . the Church must succeed in making better known . . . that support of the unborn is linked to the support of justice for women." This must include "an increasingly critical appraisal of Western economic systems," and a critique of gender discrimination such as that found in the pastoral letter, *Economic Justice for All.*[53]

CONCLUSIONS

The political, legislative, and judicial contexts of abortion in the U.S. have shifted with the change in presidential administrations. On the day after the twentieth anniversary of *Roe v. Wade*, a *New York Times* headline (1/23/93) proclaimed, "Clinton Cancels Abortion Restrictions of Reagan-Bush Era." Specifically, President Clinton lifted restrictions on abortion counseling at federally funded clinics and on use of U.S. funds in United Nations population programs that include abortion information; permitted privately paid abortions to be performed in military hospitals; and ordered review of the ban on RU-486 (a drug which ends pregnancy very early by interfering with implantation). However, President Clinton did not sign these policy changes under the aegis of "choice" as such, but in the hope that abortion in America would become "safe and legal but rare." Although some in the pro-life movement might hope to make abortion nonexistent instead, we certainly would have accomplished a major advance if abortion were to become an infrequently used last resort because less drastic solutions were more available to women.

Do President Clinton's policy changes offer any movement in this direction? It is too early to have any certain evidence. We can take a preliminary reading of the symbolic importance of President Clinton's acts and words. The *Arlington (Virginia) Catholic Herald* reported that the bans on abortion information did not prevent many abortions, but did stand for a federal refusal to endorse abortion (January 28, 1993). If this is true, then numbers of abortions will not likely increase much with the changed counseling policy. However, some may read the end of the ban as a social approval of abortion, which could increase receptiveness to permissive access policies at the state level.

Unfortunately, President Clinton also chose the day he lifted the "gag rule" as the day on which to lift the ban on federally sponsored research on fetal tissue uses. The association of fetal tissue research with permissive attitudes toward abortion was specifically the point on which a NIH panel which reviewed the matter recommended caution. In fact, it determined that such research should be permitted only if the research decision could be *disassociated* from the abortion decision, and if the possibility of donation to research in no way served as an inducement to abortion. I mention this because instituting both changes together, at a White House ceremony on the anniversary of *Roe* v. *Wade*, does not signal that President Clinton is as sensitive to the symbolic value of political acts regarding abortion, nor as interested in preserving as clear a sense of the tragedy of abortion, as someone ought to be who sincerely wants to see abortion become "rare."

On the other side, however, President Clinton signed the family-leave bill on February 5. Again the symbolic value of this bill probably outweighs its material effects. Practically speaking, the bill will serve the middle and upper classes more than the poor. To benefit from the bill's provisions, a parent would have to be employed, and to be able to afford to take an unpaid leave to care for a child. However, the bill signifies a moral stance in favor, not only of work arrangements which permit parents to combine employment and birth, but also of mothers' place in the world of work, and of the cooperation of both mothers and fathers in accommodating children within the family. Placed alongside his abortion policies, this bill expresses President Clinton's encouragement of social support for childbirth, parenthood, and the family, and signifies that he is willing to begin to take away some of the pressures which make abortion seem like the only viable alternative to an economically and socially difficult pregnancy.

One may also note the attention to health care reform which the present administration represents, and add that decent, reliable health care for all Americans would greatly enhance a context in which women could choose childbirth over abortion. The Catholic politician may elect to work in concert with other groups, not necessarily "pro-life," who are committed to social goods such as universal health coverage and policies which make it feasible rather than difficult for parents to hold down jobs and raise families. On the other side, he or she will address the serious questions Americans have about a "blank check" for abortion choice and work against legislation such as the Freedom of Choice Act, which would forbid states to restrict abortion.

In regard to the issue before us, both the past moral wisdom of Catholicism and present political and moral experience teach that abortion is a broad-based social problem demanding a multi-pronged, complex, flexible, and necessarily gradual solution. If we appreciate the cumulative and communal character of moral wisdom, we will realize that the "right" social solution to the abortion dilemma may not be easy to devise or recognize. Moreover, political and legal solutions, even when characterized by objective moral rightness, must be adequately nuanced to their situations. So, on the one hand, we recognize that our moral knowledge about abortion as a social problem may be incomplete. And, on the other hand, we see that even a complete and accurate moral solution to abortion requires going beyond abstract or general principles to deal with the human realities which a law affects. Respecting Catholicism's protective stance toward unborn life, even in its earliest stages, is consistent with a political agenda which recognizes the practical divisiveness and even destructiveness of an absolutist position on the recriminalization of abortion—and hence the possibility of its objective, moral failure as a prudent means to the worthy end of protecting human life. A comprehensive sense of social justice, grounded both in Aquinas and in Catholic social teaching, recommends, however, that the decision to abort be socially discouraged in favor of more constructive alternatives for women, children, and families. The task of the politician is to seek consensus around a supportive environment for women facing a difficult pregnancy, and to that end aid the cultivation of civic virtues of cooperation, generosity, and even sacrifice on the part of the community as a whole.

NOTES

1. The following survey is adapted from Lisa Sowle Cahill, "Abortion," in *The Westminster Dictionary of Christian Ethics*, ed. James F. Childress and John Macquarrie (Philadelphia, PA: The Westminster Press, 1986), 1-5. Also consult John T. Noonan, Jr., ed., *The Morality of Abortion: Legal and Historical Perspectives* (Cambridge, MA: Harvard University Press, 1970); and John

Connery, S.J., *Abortion: Development of the Roman Catholic Perspective* (Chicago: Loyola University Press, 1977).

2. The Sacred Congregation for the Doctrine of the Faith, "Declaration on Abortion," *Origins* 4 (1974): 385-92, at 386.

3. *Declaration on Abortion*, 389.

4. Congregation for the Doctrine of the Faith, "Instruction on Respect for Human Life in Its Origin and on the Dignity of Procreation," *Origins* 16 (1987): 697-711.

5. For a much more complete review of the entire debate than is possible here, see Lisa Sowle Cahill, "The Embryo and Fetus: New Moral Contexts," *Theological Studies* 53 (1993): 124-42.

6. Norman M. Ford, S.D.B., *When Did I Begin? Conception of the Human Individual in History, Philosophy and Science* (Cambridge: Cambridge University Press, 1988). Ford summarizes his argument in "When Did I Begin—A Reply to Nicholas Tonti-Filippini," *Linacre Quarterly* 57 (1990): 59-66.

7. Ford, *When Did I Begin?*, 64.

8. Richard A. McCormick, S.J., "Who or What is the Preembryo?," *Kennedy Institute of Ethics Journal* 1 (1991): 2.

9. *Summa Theologiae*, I, q. 92, a. 1. "It was necessary for woman to be made, as the Scripture says [Gen 2:18], as a helper to man; not, indeed, as a helpmate in other works, as some say, since man can be more efficiently helped by another man in other works; but as a helper in the work of generation."

10. John Paul II, *Familiaris Consortio, Apostolic Exhortation on the Family*, December 15, 1981 (Washington, D.C.: United States Catholic Conference, 1981).

11. John Paul II, "On the Dignity and Vocation of Women" (August 15, 1988), *Origins* 18 (1988): 261, 263-83.

12. Juliet K. Moyna, Columbia College Class of 1991, "Abortion Consent Law Creates Support System," *New York Times* (October 30, 1989): A, 18.

13. National Conference of Catholic Bishops, "Economic Justice for All: Catholic Social Teaching and the U.S. Economy," *Origins* 16:24 (1986), §71.

14. *Economic Justice for All*, §§409-56.

15. Noonan, "The Morality of Abortion," 3.

16. Alasdair MacIntyre, *After Virtue: A Study of Moral Theory* (Notre Dame, IN: University of Notre Dame Press, 1981); and *Whose Justice? Which Rationality?* (Notre Dame, IN: University of Notre Dame Press, 1988).

17. Jeffrey Stout, *Ethics After Babel: The Languages of Morals and Their Discontents* (Boston, MA: Beacon Press, 1988).

18. George A. Lindbeck, *The Nature of Doctrine: Religion and Theology in a Postliberal Age* (Philadelphia, PA: The Westminster Press, 1984).

19. Ronald F. Thiemann, *Constructing a Public Theology: The Church in a Pluralistic Culture* (Louisville, KY: Westminster/John Knox Press, 1991).

20. Stout, *After Babel*, 282.

21. MacIntyre, *Whose Justice?*, 350.

22. Martin E. Marty, "Religion, Theology, Church, and Bioethics," *Journal of Medicine and Philosophy* 17 (1992): 285.

23. J. Bryan Hehir, "Policy Arguments in a Public Church: Catholic Social Ethics and Bioethics," *Journal of Medicine and Philosophy* 17 (1992): 348.

24. John Courtney Murray, *The Problem of Religious Freedom* (New York: The Missionary Society of Saint Paul the Apostle, 1965), 29-30.

25. See M. Cathleen Kaveny, "Toward a Thomistic Perspective on Abortion and the Law in Contemporary America," *The Thomist* 55 (1991): 378.

26. Mary Ann Glendon, *Abortion and Divorce in Western Law: American Failures, European Challenges* (Cambridge, MA: Harvard University Press, 1987).

27. Daniel Callahan, "An Ethical Challenge to Prochoice Advocates: Abortion and the Pluralistic Proposition," *Commonweal* 127 (1990): 684.

28. Glendon, *Abortion and Divorce*, 61.

29. "Conscience," in Albert J. Nevins, M. M., ed., *The Maryknoll Catholic Dictionary* (New York: Grosset & Dunlap, 1965), 151.

30. *Declaration on Religious Freedom*, §3.

31. *Pastoral Constitution on the Church in the Modern World*, §16.

32. Richard A. McCormick, S.J., *Health and Medicine in the Catholic Tradition: Tradition in Transition* (New York: Crossroad, 1984), 47.

33. See Timothy E. O'Connell, *Principles for a Catholic Morality*, rev. ed. (San Francisco, CA: Harper and Row, 1990), 107-9.

34. See Josef Fuchs, S. J., "The Absolute in Morality and the Christian Conscience," *Gregorianum* 71 (1990): 700.

35. *Summa Theologiae*, I, q. 79, a. 12-13.

36. *Summa Theologiae*, I-II, q. 24, a. 3.

37. See O'Connell, *Principles*, chapter 9; and Richard M. Gula, S. S., *Reason Informed by Faith: Foundations of Catholic Morality* (Mahwah NJ: Paulist Press, 1989), also chapter 9.

38. The key figure here is the prolific Protestant theologian, Stanley Hauerwas. For Roman Catholic theologians and ethicists who appropriate the North American "pragmatist" traditions of thought about religious experience and religious affections, see Frank M. Oppenheim, S. J., ed., *The Reasoning Heart: Toward a North American Theology* (Washington, D.C.: Georgetown University Press, 1986).

39. Fuchs, "Christian Conscience," 704-5.

40. Sidney Callahan, *In Good Conscience* (San Francisco, CA: Harper San Francisco, 1991), 213-14.

41. Roger Rosenblatt, "How to End the Abortion War," *New York Times Magazine* (January 19, 1992): 56.

161

42. Steven R. Hemler, "The Pro-Life 'Sophie's Choice'," *America* 166 (February 29, 1992): 164.

43. Hemler, "The Pro-Life *Sophie's Choice*," 165.

44. See n. 23 above.

45. Kaveny, "Abortion and the Law," 364.

46. Kaveny, "Abortion and the Law," 369.

47. Kaveny, "Abortion and the Law," 379.

48. See Cardinal Joseph Bernardin, "The Consistent Ethics: What Sort of Framework?," in Patricia Beattie Jung and Thomas A. Shannon, eds., *Abortion and Catholicism: The American Debate* (New York: Crossroad, 1988), 260-67.

49. June O'Connor, "The Summer of Our Discontent," *Hastings Center Report* 22 (1992): 29.

50. National Conference of Catholic Bishops, "Putting Children and Families First: A Challenge for Our Church, Nation and World," *Origins* 21 (1991): 393, 395-404.

51. Daniel Callahan, "An Ethical Challenge," 687.

52. Daniel Callahan, "An Ethical Challenge," 687.

53. James R. Kelly, "A Political Challenge to the Prolife Movement: Toward a Post-'Webster' Agenda," *Commonweal* 127 (1990): 695.

The Public Law of Abortion:
A Constitutional and Statutory Review of the
Present and Future Legal Landscape

Basile J. Uddo

INTRODUCTION

When I was first invited to present a paper to the Saint Louis University Conference on Abortion and Public Policy, I was elated by the prospect of participating in what I expected to be the first national conference in the new era of abortion law. That new era was supposed to be one in which law and reason would reunite to erase the blemish of *Roe* v. *Wade* on American constitutional law. It was to be the post-*Casey* era, an era when a decade of "pro-life" judicial appointments, especially to the Supreme Court, would reach fruition and ameliorate two decades of pro-abortion bias within the federal judiciary.[1] As one who has unabashedly opposed *Roe* v. *Wade* and its ruinous public policy,[2] the hope of this new era fueled my enthusiasm for the Saint Louis University conference. Then the Court decided *Planned Parenthood* v. *Casey*,[3] and suddenly the prospects for a new era were thoroughly defused.

Reasonable minds can differ over the effect of *Casey* on abortion policy in this country, but not much. Any fair reading of *Casey*, especially in light of expectations, leads inexorably to the conclusion that opponents of *Roe* v. *Wade*, and more importantly, defenders of the unborn, have suffered a grave defeat. There is little good news for the pro-life movement within the many pages of the *Casey* opinions. In addition, President Clinton has made clear his commitment to undo every hard-won abortion restriction within the control of the executive branch and his support for the dismantling of all others beyond his immediate control. To this observer, twenty years of effort have dissipated with almost the same swiftness and shock that had been produced by *Roe* v. *Wade* itself.

THE CASEY OPINION: POLICY BACKGROUND

What gives rise to such pessimism over this single Supreme Court case lies in the text itself of the "joint opinion," which forms the core of *Casey*. All view this core as the controlling opinion of the Court. The measure of its inadequacy consists in the fact that all parties have found it so objectionable.

The first thing to notice is the form of the message: the joint opinion is a judicial anomaly. Unprecedented, the joint opinion purports to be the *single* opinion of Justices O'Connor, Kennedy, and Souter. The usual procedure of an opinion with concurrences was apparently unsuited for the firm voice with which the *Casey* triumvirate wished to *speak*. Justices Blackmun and Stevens were pleased to cast their votes in support of the result of the joint opinion, but not surprisingly, they would go farther.

In substance the joint opinion reaffirmed *Roe* v. *Wade* in what the justices call its "essential holdings."[4] In doing so, the joint opinion refused to reexamine *Roe* with an eye toward overruling it, as numerous *amici*, including the United States, had urged the Court to do. Ironically, the joint opinion cites the rule of *stare decisis* as reason not to overrule *Roe*, while at the same time significantly rewriting the *Roe* opinion and overruling, at least in part, two other opinions.[5] Consequently, respect for precedent seems less the cause for the Court's concern than a continuing predilection to allow abortion on demand, tempered only by the Court's reading of the public opinion polls. This seems apparent in the three main reasons given for reaffirming *Roe*, each of which reflects political more than constitutional analysis.

A major justification given by the joint opinion for reaffirming *Roe* is that it has not proven unworkable.[6] Aside from the fact that this conclusion is not correct, it is a political conclusion: why else would this Court consistently find itself addressing the issue so many times over the past twenty years, and why else would there be such a continuing flood of state and federal attempts at restrictions, unless *Roe* is truly unworkable in the sense that it has failed to solve the issue? To say *Roe* is workable is to discuss a principle of constitutional law as though it were a statute in debate before a legislature. Statutes are workable or unworkable, principles of constitutional law are enduring interpretations of our governing document. Interpretation is based upon text, structure, or history, not workability.

The second reason given for reaffirming *Roe* is that it could not be overruled without serious inequity to those who have relied upon it. Again, this is an odd standard for constitutional interpretation, as though the economic expectations of slave owners would be sufficient reason not to overturn *Dred Scott*. Moreover, it is a specious conclusion. Who in this country does not know that abortion is far from a settled "right"? Who could ignore the intense nature and persistence of the abortion controversy during these past twenty years? Who has not seen the countless marches and protests on both sides of the issue?

Then, too, what is the nature of this reliance and what price its removal? The Court attempts to answer the former question, but ignores the latter:

> But to . . . (eliminate the issue of reliance) would be simply to refuse to face the fact that for two decades of economic and social developments, people have organized intimate relationships and made choices that define their views of themselves and their places in society, in reliance on the availability of abortion in the event that contraception should fail. The ability of women to participate equally in the economic and social life of the Nation has been facilitated by their ability to control their reproductive lives.[7]

Not surprisingly the joint opinion offers no data to support this doubtful conclusion, which apparently deterred the Court from overruling *Roe*. Indeed, the joint opinion admits it has no basis for its concern:

> The Constitution serves human values, and *while the effect of reliance on Roe cannot be exactly measured, neither can the certain cost of overruling Roe* for people who have ordered their thinking and living around that case be dismissed.[8]

The third reason given not to overrule *Roe* comes from the joint opinion's concern for damage to the integrity of the Court by the appearance of yielding to public pressure.[9] But to overrule *Roe* would hardly be yielding to public pressure, especially given the fact that the amount of scholarly criticism of *Roe* is legion.[10] Yet, what harm would really result from overruling a decision that has failed utterly to garner public support?[11] Is not the greater harm in adhering to a position that the public will not accept and many scholars reject? The joint opinion seems to recognize this, because at the heart of the joint opinion is actually a desire to reflect the opinion polls. The joint opinion seems to be seeking out this accommodating middle ground supported in the opinion polls. Indeed, one of Justice Souter's clerks—a joint opinion justice—worked with Professor Laurence Tribe on his 1990 book, *Abortion: The Clash of Absolutes*,[12] which argued for an accommodating *reformulation* of *Roe* that looks very much like the *Casey* joint opinion.

Consequently, the joint opinion contradicts itself when it rejects overruling *Roe* to avoid the appearance of succumbing to public pressure while it "reformulates" *Roe* apparently to accommodate public opinion. No wonder Charles Krauthammer called *Casey* "appalling constitutional law," and the Court "a National Commission on Everything."[13] So much for the integrity of the Court.

THE CASEY OPINION: WHAT IT DOES

Despite protestations of the sanctity of *stare decisis* the joint opinion finds no obstacle to a major reformulation of *Roe* v. *Wade*. In several particulars, *Casey* rewrites *Roe*, not only preserving it, but making it an ever greater obstacle to abortion regulation.

First, the joint opinion jettisons the *Roe* trimester system, but replaces it with a "bimester" framework. Now the dividing line for various degrees of constitutional scrutiny is viability.[14] No better reason is given for this new guidepost in constitutional law than that it is "workable."[15] Nothing in the joint opinion attempts to "rejustify" the significance of viability as the dividing line in abortion regulation. Indeed, the joint opinion simply begs the viability question and again relies upon the principle of *stare decisis*:

> The woman's right to terminate her pregnancy before viability is the most central principle of *Roe* v. *Wade*. It is a rule of law and a component of liberty we cannot renounce. . . . The matter is not before us in the first instance, and coming as it does after nearly twenty years of litigation in Roe's wake *we are satisfied that the immediate question is not the soundness of Roe's resolution of the issue, but the precedential force that must be accorded to holding.*[16]

As unsatisfying as this is in the context of this long anticipated, major "rethinking" of *Roe*, it is less important than what significance is attached to pre- and post-viability decisions. In fact, had the Court applied Justice O'Connor's previous formulation of the undue burden test the effect of preserving viability may have been minimal. However, the joint opinion also reformulates the undue burden test, and while this view did not command a majority of the Court it is practically controlling since Justices Blackmun and Stevens would never support a more stringent standard, and could be expected to support the result of *Casey's* undue burden test.

As now formulated, the test is confusing and virtually unlimited. Its greatest impact comes in pre-viability regulation cases where two things seem certain: first, a total ban on abortion would be declared an undue burden and thus held unconstitutional; second, all state restrictions on pre-viability abortions now must be examined on a case by case basis and, until adjudicated, will perpetuate uncertainty in the law of abortion.

Previously, in various opinions,[17] Justice O'Connor, the chief proponent of the undue burden test, articulated it as minimally intrusive into state decision making in the abortion area. Specifically, abortion regulation would be tested by a rational relationship test if it was not determined to be a regulation that created an undue burden on the woman's abortion decision. More importantly, the original articulation of this test would find an undue burden only if the challenged regulation imposed an "absolute obstacle" or "severe limitation"[18] on the woman's decision, meaning that a vast array of restrictions, even those strongly discouraging abortion could meet the standard. Moreover, the original test would even allow for the approval of an undue burden if the questioned regulation could meet the standard of strict scrutiny, that is, if the state could justify the regulation as necessary to protect a compelling state interest. Naturally, before *Casey*, it was hoped that an increased awareness of the state's compelling interest in unborn life, throughout pregnancy, would supply the justification for a variety of otherwise "undue burdens."

However, somewhere between *Akron* and *Thornburgh*, and *Casey*, Justice O'Connor experienced a conversion to a variety of the undue burden test that transformed it from one respecting state decisions and permitting greater abortion regulation, to one that reflects a kind of imprecision rendering it available to cut down any abortion regulation that interferes with a woman's "spiritual imperatives."[19] In particular this version of the test asks whether the regulation's "purpose or effect is to place a substantial obstacle in the path of a woman seeking an abortion" before viability. If this illicit "purpose" *or* "effect" is found, the joint opinion would require a finding of undue burden not salvageable by a compelling interest of the state.

Conversely, the joint opinion purports to bolster the state's interest after viability; moving away from the undue burden analysis to a standard where the state "may, if it chooses, regulate, and even proscribe, abortion except where it is necessary, in appropriate medical judgment, for the preservation of the life or *health* of the mother."[20] The key, of course as it was in *Roe*, is a question of what constitutes the health of the mother.

The next major shift in *Casey* comes via the joint opinion's attempt to shore-up the shifting constitutional foundation of *Roe*. In what appears to be a deliberate attempt to quell the most consistent theoretical critique of *Roe*, the joint opinion grounds the abortion "right" in the concept of liberty under the Fourteenth Amendment, rather than the totally non-textual right to privacy of *Roe*. Two things are significant about this approach: first, it confirms that *Casey* is attempting to strengthen the constitutionality of the abortion right; and second, the joint opinion lacks constitutional legitimacy for what it *fails* to do.

This latter observation proceeds from a careful reading of the joint opinion, which begs the question of how a criminal act so clearly proscribed by our tradition of ordered liberty became a protected liberty under our constitution. In the end, the joint opinion offers a strange constitutional analysis:

> These matters, involving the most intimate and personal choices
> a person may make in a lifetime, choices central to personal

dignity and autonomy, are central to the liberty protected by the Fourteenth Amendment. At the heart of liberty is the right to define one's own concept of existence, of meaning, of the universe, and of the mystery of human life. Beliefs about these matters could not define the attributes of personhood were they formed under compulsion of the State.

Though abortion is conduct, it does not follow that the State is entitled to proscribe it in all instances. This is because the liberty of the woman is at stake in a sense unique to the human condition and so unique to the law. The mother who carries a child to full term is subject to anxieties, to physical constraints, to pain that only she must bear. *That these sacrifices have from the beginning of the human race been endured by women with pride that ennobles her in the eyes of others and gives to the infant a bond of love cannot alone be grounds of the State to insist she make the sacrifice.* Her suffering is too intimate and personal for the State to insist, without more, upon its own vision of the woman's role, *however dominant that vision has been in the course of our history and our culture.* The destiny of the woman must be shaped to a large extent on her own conception of her spiritual imperatives and her place in society.[21]

Note how in defining liberty to include abortion the joint opinion virtually admits that such a conclusion goes contrary to the state of affairs "from the beginning of the human race" and the "dominant . . . vision...in the course of our history and our culture." How then does something contrary to our history and culture become a constitutionally protected liberty interest? How does an act that was criminal for all but twenty years of our history become a right?[22] What historical, philosophical, religious or traditional principles or facts support making abortion a constitutional liberty? The joint opinion demonstrates no compulsion to ground this dramatic interpretation in anything more that its conclusion bolstered by a handful of modern Supreme Court decisions. These decisions, however, have no precedential value for defining liberty to include abortion, except as a leaping off point, much like a rock is a place to leap into the pond but is no part of the pond.

Finally, the *Casey* joint opinion, with the concurrence of Justices Blackmun and Stevens, and despite its concern for *stare decisis*, overruled *Akron* v. *Akron Center for Reproductive Health*,[23] and *Thornburgh* v. *American College of Obstetricians and Gynecologists*,[24] to the extent that those decisions conflict with *Casey* and its new undue burden test.

THE CASEY OPINION: THE PENNSYLVANIA STATUTE

Casey did involve a state statute that was the occasion for the Court's review. How that statute fared is significant for purposes of understanding the application of the new test. The Pennsylvania statute imposed several abortion restrictions. First, the legislature required that a woman seeking an abortion give her informed consent prior to the abortion; that she be provided with abortion related information at least twenty-four hours prior to the abortion; and that a minor have the informed consent of one of her parents, or exercise a judicial bypass option, prior to obtaining an abortion. In addition, the legislature required written spousal notification, with certain exceptions, prior to an abortion; it exempted compliance with any of the above in the event of a "medical emergency" as defined in the statute; and finally, it imposed certain reporting requirements on abortion providers.

The Court, with a variety of vote configurations, upheld each of the Pennsylvania restrictions *except* spousal notification. However, the joint opinion writers did not give a rousing endorsement to any of the provisions, and as will be discussed below, many of them might be struck down with a different factual record.

Perhaps the most important of the regulations to be upheld is the informed consent/twenty-four-hour waiting period. Opponents of abortion have long believed that given accurate and truthful information about abortion, most women would not choose to abort. Consequently, Pennsylvania, expressing its concern for the health of the woman, and for the unborn child, required that at least twenty-four hours before an abortion a woman contemplating an abortion be given information about the risks of the procedure, the probable gestation age of the unborn child, and alternatives to the abortion. It also required that the woman be given information about the medical risks of continued pregnancy, childbirth and delivery. Significantly, the information had to be given by a physician. Finally, the woman must be told that other information—about the unborn child, medical assistance for childbirth, information about child support and agencies providing alternatives to abortion—was available upon her request.

The Court rejected arguments that the waiting period and informed consent requirements effected an undue burden on the woman, it also rejected First Amendment claims on behalf of physicians who would be required to give the information. However, the subjectivity and fact sensitivity of the new undue burden test is apparent in the joint opinion language:

Since there is not evidence on this record that requiring a doctor to give the information as provided by the statute would amount in practical terms to a substantial obstacle to a woman seeking an abortion, *we conclude that it is not an undue burden.*

In theory, at least, the waiting period is a reasonable measure to implement the State's interest in protecting the life of the unborn, *a measure that does not amount to an undue burden.*

Hence, *on the record before us, and in the context of this facial challenge, we are not convinced that the 24 hour waiting period constitutes an undue burden.*[25]

Casey reached a similar result in assessing the parental consent for minors' restriction. The opinion once again notes that no such provision could survive the undue burden test if it lacked a judicial bypass procedure that allowed a minor to avoid obtaining the parent's consent, but beyond that, one-parent consent restrictions, were treated as a settled issue. What the Court did address separately was the Pennsylvania requirement that the parent's consent must be informed, similar to the informed consent provision. Nonetheless, the Court concluded that, for reasons similar to those given in the assessment of the informed consent provision, the state could require a parent's consent to be informed.

In upholding most of the health related record keeping and reporting requirements the Court again reflected the pervasive subjectivity and factual review that the undue burden test, newly formulated, will require:

171

Nor do we find that the requirements impose a substantial obstacle to a woman's choice. At most they might increase the cost of some abortions by a slight amount. *While at some point increased cost could become a substantial obstacle, there is no such showing on the record before us.*[26]

Consequently, constitutionality is reduced to a cost analysis that draws an undetermined—indeed prospectively undeterminable—line between due and undue burdens.

The final provision addressed by the Court did not fare as well. The Pennsylvania law required that, except in cases of medical emergency, no physician could perform an abortion on a married woman unless the woman signed a statement that she had notified her spouse that she was about to undergo an abortion. In addition to the medical emergency exception, the law also suspended the spousal notification requirement if the husband was not the father of the child; his whereabouts were unknown; the pregnancy was the result of rape by the husband; or there was reason to believe that notification would result in physical abuse to the woman.

The joint opinion accepted the trial court findings about *general* domestic violence statistics to declare this provision unconstitutional despite the exceptions, and despite the fact that statistically the record indicated that fewer than one percent of women seeking abortions in Pennsylvania would in any way be affected by the requirement. Nonetheless, the joint opinion concluded that:

The unfortunate yet persisting conditions we document above (on domestic violence) will mean that in a large fraction of the cases in which (the requirement) is relevant, it will operate as a substantial obstacle to a woman's choice to undergo an abortion. It is an undue burden, and therefore invalid.[27]

Finally, all nine justices upheld the statutory definition of "medical emergency" that was critical to the overall statutory scheme since many of the restrictions were premised on the medical emergency exception. The definition reads:

That condition which, on the basis of the physician's good faith clinical judgment, so complicates the medical condition of a pregnant woman as to necessitate the immediate abortion of her pregnancy to avert her death or for which a delay will create serious risk of substantial and irreversible impairment of a major bodily function.[28]

The Court noted that the Court of Appeals had given the definition a saving construction by reading it to include three conditions that the petitioners argued were not included and would, therefore, render the definition impermissibly narrow. By reading in preeclampsia, inevitable abortion, and premature ruptured membrane, the joint opinion, joined by all other justices, found that "as construed by the Court of Appeals, the medical emergency definition imposes no undue burden on a woman's abortion right."[29]

THE FUTURE OF ABORTION:
LEGISLATION AND LITIGATION

Given the controlling effect of the *Casey* joint opinion, and given its application to the Pennsylvania law, what does the future hold for opponents of abortion on demand? It is true that the joint opinion said some things that in the abstract sound encouraging. Perhaps the most encouraging comment is the clear statement that "There is a substantial state interest in potential life *throughout* pregnancy."[30] But, what good is that in the face of a highly subjective undue burden test? The reality seems quite bleak given that unprincipled subjectivity.

The stark bottom line of *Casey* is that the Court has become even more of a super-legislature than it was accused of being after *Roe*. The new undue burden test, unlike its predecessor with its deference to most state decisions, unfortunately is nothing more than a subjective tool, that easily may be wielded against state abortion legislation. In addition because the undue burden test is so dependent on the factual record, it becomes increasingly difficult to depend upon any consistency in the abortion area. For example, even though the Court upheld the twenty-four-hour waiting period, it did so in a tenuous, fact-based manner:

Whether the mandatory 24 hour waiting period is nonetheless invalid because *in practice* it is a substantial obstacle to a woman's choice to terminate her pregnancy is a closer question. The findings of fact by the District Court indicate that because of the distances many women must travel to reach an abortion provider, the practical effect will often be a delay of much more than a day because the waiting period requires that a woman seeking an abortion make at least two visits to the doctor. The District Court also found that in many instances this will increase the exposure of women seeking abortions to "the harassment and hostility of anti-abortion protestors demonstrating outside a clinic" . . . As a result, the District Court found that for those women who have the fewest financial resources, those who must travel long distances, and those who have difficulty explaining their whereabouts to husbands, employees, or others, the 24 hour waiting period will be "particularly burdensome."

These findings are troubling in some respects, but they do not demonstrate that the waiting period constitutes an undue burden. We do not doubt, as the District Court held, the waiting period has the effect of "increasing the cost and risk of delay of abortions," . . . but the District Court did not conclude that the increased costs and potential delays amount to substantial obstacles. . . . A particular burden is not of necessity a substantial obstacle. Whether a burden falls on a particular group is a distinct inquiry from whether it is a substantial obstacle even as to the women in that group. And the District Court did not conclude that the waiting period is such an obstacle even for the women who are most burdened by it. *Hence, on the record before us, and in the context of this facial challenge, we are not convinced that the 24 hour waiting period constitutes an undue burden.*[31]

Clearly, if a different record is presented, a different conclusion may be reached. Consequently, if a somewhat stronger case of alleged burdens can be made or if a new context arises, a different outcome is entirely likely. Indeed, with the recent murder of an abortionist in Pensacola, Florida, the next evaluation of waiting periods is far more likely to weigh heavily the "harassment and hostility" argument. Consequently, even the good news is uncertain.

Nonetheless, *Casey* does offer some areas for *possible* pro-life activity. In sum, I find that *Casey* promotes four kinds of activity: persuasion, contemplation, involvement, and information.

The joint opinion allows states to prefer childbirth to abortion and to try to "persuade (a woman) to choose childbirth over abortion"[32] as long as it does not impose an undue burden on the woman's choice. Consequently, even though it is impossible to tell where the undue burden line is drawn, stronger informed consent laws may be possible. This might be especially effective if state laws required greater emphasis on fetal development and methods of abortion. *Casey* also finds acceptable the states use of "philosophic and social arguments of great weight"[33] that encourage childbirth, along with information about alternatives, including sources of assistance to allow the woman to have and raise the child. All of which intertwine with the next area of approved activity, that is contemplation.

While the state may persuade, it may facilitate that persuasion by means calculated to foster contemplation by the woman of all of the consequences of abortion, including "the consequences . . . for the fetus."[34] Coupled with a waiting period this inducement to contemplation is fertile ground for state action. However, the fluid undue burden test makes it impossible to predict what length waiting period would pass muster. In *Casey* twenty-four hours was accepted, on that record, in that context, without much enthusiasm. With the loss of Justice White and the ambivalence of the joint opinion, coupled with the shifting factual record that might be needed, who knows what may happen? At a minimum any state contemplating a waiting period, especially one that pushes beyond twenty-four hours, would be well served to develop the factual record that the state's interest in encouraging childbirth is significantly promoted by the period, as against the slight burden to the woman's choice.

With respect to involvement, *Casey* clearly endorses the value of parental involvement in the abortion decision of a minor. Just how far that involvement might be pushed is very difficult to predict. Pennsylvania's law required only one parent's consent. Nothing in *Casey* expressly forecloses two-parent consent. Nor does *Casey* specify the nature of the judicial bypass that certainly would be required. Perhaps a more limited judicial bypass, reflecting only certain specific fears, such as violence or abuse, would meet the undue burden test. In any event parental involvement seems a solid principle in *Casey*.

Spousal involvement, on the other hand, seems impossible given the joint opinion's willingness to extrapolate from nonspecific factual data to strike down a restriction that would apparently have only a small impact of the kind envisioned by the Court. One can only conclude that factual data aside, the joint opinion's true intent with respect to spousal involvement is social and public policy:

> If this case concerned a State's ability to require the mother to notify the father before taking some action with respect to a living child raised by both, therefore, it would be reasonable to conclude as a general matter that the father's interest in the welfare of the child and the mother's interest are equal.
>
> Before birth, however, the issue takes on a very different cast. It is an inescapable fact that state regulation with respect to the *child* a woman is carrying will have a far greater impact on the mother's liberty than on the father's. The effect of state regulation on a woman's protected liberty is doubly deserving of scrutiny in such a case, as the State has touched not only upon the private sphere of the family but upon the very bodily integrity of the pregnant woman.[35]

The irony of using the word "child" to describe the object of an intended abortion seems to escape the opinion writers. If it is a child, how can the previously identified "equal interest" of the father suddenly disappear? Nonetheless, spousal involvement seems little prized by the majority and unlikely to be upheld in any form.

Finally, *Casey* seems to allow more information gathering than ever before. Qualifying its view, the joint opinion requires that the information gathering must be "reasonably directed to the preservation of maternal health"[36] and must "properly respect a patient's confidentiality and privacy."[37] Even slight increases in the cost of the abortion due to the information gathering is not an undue burden. However, without useful guidance, the joint opinion concludes that "at some point increased cost could become a substantial obstacle"[38] and therefore an undue burden. Consequently, states could maximize their efforts at information gathering within these fuzzy limits in order to help create the factual data necessary for future legislation and litigation.

Beyond these efforts to "fine tune" abortion regulations, *Casey* probably allows at least one total prohibition and a questionable argument for a second. The Pennsylvania statute considered in *Casey* included a sex-selection prohibition that the petitioner did not challenge. This probably reflects their wise assessment that defending sex-selection abortions is fool-hardy and probably fruitless, even under the new undue burden test. Yet, this is a small victory indeed. Such a prohibition is virtually impossible to enforce since it could never be determined that sex- selection was the reason an abortion was sought when reasons are not required to be given. Moreover, even if it was an enforceable provision, it would prohibit a very, very small number of abortions.[39]

The other "arguable" prohibition would be post-viability abortions unless done for "medical emergency" reasons as defined in the Pennsylvania statute. The definition of medical emergency approved by the Court is much more restrictive than the "health" exception requirement of *Doe* v. *Bolton*.[40] If a state were to prohibit post-viability abortions except in the defined emergency situation, the Court would ultimately have to decide if that were an adequate exception under *Roe* and *Doe*. By virtue of dicta the joint opinion seems to answer that question affirmatively. In response to the argument that the definition is too narrow because it excludes the three conditions discussed above, the opinion said:

> If the contention were correct, we would be required to invalidate the restrictive operation of the provision, for the essential holding of Roe forbids a state from interfering with a woman's choice to undergo an abortion procedure if continuing her pregnancy would constitute a threat to her health.[41]

Presumably, then, this narrower definition is consistent with *Roe* and *Doe*. Yet, *Casey* was assessing it in the context of a regulation, not a prohibition. What difference that might make remains to be seen. But, again, even if post-viability abortions could be so restricted, the impact on total abortions would be minor.

However, there is a more important point, not even addressed by *Casey*, that is, the issue of viability itself. Despite the irrationality of the viability dividing line, *Casey* did not rethink, reassess or defend viability. The joint opinion merely accepted it as *"central* to the holding of *Roe."*[42] But, as Paul Linton of Americans United for Life has pointed out, viability is far from central to *Roe.*[43] Indeed, viability was not even raised by the briefs or arguments in *Roe* v. *Wade.*[44] Sara Weddington even refused to acknowledge *any* point at which abortion might be proscribed, much less at viability.[45] The viability issue was introduced by Justice Harry Blackmun and occupies all of three lines of the book-length *Roe* opinion. How can this be so central to *Roe*, especially when the trend is clearly contrary in other areas of law, and medical technology? In the development of public policy on this issue, laser sharp focus must be directed at the illegitimacy of the viability dividing line. The Court must be forced to confront its illogic. Perhaps, one mechanism would be an abortion ban taking effect earlier than the 23-24 weeks mentioned in *Casey*, with the medical emergency exception from the Pennsylvania statute. This would force the Court to confront both the legitimacy of viability and the scope of the mandated health exception.

This, however, raises another very important and difficult issue. How much can we ask states to do to test the limits of *Casey*? Perhaps the most devastating effect of *Casey* is to dash hopes that continuing to legislate beyond the Pennsylvania statue makes sense and can be productive. The subjectivity of the undue burden test makes it virtually impossible to argue that we can predict what will happen to any given abortion law. Ordinarily, this would not be reason enough to avoid legislating to map-out the constitutional limits of abortion regulation. However, the existence of the federal fee shifting statute,[46] which places the costs of litigation upon the loosing party, makes such litigation extremely risky for state legislators. In an era of strapped budgets it is difficult to persuade even the most pro-life legislator to test the limits of *Casey* when the unavoidable challenge that will be raised will not only cost the state a great amount in direct defense costs, but will burden it with the legal fees of *challengers* and *intervenors.*

Consequently, if one thing could be changed to allow states to continue to shape public policy in the abortion area, it would be to exempt abortion litigation from the fee shifting provisions. Otherwise, states will be hard-pressed to test the limits of *Casey.*

CONCLUSION

After twenty years of debate, political battles, and perceived political victories leading to a Supreme Court that was supposed to be solicitous of the original intent of the constitution, we measure our grand victory in increments of fine-tuning of the abortion "right." Given that assessment, I find it is impossible not to have a pessimistic reaction to the *Casey* decision.

Moreover, the future holds little promise. *Casey* creates a mercurial standard that is unlikely to permit any legislation that actually affects the massive U.S. abortion business. Indeed, we may have seen all that *Casey* will allow in those provisions of the Pennsylvania law upheld. With the loss of Justice White and the likelihood of a pro-abortion rights nominee, the Court may become even more supportive of *Roe* with its *Casey* gloss.

Yet, my greater fear is that *Casey* could succeed in quelling the public policy debate. Touted as a Solomonic compromise reflective of public opinion, it will be wielded as a good reason for doing nothing and assuming the issue is settled. However, *Casey* does not reflect public opinion. True, the Pennsylvania statute reflected restrictions that are overwhelmingly supported by the American people; but the best polls[47] also show they reject abortion on demand and any abortion performed in the absence of a compelling reason or exceptional cause. But abortion on demand without compelling justification is precisely what *Casey* maintains, for that is the core holding of *Roe*.

Therefore, still now twenty years later, pro-life public policy continues to rest on education, massive and pervasive education, which attempts to tell the truth about abortion in the face of so much strident misinformation. The likely debate of the Freedom of Choice Act may be one occasion for such education, yet passage of the Act in some form is likely. Health care reform may be another, since the Clinton administration has indicated that full coverage for abortion on demand is likely to be included.

For the past 12 years the receptiveness of the Oval Office to the pro-life position was critical in preserving some respectability for the issue, and for adding the strength of the veto pen to the pro-life movement. Now, the pro-life position faces a radically different situation in that office. For example, in his first week in office and on the 20th anniversary of *Roe* v. *Wade*, President Clinton signed executive orders that lifted a federal ban on abortions on military bases[48] and ordered the liberalization of federal policy on fetal tissue and embryo research regulations.

Notwithstanding these difficulties, the effort to minimize the occurrence of the tragedy of abortion must continue. Sound public policy on any issue can effectively be shaped by truth. And that is the good purpose of this conference. Unfortunately, the search for the truth about abortion outside of settings like this one requires an open and honest debate; but that conversation rarely occurs in public. The 1992 Democratic National Convention's refusal to allow Governor Casey to speak because of his pro-life position illustrates just how very disordered public discourse on this subject has become. Consequently, for all who are concerned about the union of truth and public policy on this issue, every effort must be made to reopen the debate and rigorously to confront the act of abortion as a complex social evil.

NOTES

1. Basile J. Uddo, "A Wink From The Bench: The Federal Courts and Abortion," *Tulane Law Review* 53 (1979): 398.

2. Basile J. Uddo, "A Wink From The Bench," 398. Also see, Basile J. Uddo, "The Human Life Bill: Protecting the Unborn Through Congressional Enforcement of the Fourteenth Amendment," *Loyola of New Orleans Law Review* 27 (1981): 1079; "The New Pro-Abortion Rhetoric," *Human Life Review* (1981): 48; "Manipulating 'The Choice' on CBS," *America* 144 (March 21, 1981): 230-32 at 230; "Pregnancy Due to Rape and Incest," in, *Restoring the Right to Life: The Human Life Amendment*, ed. J. Bopp (Provo, UT: Brigham Young University, 1984), 175; Basile J. Uddo and Ann Neal, "The Human Life Amendment . . . Two Views," *National Catholic Reporter* (April 24, 1981): 10-11.

3. *Planned Parenthood of S.E. Penn. et al.* v. *Robert P. Casey et al.*, 112 S. Ct. 2791 (1992). (Hereafter, *Planned Parenthood* v. *Casey*.)

4. *Planned Parenthood* v. *Casey*, 2804.

5. *Planned Parenthood* v. *Casey*, 2816, wherein the Court partially overrules *City of Akron* v. *Akron Center for Reproductive Health*, 462 U.S. 416, 103 S.Ct 2481 (1983) and *Thornburgh* v. *Am. College of Obstetricians and Gynecologists*, 476 U.S. 747, 106 S. Ct. 2169 (1986).

6. *Planned Parenthood* v. *Casey*, 2809.

7. *Planned Parenthood* v. *Casey*, 2809.

8. *Planned Parenthood* v. *Casey*, 2809. (Emphasis added.)

9. *Planned Parenthood* v. *Casey*, 2798.

10. See, for example, John T. Noonan, Jr., *A Private Choice: Abortion in America in the Seventies* (New York: The Free Press, 1979); Robert A. Destro, "Abortion and the Constitution," *California Law Review* 63 (1975): 1250; John Hart Ely, "The Wages of Crying Wolf: A Comment on Roe v. Wade," *Yale Law Journal* 82 (1973): 920.

11. For a recent and thorough analysis of American public opinion on abortion, conducted by The Gallup Organization, which confirms the lack of support for *Roe* v. *Wade* almost 20 years later, see, "Abortion and Moral Beliefs: A Survey of American Opinion" (Chicago, IL: Americans United for Life, February 28, 1991).

12. Laurence H. Tribe, *Abortion: The Clash of Absolutes* (New York: W. W. Norton, 1990).

13. Charles Krauthammer, "Good Policy, Bad Law," *Washington Post*, (July 3, 1992): OP-ED.

14. *Planned Parenthood* v. *Casey*, 2816.

15. *Planned Parenthood* v. *Casey*, 2817.

16. *Planned Parenthood* v. *Casey*, 2817. (Emphasis added).

17. See, for example, *City of Akron* v. *Akron Center*, 2481.

18. *City of Akron* v. *Akron Center*, 2510.

19. *Planned Parenthood* v. *Casey*, 2807.

20. *Planned Parenthood* v. *Casey*, quoting *Roe* v. *Wade* 410 U.S., 164-65. (Emphasis added).

21. *Planned Parenthood* v. *Casey*, 2807. (Emphasis added).

22. For an excellent discussion of the history of abortion, especially its status as a common law, and then, a statutory crime, see, John T. Noonan, Jr., *A Private Choice*, 33-68.

23. *City of Akron* v. *Akron Center*, 2481.

24. *Thornburgh* v. *Am. College of Obstetricians and Gynecologists*, 2169.

25. *Planned Parenthood* v. *Casey*, 2824-25. (Emphasis added).

26. *Planned Parenthood* v. *Casey*, 2833. (Emphasis added).

27. *Planned Parenthood* v. *Casey*, 2830.

28. *Planned Parenthood* v. *Casey*, 2822.

29. *Planned Parenthood* v. *Casey*, 2822.

30. *Planned Parenthood* v. *Casey*, 2820. (Emphasis added).

31. *Planned Parenthood* v. *Casey*, 2825-26. (Emphasis added).

32. *Planned Parenthood* v. *Casey*, 2826.

33. *Planned Parenthood* v. *Casey*, 2818.

34. *Planned Parenthood* v. *Casey*, 2818.

35. *Planned Parenthood* v. *Casey*, 2830. (Emphasis added).

36. *Planned Parenthood* v. *Casey*, 2832.

37. *Planned Parenthood* v. *Casey*, 2832.

38. *Planned Parenthood* v. *Casey*, 2833.

39. By all estimates no more than 1% of abortions are sex-selection or third trimester abortions.

40. *Doe* v. *Bolton*, 410 U.S. 179, 93 S. Ct. 739 (1973).

41. *Planned Parenthood* v. *Casey*, 2822.

42. *Planned Parenthood* v. *Casey*, 2817.

43. Paul Linton's comments were made during a speech given at the Legislator's Educational Conference, held on July 31-August 2, 1992. The conference was sponsored by Americans United for Life. Linton's comments appear in written form in AUL reprints of the speeches available from Americans United for Life, Chicago, IL.

44. Paul Linton, see note 42, *supra*.

45. Paul Linton, see note 42, *supra*.

46. 42 U.S.C., §1988 (West 1991).

47. See note 11, *supra*.

48. "Clinton Orders Reversal of Abortion Restrictions Left by Reagan and Bush," *New York Times* CXLII (January 23, 1993): 1.

De Officiis: Catholics and the Strains of Office

Hadley Arkes

There is always a point to be made in recalling that story about the philosopher Wittgenstein, asking a friend, "Tell me, why do people always say it was *natural* for men to assume that the sun went round the earth rather than that the earth was rotating?" His friend replied, "Well, obviously, because it just *looks* as if the sun is going round the earth." To which Wittgenstein responded, "Well, what would it have looked like if it had looked as if the earth was rotating?" The question has been posed ever more urgently over the last twenty years as to the responsibility of Catholics, in public authority, to honor the moral understanding that makes them Catholics, even when that understanding puts them at odds with currents of opinion that may be dominant in the community. But I would take that question at first from a different angle, by asking a version of the question, What would it have looked like if it were thought that the earth was rotating, rather than the sun? What would the problem appear to be if the question of moral conflict were viewed from the perspective of a politician who was not Catholic? What would the tension seem to be, and what properties would be drawn into the claims of "belief," "conviction," or "moral judgment"? We would find, I think, that there are no novel tensions imported into this problem for Catholics. On the other hand, we would find that the Catholic tradition has already set in place the precise moral groundwork that is necessary in addressing this problem. And in fact, once that groundwork is understood, there should be no special strain, for the Catholic, between the principles that govern his moral judgment as a Catholic, and the law he would install for a community of people who are not joined with him in the body of the Church.

But before I set off on that path, it is worth mentioning that this problem of moral conflict has been posed with more urgency over the last twenty years, since the freedom to order an abortion has been made into nothing less than a constitutional right. I would not announce anything new or provocative to point out that this novelty in the law could not have claimed the acceptance it has gained if Catholics at the highest reaches of American government had acted with the moral reflexes of Catholics. Instead, men such as Justice Brennan, and Senators Kennedy, Moynihan, Leahy, and Biden, have reacted to embrace the change, as a rule of law quite tolerable and fitting for a community that is not wholly Catholic. But then, more than that, to celebrate this new rule as a rule of justice and right for women. Of course, in the sweep of this celebration, these public men have moved beyond the matter of tolerance for a law not tailored to the demanding requirements of Catholicism. They have moved to the point of proclaiming the rightness of abortion for Catholics as well. That is to say, they have proclaimed nothing less than the wrongness of a teaching that has been central to the moral teaching of the Church, and they have deepened the problem by suggesting that there is nothing in this rejection, of the deepest teaching of the Church, that should alter in the slightest degree their standing as "good Catholics." These Catholics have helped, in fact, to tutor the public mind, to build the acceptance of abortion among Catholics and non-Catholics alike, and so they have sharpened the ancient problem. These Catholic politicians have placed an even heavier burden on any Catholic in office who would accord his own judgments with the teachings of the Church. And indeed, the serious Catholic in public office is more likely to appear sectarian and partisan, the agent of religion in a secular community.

And so, back to the point I proposed: to view the problem from the perspective of the politician who is not a Catholic. At this moment, President Clinton may be taken as the most notable example of a non-Catholic in high office. He is also the product of a Catholic College; still, that connection does not spoil the point, for Georgetown did not seem to make a deep impression on him in its Catholic character. He expresses a certain public piety toward the notion of religious belief. He is not inclined to challenge the things people claim as their religious convictions, and he professes a willingness to avoid those straining cases in which the law imposes on people a policy at odds with the commands of their religion. And so, Mr. Clinton has staked out an advanced position on "gay rights," but he has suggested so far that the law ought not be imposed on people whose aversion to homosexuality may be

184

drawn from their religious traditions. Clinton has taken the initiative in establishing a new policy on gays in the military, and he has intimated that he would support some version of a "gay rights" bill. Presumably, that bill would bar a wide range of discriminations against gays in private employment, or even in private housing. And yet, he has suggested that he would be wary of imposing any such regulations on religious institutions or religious schools. A public school might come under the law if it barred homosexuals from positions as teachers, but apparently, in Mr. Clinton's understanding, that policy might not be applied in the same way to Catholic schools.

Mr. Clinton has made it clear that he regards this policy on gays as a matter of fairness, decency, and justice. Some of us would point out that these are moral terms, and it is with a moral voice, with the overtones of right and wrong, that Mr. Clinton seems to speak on this question. And yet, Clinton evidently marks off an important moral gradation: discrimination against gays is something he proclaims to be wrong, and yet apparently he does not regard it as a wrong on the same plane as discrimination on the basis of race. For with racial discrimination, there is not the least allowance for religious conviction. We have a full body of laws now that forbid discriminations based on race, and there has not been the least suggestion that these laws may not be enforced, in their full stringency, on religious schools. And Bill Clinton has not made any gesture toward extending, on this issue, the kind of immunities he is willing to cede to churches and religious schools on the treatment of gays. For Bill Clinton, both policies have a moral standing, but he seems to make a division between two tiers of moral commitments: certain wrongs seem indeed to be universal, and the law that forbids them sweeps universally, with no allowances made for people who disagree with the law, and claim, as the ground of their objection, their religious beliefs. On the other hand, certain kinds of wrongs are not regarded as universal in the same way. They might be applied generally, but not to people who object on grounds that may be called "religious." But what may be called "religious" in America may be just about anything: the strong presumption in American law is that people in official authority should not be rendering judgments about the beliefs that count as legitimate or spurious religions.

When legislators are willing to accommodate such a vast area of exemption from their policy, they suggest, at the very least, that they have a lesser sense of urgency about the need or the justification for applying their policy universally, to everyone who may come within its terms. And it is hard to avoid the sense that the lesser urgency must be connected with a lesser conviction, or a lesser surety about the grounds of their policy.

Why, after all, is it more important that the ban on racial discrimination be applied with the full moral sweep, to every pocket of discrimination, whether it is in private corporations, private restaurants, even private clubs? Why is there no willingness to break that universal sweep by accommodating some of those fundamentalist groups that have claimed a certain aversion, on doctrinal grounds, to racial integration? The answer seems to be that it is just that much harder to accord even a shred of plausibility to anyone who contends that it is indeed legitimate to draw moral inferences about people on the basis of their color. We could show that the case in principle against racial discrimination is grounded in axioms of reason that hold true as a matter of necessity. They involve propositions of this kind: that we may not hold people blameworthy or responsible for attributes they were powerless to affect; that attributes such as race or color, or height or weight, are utterly without moral significance, in the sense that none of these attributes can exert a controlling or "deterministic" force in molding the moral conduct of any person. From knowing that a person is tall or short, dark or fair, we can draw no moral inference as to whether he is a good or a bad man, whether he deserves praise or punishment, whether his presence should be welcomed or shunned. These conclusions simply flow out of the nature of a moral agent and the logic of morals itself, and we would find ourselves falling into contradiction if we sought to reject them. No theology that has any serious claim to credence would reserve a claim, say, to reject the law of contradiction in the name of belief or revelation. And for the same reason, no serious body of theology will set itself against propositions that express necessary truths or axioms of reason—e.g., that there is no effect without a cause, that there cannot be responsibility or blame without a causal agent. No respectable theology then will associate itself with the proposition that "race" may indeed govern or control the moral conduct of any person.

Aristotle understood that there was something divine about reason itself, and we have long come to understand that there need not be a tension between reason and belief. As Aquinas remarked at one point, if

God wished us to be governed in everything by faith, He would not have given us the gift of reason. We act in accord with the design of our natures when we explore rigorously the commands of reason; and therefore, we are not inclined to grant any casual exemptions from the law, or strain our credulity by seeking a release from propositions that stand among the laws of reason.

In the case of discriminations based on race, we make no concession to the claims of belief, but in the case of discrimination against gays, Bill Clinton is willing to make that concession, and I would suggest that the divergence marks a serious difference of conviction. In the face of people who will not accept a homosexual couple as a marriage, the case for gay rights has many more challenges to answer, and the proponents of gay rights simply may not be confident that they can reply with an account as compelling as the case they could make on racial discrimination.

But regardless of the source of this diffidence, there is evidently a lesser certainty or lesser conviction, and it must give way to this further question: if we admit doubts about the rightness of imposing this policy on religious people who cannot accept it, why should we be any more willing to impose the law on other people who cannot accept it? What if we found people who objected to homosexuality on grounds they regarded simply as "moral," without appealing to sources in scripture? They might bring forth many plausible grounds for refusing to credit homosexual sex as something that can be "sex" at all in the strictest, biological sense. My point is not to canvass the reasons or weigh them, but merely to note them—to note that there may be objections founded simply in reasons about the justification or rightness of homosexual sex. There may indeed be a difference between the people who think that their objections to homosexuality are commanded by God, and the people who think that the objections are commanded by reason. But it is not clear that this difference can justify a different treatment in the law for these people when it comes to granting a release from the obligations of law in the treatment of gays.

Let me recall that we saw this problem not long ago in the dispute that blocked, for several years, the passage of the Civil Rights bill of 1988. That bill overrode the so-called *Grove City* case, decided by the Supreme Court. The bill offered the prospect of applying the full panoply of federal regulations to any educational institution that received funds from the federal government. But as the pieces of that bill fell into place, a grotesque possibility had emerged: it was possible for a Catholic university, such as Georgetown, to have students receiving loans from the federal government, and in that event, Georgetown could be compelled to permit abortions in the hospital run by the University. The objection to that prospect held up, for several years, a bill that had wide support in the Congress. Initially, there was an attempt to deal with the objection simply by granting an exemption, for abortion, to all colleges with a religious character, represented in their corporate structure. And yet, opposition arose on a broad front to that kind of settlement. For there were many hospitals with doctors and staffs who bore a moral objection to abortion, even though they were not religious hospitals and the objectors did not invoke a religious ground for their objections. Would abortion become a compulsory policy then for all hospitals except the religious? If doctors and staffs bore moral objections to abortion, why should they be compelled nevertheless to perform abortions because they did not claim to be animated by religious convictions? The matter was finally resolved through the passage of the Danforth Amendment, which simply declared that the legislation was creating no right to an abortion in schools or facilities funded by the federal government. If we were dubious about making the performance of abortions compulsory for Catholic doctors, we were dubious about the grounds on which we would impose that policy on other doctors as well. That is to say, we run the risk of obscuring the moral grounds of our judgments and objections when we fly to the assumption that the objections of the religious are wrapped in a haze of faith that may not be accessible to people who do not share their faith. It may be, in fact, that their objections depend on points of evidence and reasoning that are as valid for people outside their faith. In that event, their objections do not merely challenge the aptness of enforcing the law on people like themselves, people with their beliefs. Their objections would call into serious question the very justification for the law—and therefore the justification for imposing that law on anyone.

But when we discover these things anew, we rediscover an understanding as old as politics and law: a law that is binding on everyone should have as its end a good that is applicable to all, and it should find its ground in an understanding of right and wrong that holds, in principle, for everyone. We were taught by the classics, by Plato and Aristotle, that political authority was public in its nature and its ends. That nature was perverted when this authority over the whole was placed in the service merely of private interests, which might not be publicly expressed, and private beliefs, which may not be publicly shared. But that is to say, the problem of politics points us to a distinct moral ground for the making of law, and it brings us back to distinctions that have always been bound up with the natural law. Aquinas touched the core of the matter when he invoked the words of Paul in Romans that when the Gentiles, who have not the law, do by nature the things of the law, they are as a law unto themselves (Rom 2:14). Aquinas himself was quite clear in explaining that the divine law we would know only through revelation, but that the natural law was the law that was accessible to human beings, as human beings, through the reason that marked our essential nature as human beings.

In our own founding generation, we had a political class that understood, quite precisely, the grounds of natural law in the "laws of reason." Men like John Marshall and Alexander Hamilton showed an awareness, quite precisely, of certain axioms, or indemonstrable first principles, which formed the groundwork for all moral judgments. Hamilton conveyed the point elegantly in the Federalist No. 31:

> In disquisitions of every kind there are certain primary truths, or first principles, upon which all subsequent reasonings must depend. These contain an internal evidence which, antecedent to all reflection or combination, command the assent of the mind.... Of this nature are the maxims in geometry that the whole is greater than its parts; that things equal to the same are equal to one another; that two straight lines cannot enclose a space; and that all right angles are equal to each other. Of the same nature are these other maxims in ethics and politics, that there cannot be an effect without a cause; that the means ought to be proportioned to the end; that every power ought to be commensurate with its object; that there ought to be no limitation of a power destined to effect a purpose which is itself incapable of limitation.[1]

The Founders understood that the American regime was established on an axiomatic truth of that kind, that "all men are created equal." Or to put it another way, beings who are capable of giving and understanding reasons deserved to be ruled through the rendering of reasons, in a government of consent. The Founders regarded that proposition, in all strictness, as a necessary moral truth. But in our own day, of course, in the circles of the educated, it has become unfashionable and even unsettling to speak about moral truths or to suggest that our judgments on matters moral can ever be anything more than tentative. Whether we are dealing with the Left or the Right, the dominant view in our political class is that moral judgments do not find their ground in necessary truths. They come to rest, finally, on beliefs, stronger or weaker beliefs, more or less plausible beliefs, but in the end, nothing that claims any higher standing than a "belief."

That sentiment has now become familiar, but few people have completed the translation: if all of our judgments on right and wrong—and if all of the judgments incorporated in our laws—come to rest on nothing more than "beliefs," then why should "religious belief" stand on a lower plane than any other beliefs that animate people in our politics and seek their enactment in our laws? After all, we are asked to credit "beliefs" precisely because there are no moral truths: could the claim be made now that certain kinds of beliefs—say, religious beliefs—are knowably less true or plausible, or less fitting, as the ground of a public policy? Our political class has not seemed to take hold of that question, and while it eludes them, our politics show the notable signs of inversion: It is taken as quite legitimate that certain "high tech" companies should seek to have their industries promoted by the government through policies on taxation and investment. But if the Catholic Church lobbies for the sake of resisting euthanasia, that is taken as an illegitimate intrusion of religion into politics, as though there were something about these ends that were immanently less wholesome for our political life. With the same state of mind, we may make public funds available to a private secondary school such as Andover Academy, but we could not make them available to a Catholic secondary school. And yet, if everything reduces finally to a matter of belief, how could we say that there is anything more valid, more legitimate, more wholesome, about the ethic that informs Andover than the ethic that pervades a Catholic school?

But these distinctions continue to be made, with this touch of irony: that the people who cling to them do not apparently recognize that they are backing into the logic of natural law. For in one way or another, they must insist that we are possessed, after all, of some truths, some standards

190

of moral judgment, which permit us to make distinctions among the beliefs that are more or less plausible, or more or less legitimate for a republic.

And yet, whether we are dealing with conservatives or liberals, we have seen the tendency, in our own time, to reject natural law and identify the natural law with revelation. That curious understanding has been part of the commentaries put forth by Judge Bork, as well as by that premier commentator on the natural law, Senator Biden.[2] The suggestion is made that anyone who appeals to natural rights is appealing to religious faith or revelation, and those who profess some ground of judging between right and wrong are branded with the suggestion that they claim to have inside information about the will of God. Within this setting of opinion, the one who professes to know something about natural law will appear—in Tom Stoppard's phrase—like "a variety of crank, haranguing the bus queue with the demented certitude of one blessed with privileged information."

But the point, precisely, about natural law was that it would not depend on revelation or belief. It would depend on the kind of reasoning that is accessible to human beings as human beings, and it would work through a language that is available to all persons, quite apart from the language that furnishes their minds as Catholics and Baptists, Geologists and Chiropractors, computer mavens and Redskins fans. In this, compelling form, natural law may appeal to the deepest stratum of understanding in our common natures. And on that head, there are few examples more telling than that fragment Lincoln wrote for himself on the matter of slavery. Lincoln imagined himself to be in a conversation with the owner of slaves, and he put the question of why the master was justified in making slaves of black people.

> You say A. is white, and B. is black. It is color, then: the lighter having the right to enslave the darker? Take care. By this rule, you are to be slave to the first man you meet, with a fairer skin than your own.

> You do not mean *color* exactly?—You mean the whites are *intellectually* the superiors of the blacks, and therefore have the right to enslave them? Take care again. By this rule, you are to

191

be slave to the first man you meet, with an intellect superior to
your own.

I would note that nothing in this chain of reasoning depended on any
appeal to revelation, or to matters of religious belief. Lincoln's argument
could be understood by people of any religious persuasion, who had
access simply to the "laws of reason." People of almost every age, and
every variety of education, seem able to understand that fragment written
by Lincoln. And some of us have drawn on that analogy for the
argument over abortion. With the same style of principled reasoning, we
could simply put the question, Why do you regard the child in the womb
as anything less than a human being? Is it because she cannot speak?
Neither do deaf mutes. Is it because she seems to lack arms or legs? Well,
other people have been born missing one or more of their limbs, or they
have lost control over their limbs, and we have not thought that they
have lost anything necessary to their standing as human beings. As
Lincoln pursued the logic of his fragment on slavery, the general lesson
seemed to be that there was nothing one could cite to disqualify the black
man as a human being that could not apply to many whites as well. And
in the same vein, as we have employed the same reasoning about the
matter of abortion, we would point out that there is nothing one could
say to disqualify the child in the womb as a human being that would not
apply to many people moving about, well outside the womb.

Again, the point is that there is nothing inscrutable or mysterious in
this exercise; it is simply a matter of principled reasoning. There is no
need to fly to the most exotic realms of belief or theology, cut off from
the prospect of giving and judging reasons. And what seems to come as
news to people—even to Catholics—is that the Catholic tradition has cast
up the clearest tools, or offered the clearest guidance, so that people in
public office need not be confused by these distinctions: they need not
fear to engage in deliberation on matters of moral consequence for fear
that they will be drawn into a discourse that is theological and
unfathomable. And yet, that is precisely the line that has been retailed to
us, by Catholic as well as non-Catholic politicians. If it is possible to find
the most crystalline examples of distraction, this species of confusion was
exemplified for us in the most telling way by President Clinton when he
was speaking in a high school gymnasium in Ohio. One youngster asked
the President if he did not think that life began at conception. Mr.

Clinton drew on something he might have recalled dimly from his days at Georgetown and reminded this young man that controversies had flared long ago over the question of ensoulment, the question of when the soul enters the body and converts the embryonic material into a distinctly "human" life. That question, said the President, had never been settled, and would never be settled, and he was not about to have the laws shaped according to religious beliefs so murky or ineffable that they may never be judged for their truth or falsity.

We may leave aside here the question of whether Mr. Clinton understands the notion of the soul as the "substantial form" of the body. Theologians do not seem to be vexed by this problem today, since it is taken for granted that ensoulment virtually coincides with the existence of the body and the emergence of life. No one, that is, seems to think that the body is around very long waiting for a soul to arrive,[3] although some artful biologists recently have been presenting arguments on "delayed hominization."[4] But putting all of that aside, it has been well understood in the Catholic tradition, at least since Aquinas, that the law involves practical reason; that it proceeds from the indemonstrable principles of the natural law to the conclusions cast on contingencies, on the circumstances of our real lives.[5] The question may be asked of Mr. Clinton: is it only on the matter of abortion that the civil law must come to a judgment on the question of when human life begins? Under the laws of Arkansas, when does a child qualify to receive the support of the State in welfare if her parents are poor? When would she have a claim to receive the pre-natal care that is supported by the federal government? When would that child have standing as an heir to inherit property? When would it have standing to sue against a negligent driver or a malpracticing physician? The answer, in most of these cases, is that the child would have standing in the law as soon as she is shown to exist.[6] And the procedure established now for this critical test is not "quickening," but what we call these days a "pregnancy test." But with the requirement of a pregnancy test, the civil law does nothing less than "legislate a theory" about the beginning of human life. Now, we might plausibly ask, How could a child in the womb have standing, as a human child, or a moral agent, with a claim to receive the protection of the law, or have standing to press claims in a court, when it comes to welfare or pre-natal care—and yet, have no standing at all as a human child, and no claim even to the minimal protection of the law, when it comes to the matter of extinguishing its life in an abortion? If Mr. Clinton is truly perplexed about the beginning of human life, then to take a line from Henry James, he seems to be the victim of perplexities from which a single spark of direct perception might have spared him. But if he is truly perplexed, we can dissolve his problem instantly, with this instruction: why don't you see what judgment you have been willing to settle upon in other parts of the law for the beginning of human life? Those of us who would seek to protect the child would be pleased to start there, at least, as a promising place to begin.

But if the discussion manages to advance to this point, one other recognition may break in on us: it is only a pregnancy test that provides the predicate for the surgery known as abortion. Without that test, we would not know that any woman was in a condition that was even relevant to the performance of an abortion, as opposed to an appendectomy. The very condition that defines the appropriateness of the abortion is the condition that establishes, unequivocally, the decisive points that President Clinton and others pretend are in serious doubt: namely, there is a living being, a separate life, launched now on a self-sustaining process of growth; and in the nature of things that being will not be an orange or a canary. If it were, then an unwanted orange would not present us with the kinds of problems that surround an "unwanted pregnancy." The matter is freighted with moral significance because we understand that we are dealing with an unwanted human child, and we could not be free to rid ourselves of a human child on any other occasion by selling her, giving her away, or simply discarding her. In short, we mark, in a pregnancy test, the very predicate of abortion, an understanding that should be decisive in settling the things that Mr. Clinton finds shrouded in mystery.

That question seems to have been shrouded in mystery also for Governor Mario Cuomo. And yet Governor Cuomo has acknowledged that even a radically secular world must address the question of "when life begins, under what circumstances it can be ended, when it must be protected, by what authority." Even if people in office were wholly detached from Catholicism or any variety of religious conviction, the law would still have to work out its position on when life begins and ends. If legatees may inherit their legacy only when Uncle Julius has died, it makes a difference as to when, precisely, Uncle Julius may be pronounced dead.

Cuomo understands that even a government of atheists would have to legislate an understanding about the beginning and end of human life. And in addressing this question, the Church has not begun from any inscrutable or mystical point. It has begun with the things that are nearest to sight, in the experience that is accessible to all; and it may amplify that experience through the testimony of science and the findings of embryology. A liberal legislator in Maryland complained not too long ago that the old laws that restricted abortion would encumber women with a medieval understanding. But it could be said, more truly, that the proponents of the new laws on abortion seem mired in a medieval view of embryology. Aristotle might have thought that the embryo moves through a vegetative and animal stage before it becomes human; and Aquinas might have thought there was a notable interval before the embryo is invested with a distinctly human soul. But no one who is informed by modern genetics should hold back for a moment, in medieval superstition, and suffer the least doubt that the zygote, or the conceptus, is a genetically distinct human being, and nothing other than a human being, from its first moments.

We have not thought in the past that it requires any special flexing of imagination, or religious belief, to say that the laws of homicide cover Jews or Koreans, left-handers or backgammon players. We do not need any special mention of those humans; why should we need then any special mention of the human beings who happen to be resident for several months in the wombs of their mothers? The Church has simply raised these questions and insisted on these points; and in making this argument, the Church has not had to invoke any perspective that has been narrowly or distinctly Catholic.

Governor Cuomo has dimly recognized that point, but without quite grasping its significance. He has complained that "abortion is treated differently" by the Church. The Church does not seek to legislate, for the community at large, the exacting view of the Church on the matters of divorce or contraception. In those domains, the Church has been appealing for a special regimen of self-denial, and it offers an invitation to people who are willing to share in that demanding life of belief and practice. But on abortion, the Church has been insistent, unyielding, and willing to assert its position, without apology, in the political arena, because it understands that it has been offering a distinctly moral argument, drawn from natural law, and accessible to all beings of reason, even if they are not Catholic.

These distinctions are hardly novel, then. They have been cultivated in the Church from its beginnings. And so my main argument today has been that Catholics should be in a better position to deal with the tension between public authority and religious belief, because they should be equipped with an even clearer sense of the distinctions that mark the boundary between private belief and public law. They have also been tutored on the prudence that ought to restrain people in office, even when they are seeking the best of ends. They have been taught by Aquinas that the "purpose of the law is to lead men to virtue, not suddenly but gradually." As Aquinas remarked, we should not impose upon the multitude of imperfect men the burdens of those who are already virtuous, namely that they should abstain from all evil.[7] The law is made, we know, for beings who are between animals and angels. We may say, with Disraeli, that we prefer to regard them as on the side of the angels; but we cannot expect from human beings, or human law, a regime of perfection. Or, as Aquinas put it, citing Augustine, we may expect the human law to leave unpunished many things that are punished by a divine providence.[8] But that is not because the ends of human law are wholly different from the ends of a divine, eternal law. Human laws may be a scaled down version of law, reduced to more modest ends, but we understand the model from which they have been scaled. The wondrous arrangement of law did not spring from a random numbers table, any more than the universe that contains the law. Even the most modest efforts at law proceeded from the understanding of "law" and lawfulness, and as Aquinas understood, they were ultimately drawn from first Author of all laws and lawfulness.[9]

But if the law must be more modest in its ends, it must still be directed to the *rightful* ends, and people in positions of authority would still have an obligation to teach. The Church has not sought to enact all of its teachings into public law; and yet, as I have suggested, those teachings have not been woven entirely out of faith. They have been composed for the most part of moral reasoning, amplified by faith, or of arguments completed by faith in the places where arguments are necessarily incomplete. The teaching of the Church on contraception may be the most intriguing case in point. It is evident that, with the current habits and temper of Americans, there would be no prospect of enacting into law the teaching of the Church on contraception. It is not even clear that the Church could command, on this matter, a majority of the American Catholics, let alone a majority of people in the country. And yet, the teaching of the Church is grounded in an understanding of the natural end of sexuality, of the natural form it offers for a distinctly human love. The departures from these understandings will be marked by a disfiguring of love and a disordering of relations among persons. Many people will sense that something is wrong, but very few will be able to trace these maladies back to their source, or recognize that they may have something to do with the understandings that were overthrown when the country absorbed, with enthusiasm, the ethic of contraception.

And yet, it is precisely because the disorders keep cropping up in different places, in new forms, that it may be possible to respond, in different settings, with measures that reflect an older, Catholic understanding. The Catholic official who understands something of the teachings of the Church on contraception may not be in a position to enact a ban on contraception. But he might draw on that older understanding in a variety of cases, dealing with some of the moral novelties of our age: condoms distributed in schools, or an arrangement of making condoms available to students and unmarried people through the undiscriminating device of vending machines in inappropriate places such as restaurants and theaters. The distribution of condoms in these settings, under these conditions, implies an indifference to the age and condition of the users. It seems to be an endorsement, or even an encouragement, of sex as an adjunct to a night out, on the part of people who should not evidently be expecting such liberties. Catholics clothed with public authority could find themselves in a position to express, in these instances, a moral aversion that is shared widely in the community. And if they were touched with some imagination, they might have something quite suggestive to say about the willingness to view sex as a form of recreation on the plane of bowling or billiards. Catholic politicians might have the chance here to put in place some minimal regulations, designed to deal with the problem of youngsters, and yet they might take the opportunity to plant some interesting lessons, which may be absorbed by grownups and by people who are not Catholic.

During those notorious hearings in 1987, over the nomination of Robert Bork to the Supreme Court, Senator Biden kept taunting Judge Bork over the case of *Griswold* v. *Connecticut*; he kept up a drumbeat for a right to contraception as a kind of first step in a right to privacy. Biden asked the Judge: could you even imagine a case in which legislators could plausibly legislate to forbid the use of contraceptives, or even restrict their use for mature adults? During the mean days of those hearings, that was the only moment in which I ever wished to change places with Robert Bork, to take that question. I would have been tempted to respond by saying: yes, Senator, I *can* imagine such a case and such a statute, and it is the kind of statute that you are likely to support. The case might involve a woman who has used the Dalcon shield in the past with no troubles, and she finds now that this device has been removed from the market by a regulatory commission, working under a statute you have sustained, to police drugs for their safety and take certain products or devices off the market. She complains now that she has used the Dalcon shield with no ill effects, that it is, for her, inexpensive and effective. And she argues now that she should be free to make her own decisions about the risks she is willing to take with her own body in making decisions on reproduction. On what ground would the government presume to remove from the field of choice a product that she is willing to use upon her own body?

The fact of the matter is that legislatures and courts are persistently making decisions to restrict contraceptive devices, even from the hands of mature adults. But these cases do not seem to break through the clichés that make up the jurisprudence on privacy and sex. They never seem to make the Bidens among us look again at the propositions they have put forth as jural principles. Just this past summer, in the *Casey* case, Justice Anthony Kennedy signed on to an extravagant example of solipsism as a new principle of constitutional law, in a passage that has also been attributed to his authorship. That is the passage, quickly becoming famous, in which Justice Kennedy and two of his colleagues proclaimed that the right to order an abortion is a right that must stand at the core of our being; that it is bound up with nothing less than "the right to define one's own concept of existence, of meaning, of the universe, and of the mystery of human life."[10] Each person, apparently, has the freedom to conceive the cosmos anew according to his own angle of vision on his sexuality. Students of the courts, who observe the judges closely, were inclined to take that passage as a signal that the Court would have to abandon its decision of several years earlier, to uphold the statutes of a State on sodomy.[11] If the decision on sexuality was at the core of our personal being, of our identities as moral agents, then any restrictions on those private sexual lives would be called immanently into question. And yet, just a few weeks ago, a panel in New York State offered another glimpse of the law, which points in a radically different direction. It turns out that, between 1985 and 1987, New York City ordered the closing of seven businesses, involving gay bathhouses and so-called "swingers clubs" for heterosexuals. The closings were ordered after inspectors had observed patrons paying entrance fees and then engaging in oral and anal sex, evidently with strangers or with acquaintances newly formed.

The closures were ordered under the authority of a public policy, adopted in 1985, to prohibit "high risk" sex in public places. But of course, these were not public places; they were private establishments, and any of these activities could readily occur in private homes, in the guise of parties. And yet, that does not seem to have diminished the conviction on the part of the authorities that they can reach these sexual engagements taking place in private settings. For a panel that advises the City Health Commissioner has strongly advised a more strenuous regimen of enforcement now to deal with the special dangers posed over AIDS. At the end of February, the advisory council recommended that the law be amended to add to the prohibited activities "vaginal inter-course without a condom," and to define sex without a condom as "high risk" sex.[12]

Chairman Biden, where are you now? Several years ago, Senator Biden thought it was unthinkable that public authorities could touch the matter of contraception, as the most private of private decisions. And now, an official panel in New York thinks that the law can enforce a policy on *compulsory contraception*, or compulsory condoms, a policy that could reach heterosexual or homosexual acts, in the most private of settings, if they sin against the policy of prescribing condoms.

The question should earnestly be put to Biden and Justice Kennedy: does this kind of policy not stand in radical opposition to those principles you have proclaimed so gravely on the privacy of these decisions about sex? The answer, in either direction, cannot help but be illuminating. If Biden and company agree that this policy, undertaken with the tenderest liberal sentiments, violates the principles of privacy, then they can speak the words that establish a barrier in the law to any policy of compulsory contraception. But if they are willing to cede to local government some room to regulate these matters of sex in the name of health, then they may do us the service of helping to dismantle some of the worst cliches they have helped to build into doctrines of our law. They would remind us that the walls of privacy establish no barrier to the reach of the law. Murders undertaken in private quarters are every bit as much of a concern to the law as murders performed in the public streets. Rapes, or sexual assaults, may not be insulated from the reach of the law if we think we can judge them as wrong. They are not placed beyond the reach of the law merely because they take place in private settings or because they may take the form of sexual acts. In the same way, these acts of anonymous sex, among strangers, may not be any more insulated from our judgment, or the reach of public law, than acts of prostitution carried out in private apartments.

But for the law to reach these acts, it will be necessary for people in positions of authority to explain the nature of the wrong described in these acts. They will have to explain the grounds on which they can cast judgments on people, even in private settings, even in acts of sex. As they explain the nature of the wrong in these anonymous acts of sex, or explain why people may not indeed have a sovereign claim to degrade the health of their own bodies, they will be compelled to make their way back to some ancient ground. They will be compelled to speak again a language that has fallen into disuse, and discover again understandings that they never quite incorporated in the past, because they never quite took them seriously. If the people clothed with authority happen to be Catholics tutored in their own tradition; if they have a comic touch, or a bit of poetry in them; they may use the occasion to plant suggestions and begin to lead people back, without strain, to a moral tradition they may be surprised to find rather plausible and compelling after all. But an even further surprise may await the people in authority who are not Catholic. For they may discover that these old lessons, as Plato suggested, are simply locked away in our souls; that it is mainly a matter of remembering; and that, in unlocking these old recognitions, it is not even necessary to be Catholic. And that, too, has been one of the abiding teachings of the Church.

NOTES

1. *The Federalist*, No. 31 (New York: Random House, n. d.), 188.

2. See, for example, Senator Joseph Biden, "Law and Natural Law: Questions for Judge Thomas," *Washington Post* (September 8, 1991): C1, C4.

3. Frs. Benedict Ashley and Albert Moraczewski have recently put the matter in this way: "The purely spiritual functions of the soul, namely, the powers of abstract intelligence and of free will, since they transcend material processes (abstract thought cannot be reduced to material images, and free will cannot be determined by physical laws) do not have a physical organ, and thus are not, as so many today suppose, functions of the brain. Nevertheless, as long as the human soul informs the body, it cannot operate in its natural manner without the instrument of the brain which supplies it with the raw data of intellection and therefore of free willing. Hence we must conclude that God immediately creates the human soul at that moment when a body suitable for organization by the soul as its substantial form is proximately prepared as far as purely biological forces can effect this preparation. By the creation of the human soul God completes the act of organizing the matter of the body and produces a unique human being who is at once bodily and spiritual." "Is the Human Person Present from Conception?" Draft prepared for the Pope John XXIII Center, Project on Fetal Tissues, November 23, 1992, 30-31.

4. See Carles A. Bedate and Robert C. Cefalo, "The Zygote: To Be or Not Be a Person," *Journal of Medicine and Philosophy* 14 (1989): 641-45, and Norman Ford, *When Did I Begin? Conception of the Individual in History, Philosophy, and Science* (Cambridge, MA: Cambridge University Press, 1988). See, also, my own critique of some of these arguments, On "Delayed Hominization: Some Thoughts on the Blending of New Science and Ancient Fallacies," in *The Interaction of Catholic Bioethics and Secular Society: Proceedings of the Eleventh Bishops' Workshop, Dallas, Texas,*ed. Russell E. Smith (Braintree, MA: Pope John Center, 1992).

5. See Thomas Aquinas, *Summa Theologica*, II-I, q. 91, a. 3; q. 94, a. 4.

6. The laws on welfare begin these days with the provisions of federal law, and the program of Aid to Families with Dependent Children offers coverage to pregnant women ("at the option of the State") "if it has been medically verified that the child is expected to be born in the month such payments are made or within the three-month period following such month of payment." See 42 U.S.C., §606 (West 1991). And under the programs for Maternal and Child Health, the federal government is willing to extend pre-natal care, for the child as well as the mother, as soon as a woman is pregnant. See 42 U.S.C., §701 (West 1991).

7. Thomas Aquinas, *Summa Theologica*, II-I, q. 96, a. 2.

8. Thomas Aquinas, *Summa Theologica*, q. 96, a. 3.

9. See Thomas Aquinas, *Summa Theologica*, II-I, q. 93, a. 3: "Law denotes a kind of plan directing acts towards an end. Now wherever there are movers ordained to one another, the power of the second mover must needs be derived

from the power of the first mover, since the second mover does not move except in so far as it is moved by the first. Therefore we observe the same in all those who govern, namely, that the plan of government is derived by secondary governors from the governor in chief. . . . Since, then, the eternal law is the plan of government in the Chief Governor, all the plans of government in the inferior governors must be derived from the eternal law. But these plans of inferior governors are all the other laws which are in addition to the eternal law. Therefore all laws, in so far as they partake of right reason, are derived from the eternal law. Hence Augustine says that *in temporal law there is nothing just and lawful but what man has drawn from the eternal law.*"

10. *Planned Parenthood* v. *Casey*, 120 L Ed 2d 674 (1992) at 698 (Joint opinion of Justices O'Connor, Kennedy, and Souter).

11. See *Bowers* v. *Hardwick*, 478 U.S. 186 (1986).

12. See, "State Panel Urges Regulations for Sex Clubs," *New York Times* (February 26, 1993): B3.

The Church and Abortion in the 1990s:
The Role of Institutional Leadership

J. Bryan Hehir

This chapter will examine the role of institutional leadership which the Roman Catholic Church in the United States has played and should play on the question of abortion. The *fact* that the Church has been a major institutional force in the twenty year struggle over abortion is acknowledged by all commentators. The objective of this chapter is to evaluate *how* that institutional role should be exercised and *whether* the Church's public role should change either in its long-term strategy or its specific tactics.

Assessing the institutional posture and policy of the Church on a moral issue is not a purely tactical question. It requires an analysis of the theological foundation of institutional leadership in the Church and a testing of which choices are open to the Church in moral, legal and social terms. To examine these questions today is to face a changing landscape. The consequences of the *Webster* and *Casey* decisions by the Supreme Court and the election of President Clinton shifts the political-legal context significantly from that confronted throughout the 1980s. While the fundamental moral-legal challenge posed by the *Roe* and *Bolton* decisions of 1973 has not substantially changed over the last twenty years, the perspective, resources and tactics needed to continue the struggle today may well be quite different than those used in the 1970s and 1980s.

The argument will move in three stages. First, it will examine the nature of the Catholic Church as a social institution. Second, it will assess the character of the abortion challenge and the kind of response made to it by the Church in the United States. Third, it will analyze the changing dimensions of the abortion question in the 1990s. The assessment of Catholic institutional leadership will be both retrospective (1973-93) and prospective, seeking to propose strategy for this final decade of the century.

THE ROMAN CATHOLIC CHURCH:
SOCIAL AND INSTITUTIONAL CHARACTER

The proposition argued in this section of the paper is that the theological and social premises of the Church's response to the abortion question in the United States were in fact determined centuries ago, have been reaffirmed in terms of the political conditions of the twentieth-century, and have been quite remarkably followed by the bishops of the United States not only on the abortion question, but on a range of social issues. To fill in the lines of this argument, I will use three snapshots of the Church's institutional character: the first from the Protestant historian, Ernst Troeltsch, the second from Vatican II, and the third from the public record of the U.S. Catholic Conference of Bishops in the 1980s. Needless to say these are three quite different sources; Troeltsch's historical-sociological account of Catholicism provides perceptive insight, but is clearly the view of an outsider who misses much of the substance of the Catholic vision; the conciliar text is a theological document, a normative account of Catholicism, strikingly different in tone from Troeltsch's phenomenological account of Catholic history; the third source is a policy narrative of the Church in action in the setting of a secular, pluralistic democracy.

TROELTSCH: THE CHURCH-TYPE DEFINED

In his two volume study, *The Social Teaching of the Christian Churches*, Ernst Troeltsch (1866-1923), the Lutheran philosopher-historian and pre-eminent representative of Liberal Protestantism, set out to confront the Protestant Churches of his day with a profound challenge. In Troeltsch's view the combined effects of the Enlightenment and the Democratic Revolutions had created for the Church in Europe a new "social question" which required a thorough reexamination of how the Church addressed the world of its time. Troeltsch was less concerned with defining what the new strategy for the Church should be, than he was interested in depicting the depth and scope of the new question it faced. In addition to defining the challenge, Troeltsch sought to outline the resources which the Church brought to the social question. This goal led him to an extensive historical commentary from which his famous typology of ecclesial polities was constructed.

Without entering the complex terrain of Troeltsch's methodological premises or his detailed historical account of ecclesiastical history, it is sufficient for the purposes of this paper to summarize his account of Roman Catholicism's style of social presence and social teaching.[1] For Troeltsch, Catholicism is the embodiment of the "Church-type," a depiction which includes the internal polity of the Church and its way of relating to the society and state which it encounters in the world. *Ad intra*, the Church-type is characterized as a large, diverse community which people enter through infant baptism and familial tradition; it is shaped by a "high Church" ecclesiology with a developed sacramental structure and a hierarchial teaching authority; while the boundaries of the community's existence are well defined, there is more room for pluralism of views and practice within the community than its structured existence at first conveys.

Ad extra, in its relationship with the world (Troeltsch's real interest), the Church-type is guided by a strong sense of apostolic responsibility for the world; this takes shape in a conviction that the Church is responsible not only for the personal welfare and moral character of its members, but also for the moral fabric of the institutions of civil society. This basic principle of Church-type ecclesiology is critical to an understanding of how the U. S. Bishops have responded to the abortion challenge. The social responsibility of the Church extends to a care for the major institutions of society: Church-state relations, the moral character of the civil law, the structure of family life and the issues of wealth, poverty and the economic structure of society. This quite expansive conception of social responsibility can be fulfilled while acknowledging and accepting the secular character, origin and purpose of social institutions. In other words, the Church-type ecclesiology does not inevitably lead to a hierocractic conception of authority in which the state's authority to govern is derived from the Church. The Church-type can follow quite strictly the classical principle of Pope Gelasius (+496): all authority is from God, but it is bestowed for spiritual purposes directly upon the Church, and for temporal purposes it is bestowed upon the state.

The Church-type ecclesiology not only accepts responsibility for society, it presumes that collaboration with the state and other civil institutions is possible and necessary. Collaboration is not inevitable or simple; both the history and the theory of Church-state relations attests to the possibilities for conflict. Conflict is always regarded as a failure of the system; what Pope Leo XIII (1878-1903) consistently described as *concordia* is the norm which both church and state should pursue.

In pursuit of collaboration with civil society and in fulfillment of its exercise of pastoral responsibility, the Church-type model adopts a teaching style guided by natural law. The natural law ethic allows the Church to extend the basic values of the faith into the complex domain of civil polity, and it provides the Church with an ethic which can be addressed to those outside the community of faith.

While Troeltsch found this Church-type ecclesiology and ethic in the mainline Protestant Churches (particularly the Lutheran and Reformed Traditions), it was the Catholic Church, especially during the Middle Ages, which embodied the theory and practice of the model. A Catholic reading of Troeltsch's understanding of the Church will find much that fails to persuade, particularly his interpretation of the role of the sacraments. But in broad strokes he provides a structurally accurate conception of how Catholicism conceived and fulfilled its public role.

VATICAN II: THE CHURCH-TYPE REAFFIRMED

A more satisfying theological interpretation of that public role is found in Vatican II's document, *Gaudium et Spes*. This text, the most expansive articulation of Catholicism's social ministry in this century, provides a view of the Church's role in society which is rooted in ecclesiology, christology and theological anthropology. For the purposes of this paper, the significant point is that the Council's expression of how the Church should address civil society corresponds strikingly to the main characteristics of Troeltsch's interpretation.

The conciliar text defines its purpose as explaining to the human family "how it conceives of the presence and activity of the Church in the world today."[2] The explanation can be summarized and assessed in terms of its style, structure and substantive vision of the Church's ministry. The style of the document follows the lead of Pope John XXIII's *Pacem In Terris*; it is addressed to all in the human community, not primarily to the community of faith. The style of the text repeats the Catholic conviction that the Church should accept—in accord with its ministry—a responsibility for the welfare of human society at the local, national and global level. The method of fulfilling this responsibility is summarized in this passage: "this Council can provide no more eloquent proof of its solidarity with the entire human family with which it is bound up . . . than by engaging with it in conversation about these various problems."[3]

The method of *Gaudium et Spes* is dialogical and dialectical. Dialogue is possible because of the Church-type assumptions which the conciliar text brings to the Church's understanding of its role in society. Both the theological anthropology of the text and its ecclesiology sustain confidence that an objective foundation exists for Church-society cooperation and collaboration. The distinctive character of revelation does not prevent the content of the Church's social message from being a usable wisdom in the arena of politics, economics, law and international relations. The conciliar text envisions the work of the kingdom of God being accomplished in and through the institutions of human history. The title of the new document, "the Church in the world" (not "Church and world"), situates the Church in the midst of the *saeculum* and initiates a dynamic exchange about the problems of our time and the resources of the Church to contribute to them.

These Church-type assumptions tie the Church to the world, but they do not collapse the two into a single reality. The dialogue has a dialectical character: the Church has something to learn from the world and it has something to teach. The appreciation the conciliar text shows for the scientific, technological and political accomplishments of modernity does not yield an uncritical acceptance of all that is implied by that term. In a style which will be adopted and sharpened by Pope John Paul II, the conciliar text sees the Church as a full participant in the history of societies and states, but one which must continually teach that fulfillment of the human project lies beyond history. Hence, there is always a transitory and imperfect character to secular accomplishments. The teaching of a Church-type community should acknowledge the intrinsic worth and value of human institutions and agencies, should bring a critical normative perspective to bear upon them, and should point the way to the perfecting of human effort in the mystery of God's kingdom:

> Therefore while we are warned that it profits a man nothing if he gain the whole world and lose himself, the expectation of a new earth must not weaken but rather stimulate our concern for cultivating this one. For here grows the body of a new human family, a body which even now is able to give some kind of foreshadowing of the new age.
>
> Earthly progress must be carefully distinguished from the growth of Christ's kingdom. Nevertheless, to the extent that the former can contribute to the better ordering of human society, it is of vital concern to the kingdom of God.[4]

The structure of the Church relationship to the world is established in paragraph 76; the Church's task is to stand as "a sign and safeguard of the transcendence of the human person."[5] The defense of the human person provides the rationale for the Church's role in civil society. The significance of this sentence in the conciliar text is that it ties the Council's definition of the proper work of the Church to the entire corpus of Catholic social teaching developed by the popes in the last hundred years. Each of those documents was rooted in a conception of human dignity, human rights and a series of proposals about the political, economic, and legal order needed to protect the person in society.

Two characteristics of this rationale for ministry are pertinent. First, taking the defense of human dignity as the basis for ministry engages the Church in virtually every aspect of the socio-political order; it is a synthetic statement of the idea of universal responsibility for society which Troeltsch saw as inherent in the Church-type. Second, the concept of human dignity provides the Natural Law foundation for the rest of Catholic social teaching. On both counts, the scope of ecclesial responsibility and the style of articulating a social ethic, the conciliar text reflects the idea of Catholicism which Troeltsch saw as its distinctive social significance.

The substantive ministry which flows from a commitment to protect human dignity is described at length in the chapters on political, economic, cultural and international life as well as in the chapter on marriage and the family. The Council is at pains to distinguish the

Church from any political institution, while at the same time legitimizing an activist role in society. The style of the conciliar argument is Augustinian in structure, reflected in the following passage:

> That the earthly and the heavenly city penetrate each other is a fact accessible to faith alone. It remains a mystery of human history, which sin will keep in great disarray until the splendor of God's sons is fully revealed. Pursuing the saving purpose which is proper to her, the Church not only communicates divine life to men, but in some way casts the reflected light of that life over the entire earth.[6]

The famous "two cities" imagery grounds the conciliar text, but the tone of the document carries a more positive conception of the Church-world relationship than the classical Augustinian statement. *Gaudium et Spes* takes pains to set the Church off from any political institution and from direct political engagement in the world: "Christ, to be sure, gave His Church no proper mission in the political, economic or social order. The purpose which he set before her is a religious one."[7] But the conciliar text defines the Church's mission as one in support of protecting human dignity, promoting human rights and fostering the unity of the human family. To use a classical formula drawn from Catholic theology of church and state, the Church's ministry is "directly" related to the kingdom, but is also has an "indirect" impact on civil society:

> Out of this religious mission itself come a function, a light and an energy which can serve to structure and consolidate the human community according to the divine law.[8]

The indirect influence of the Church is to be used in protecting human dignity, promoting human rights and fostering the unity of the human family.

The conciliar text is a milestone in Catholic theology. Troeltsch's history amply illustrates the pervasive role of the Church in society, but *Gaudium et Spes* provides a theological foundation for this role which is unparalleled since the Reformation. The significance of the document is due to its content and to the catalytic role it played in the post-conciliar period. The renewed impetus given to the social ministry has been evident in the Church of Latin America, the Philippines, Eastern Europe and in the United States. The consequences have been noted by a wide range of social scientists and political commentators. Professor Samuel Huntington's analysis of Catholicism's post-conciliar role in promoting democracy and human rights is representative of this commentary:

> In the 1960s, the Church changed. Those changes brought a powerful social institution into opposition to dictatorial regimes, deprived those regimes of whatever legitimacy they might claim from religion, and provided protection, support, resources, and leadership to pro-democratic opposition movements. Before 1960 the Catholic Church usually accommodated itself to authoritarian regimes and frequently legitimized them; only rarely did it oppose such regimes. After 1970, the Church almost invariably opposed authoritarian regimes; and in some countries, such as Brazil, Chile, the Philippines, Poland, and in Central America, it played a central role in the efforts to change such regimes. This repositioning of the Church from a bulwark of the status quo, usually authoritarian, to a force for change, usually democratic, was a major political phenomenon of the 1960s.[9]

THE U.S. BISHOPS: THE CHURCH-TYPE IN ACTION

In the U.S. case, the public role of the Catholic bishops in the 1980s was rooted in *Gaudium et Spes* and reflected Troeltsch's conception of how a Church-type polity would engage the world. In the course of the decade, the bishops addressed four major issues of social policy in the United States: nuclear strategy, economic policy, Central America and abortion. Timothy Byrnes notes the fact that these issues were not "institutional concerns" of the Church but broad national issues:

> The National Conference of Catholic Bishops (NCCB) demonstrated an ability to articulate morally grounded positions on a wide range of national issues. And a number of individual bishops exhibited a willingness to lend their moral authority, and that of their Church, to politically sensitive issues and movements.[10]

Despite the enormous differentiation of these issues, the role of the episcopal conference exhibited a similarity of style in each case, one which reflected Church-type convictions.

First, in each instance the bishops spoke and acted as teachers, seeking to explain relevant Catholic moral teaching, applying it both to public policies and to personal conscience formation.

Second, in each instance their teaching was intended to engage the whole society. While recognizing a primary responsibility to the community of faith, the bishops were constantly aware of the need to build a broader constituency and to collaborate with others if issues of this magnitude were to be engaged. This awareness in turn shaped the content of their teaching. Part of the legacy of Vatican II for the Church's social teaching was a more explicitly theological and biblical content than one found in the papal social teaching. The U.S. episcopal statements reflected this theological turn particularly as they addressed their own constituency in the Church. But they also took pains in their pastoral letters and their teaching on abortion to address in non-theological terms each of the issues they faced. In the pastoral letters the shift in tone, language and ideas was particularly evident and at times criticized for being insufficiently integrated with the theological themes. But the decision to incorporate both styles of social teaching in one document was a conscious choice, lest the impact of the texts be limited only to the believing community.

Third, on all four issues the bishops sought to catalyze a wider public debate and to help forge a moral consensus for policy. This activist conception of episcopal leadership could only be sustained by a Church-type understanding of social responsibility. Among others, Robert Bellah took note of how accurately the Church-type was embodied in American Catholicism of the 1980s.[11]

THE NATURE OF THE ABORTION CHALLENGE: 1973-93

How did the presumptions of a public-Church shape the approach of Catholicism to the abortion question? We need first to understand the scope and depth of the challenge which the 1973 Supreme Court decision on abortion in *Roe* v. *Wade* presented to the Catholic Church. Three different voices—a Protestant ethicist, a Catholic judge and a Catholic legal scholar—taken together provide a narrative of the abortion challenge. Their contributions span the two decades of the abortion debate.

THE MEANING OF *ROE* V. *WADE*

Professor Ralph B. Potter provided a penetrating—and ultimately prophetic—survey of the status of the American debate on abortion five years before the *Roe* v. *Wade* decision. The value of the Potter essay is that it allows us in retrospect to chart the speed and depth of the structural change which the Supreme Court decision effected. Potter's objective was to provide a descriptive account of the major philosophical and religious voices in the abortion debate of the 1960s:

> If rational debate is to be promoted, careful distinctions must be made along the broad spectrum of recommendations put forward concerning abortion law reform. The spectrum may be divided into three major segments, three broad bands marking fundamentally different approaches to the issue.[12]

Potter distinguished the three positions as Left, Center, and Right, providing for each a description of the central values at work and the mode of moral reasoning employed by each position on the abortion spectrum. The Left ("abortion on demand") shaped an argument in the 1960s by combining a central role for the value of self-determination (for the woman) and a conviction that abortion was an issue of private, not public, morality. The Center ("justifiable abortion") began with a presumptive opposition to abortion, then sought to identify "indications" which would justify overriding the prohibition in specific cases. Potter observed that "the framework which determines the structure of argument about the limits of 'justifiable abortion' is a legacy of the style of moral theology that has flourished among Roman Catholics on the right. The intellectual framework of debate is similar in form to the apparatus employed by moral theologians in assessing the claim that a particular resort to armed force represents an instance of 'justifiable warfare.'"[13] The Center approximated in style and content the position being advocated by the American Law Institute in its Model Penal Code. It would have sustained a barrier against abortion as an accepted medical practice, but permitted it in instances of rape, incest and known deformity.

The Right ("no abortion") rooted its position in "the right to life" and then argued its case as an issue of public morality. In brief, abortion was seen as an act which was *ultra vires*, a violation of the proper human and Christian stewardship of life. Because directly intended abortion violated the right to life, the state was invoked as the proper agency responsible for restricting access to abortion. The public character of the abortion issue was simple and stark: "the condoning of widespread resort to abortion would undermine civilization."[14]

Potter's concern was to probe the moral logic of each position in detail, bringing the principal arguments into dialogue. His article can fulfill a more limited purpose in this essay. Its role is to illustrate that the fault-line in the abortion debate five years prior to *Roe* v. *Wade* defined a "Center-Right" argument. Most state laws reflected the Right's strong resistance to abortion; but by 1968, in Potter's words: "The drift of the abortion debate is clearly to the left."[15] The drift, however, was not from the Right to the Left, but from the Right to the Center. Polling data of the time, cited by Potter, showed majority support for abortion if a woman's health was endangered; if pregnancy resulted from rape; or if a strong chance of fetal deformity existed. Beyond these three cases, support for abortion in the general public declined sharply: e.g., for economic reasons or in cases of pregnancy outside marriage.[16] To summarize, the drift was to the Left, but the pace was incremental.

The Supreme Court decisions of 1973 in *Roe* v. *Wade* and *Doe* v. *Bolton* radically changed the situation described by Potter. In one sweeping act of judicial fiat the status of abortion shifted from a legal regime rooted in the Right's prohibition of abortion (with exceptions allowed for the life and health of the mother) to the Left's presumption that the state had little interest in and even less reason to restrict through the civil law a decision to abort.

The radical nature of the change effected in law and policy by the 1973 decisions can best be illustrated by consulting the analysis of Judge John T. Noonan, Jr. and Professor Mary Ann Glendon. John Noonan grasped the depth of the Court's challenge immediately and has returned to the topic often over the last twenty years. Within weeks of the 1973 decisions, Noonan wrote: "By virtue of its opinions, human life has less protection in the United States today than at any time since the inception of the country."[17] In congressional testimony presented in 1980, Noonan described the right to abortion in the United States as "the most radical in the civilized world."[18] The effect of the Court's decisions was to deny any protection to the fetus in the first six months of pregnancy, and to provide marginal defense of fetal life in the third trimester—a defense which could be overridden easily by a broadly defined appeal to maternal health. In his commentary on *Roe*, Noonan consistently sought to illustrate that it was devoid of constitutional or judicial precedent, that it failed to give *any* legal weight to fetal life and that its far reaching effects on the family and society vitiated the claim that abortion could be considered a private choice.

During the 1980s, opponents of abortion sought through law, policy and the courts to reverse the basic premise of the *Roe* decision or at least to limit its lethal consequences for fetal life. The two major court decisions of the decade, *Webster* and *Casey*, provided possibilities for restricting the right to abortion through state legislatures, but the legal regime established by *Roe* was clearly reaffirmed by the court in *Casey*. Writing after the *Casey* decision, and drawing on her work on comparative family and abortion law in the United States and Western Europe, Professor Glendon described the regime established from *Roe* through *Casey* as the most permissive abortion law in the Western world. Glendon faulted the regime on two counts: it was procedurally unsatisfactory in its reliance on the courts rather than the legislative process to decide a deeply divisive social issue; and it was substantively problematic since it did not reflect the public opinion of the nation. Majorities *did* support the principle of access to abortion, but they did not support the absence of any restraint on the exercise of the right to abortion.[19]

If the post-*Roe* pattern was in tension with the dominant stream of public opinion in the United States, it constituted an affront and a moral contradiction for the Catholic Church. Both Noonan and Glendon focused on the radical content of the *Roe* ruling; the full significance of the court's action, however, must be assessed in light of its systematic consequences. The 1973 decisions reverberated through American society; the questions individuals faced, in their personal lives, in their professions and in their public role as citizens, changed dramatically. At the level of personal choice, abortion became standard medical practice; it now confronted many women as a question which in the pre-*Roe* era might never have been asked. Joined with advances in fetal medicine and with the technique of amniocentesis, abortion decisions became for many part of the narrative of pregnancy. In the health care profession, and particularly in medical education, the *Roe* decision introduced entirely new standards, new choices and new dilemmas of conscience for physicians and nurses. Some health care professionals welcomed the new order; others either avoided the issue or were driven to resistance.

The most visible focus of change was in the realm of law, policy and politics. For twenty years the abortion conflict has been fought out at every level of the judicial and political system. Few issues, save race, have been as contested or as divisive over such a length of time. Laws were passed and policies implemented on the constitutional basis established by *Roe*, but the moral foundation of the entire enterprise was under constant criticism. As we shall see, some argue that the political-legal question has now been resolved in the 1990s, but the degree of moral and cultural conflict which persists today places such a confident assertion in doubt. Admittedly, there are different levels of the political-legal issues, but the conflict in 1994 surrounding the abortion issue in the health care debate is a good example of the way in which a disputed moral foundation continues to erupt throughout the American political process.

The Nature of the Challenge to Catholicism

The challenge which the abortion issue has posed for the Catholic Church since 1973 has gone quite beyond a moral and legal issue. It has raised ecclesial questions which are rooted in the posture and strategy of a Church-type community. A public Church, one which defines its social identity in Church-type terms, expects social conflict and controversy about its teaching but presumes that it will be an "insider" in the public debate. The *Roe* decision drove the Catholic Church into a *de facto* sectarian position. It caused a rupture between the Church's moral-legal conception of abortion and the new constitutional order of 1973. Noonan, again, best summarizes the degree of moral and legal resistance which *Roe* evoked from a scholar shaped by Catholic moral teaching:

> In terms of almost two centuries of constitutional adjudication, the right to abortion proclaimed in 1973 was a right created out of the air by the will of a majority of the court in 1973. It was

215

without basis in the text of the Constitution, without basis in the traditions of the American people and without basis in judicial precedent. Its creation was by fiat.[20]

Although Noonan states his case in universalistic terms, focused on the legal order, it was within the Catholic community that this kind of indictment of *Roe* found early and enduring support.

The question which *Roe* raised was how the resistance to *Roe* should be conceived and carried out. What kind of institutional leadership should the Church provide on the abortion issue? One way to define the ecclesial challenge the Church faced since the 1970s is to say that the epistemological assumptions and the social theory of a Church-type community outlined above produce an expectation that compromise (a positive term for Troeltsch) is possible between the Church and secular culture.

Such an expectation stands in contrast with the other major form of ecclesial community which Troeltsch analyzed in *The Social Teaching of the Christian Churches*. The "sect," as Troeltsch described it, stands in contrast to the "the Church" on almost every characteristic. It is a small, tightly knit community, usually devoid of hierarchial structure and shaped by its commitment to the scriptures, but with a minimal sacramental basis. The sect is maintained as small by the standards of its teaching and its practice of adult baptism.

Most significantly, for our purposes, the sect has none of the Church-type's commitment about positive responsibility for society and its institutions. Its strong sense of distance from the public life of society is rooted in a conviction that the demands of the Gospel will neither be understood nor observed in the wider civil society. The sect understands its responsibility for the society primarily as that of providing a counter-model, a dramatic alternative to prevailing social convictions. Rather than stressing the Christian's citizenship in two cities and seeking to build common ground on which Christians and others can stand, the sectarian theology calls the Christian to choose between the cities.

The abortion decisions placed Catholics in the situation of *de facto* sectarians; the Church as an institution and Catholics as citizens encountered the kind of societal opposition on abortion which classical sectarians (e.g. Mennonites) have always expected on issues of war and peace. Catholic citizens, health care institutions, health care professionals and politicians, all were faced with new and profound choices because of the change in the culture, the law and the policy of American society. In addition both friendly and hostile advisors encouraged the Church to confront the abortion issue in sectarian fashion. Three disparate examples will illustrate the point.

First, the ecumenical dialogue which Professor Stanley Hauerwas has conducted with Catholic theology for many years has consistently included a call for Catholics to rethink their public posture in society. Hauerwas is committed to a conception of the Church's role in society as a witness against the culture. Supporting this position is his view that the purpose of social ethics is not to formulate the Church's message for civil society, but to shape the life of the Church itself in a distinctive mode of moral witness. On epistemological and theological grounds, Hauerwas holds that the Church cannot and should not try to build common ground in a pluralistic society. The effort is appealing but in fact results in a dilution of the Christian position and little or no acceptance by the wider society. For Hauerwas, liberal democratic societies pose a special challenge because it seems *prima facie* to be possible to find common ground between Christian premises and the culture of democratic societies.

These premises and themes are brought together by Hauerwas in an essay, "Abortion: Why the Arguments Fail."[21] The argument is a call to the Church to forsake the quest for a universalistic ethic and to recognize that the conclusion held by the Church on abortion is tied intrinsically to a broader pattern of life. Only by drawing explicitly on theological premises can the Church hope to make intelligible its own position and call the society to the kind of change which would be needed to sustain a commitment to fetal life.

> For the Christian prohibition of abortion is a correlative to being a particular kind of people with a particular set and configuration of virtues. Yet we have tried to form our moral arguments against abortion within the moral framework of a liberal culture as though the issue could be abstracted from the kind of people we should be. . . . As a result Christian arguments about abortion have failed. They have not merely failed to convince but have failed to suggest the kind of "reorientation" necessary if we are to

be the kind of people and society that make abortion unthink-able.[22]

Hauerwas proposes the same advice to Catholics on war as on abortion, i.e., that they shift the focus of social teaching from seeking to influence society to definitively shaping the life of a witnessing ecclesial community. In both cases, Hauerwas is rooted in distinctly theological arguments, and his critique flows from respect for a Catholic tradition which he believes is less effective than it could be because it is tied to a Church-type (Christendom) mentality.

The second voice urging the logic of a sectarian strategy is rooted in more pragmatic soil. New York Governor Mario Cuomo maintains a deep personal abhorrence of abortion with a public posture which supports funding for abortions and refuses to lead an effort to reverse the consequences of *Roe*. When Governor Cuomo addressed the abortion issue and his responsibility as a public official at Notre Dame University in 1984 he combined two distinct arguments in his position. At times Cuomo set forth the Church-type case: the moral content of civil law should be expressed in the language of public morality and designed to cement an alliance of believers and unbelievers around core moral premises. At a crucial point in the speech, however, Cuomo shifted ground and seemed to give priority to a witness ecclesiology:

> I think our moral and social missions as Catholics must begin with the wisdom contained in the words "Physician heal thyself" . . . unless we set an example that is clear and compelling, then we will never convince this society to change the civil laws to protect what we preach is precious human life.[23]

This paragraph is surely not alien to a Church-type strategy, and it also could have been a quite subordinate part of Cuomo's larger public position; but I cite it because it could well be read as the practical counterpart to Hauerwas' theological position. Both in principle and in practice such a position would call the Church to create a zone of care and compassion in the wider society, within which different principles prevail as a way of life. But either on theological or political grounds, the conclusion is drawn that extending the zone of opposition to abortion will either fail or will compromise the Church's position.

A third—very different—kind of advice is contained in a bumper sticker which one sees often today as part of the American debate on abortion. It reads "If you oppose abortion, don't have one." The logic of the position is that abortion is a purely private affair—that no *public* harm follows from it. Therefore, opponents of abortion—including the Church—should contain their efforts to maintaining integrity between what they believe and what they do. This position is hardly theological but it illustrates how a sectarian position may find complementary support in civil society from those who diametrically oppose the Church's position.

These voices certainly do not exhaust the range of opinion which the Church has encountered in its opposition to abortion, but they do highlight the multiple ways in which it has been invited, urged and pressured to restrict its advocacy to a sectarian model of witness. In the face of these multiple appeals, the striking characteristic of the Catholic position over the last twenty years has been its classically Catholic style. From the first responses to *Roe* in 1973 through its response to *Casey* in 1992, the Church refused to reduce the issue of abortion to "a Catholic question," i.e., one which should be the concern of a single faith perspective. Ralph Potter had argued that the logic of the "Right's" response to abortion was that its constituted both a personal and a social issue, that it threatened the moral fibre of society as well as the moral character of those directly involved in an abortion. From *Roe* through *Casey*, the Church maintained that abortion was a public policy issue which demanded a response in law and policy, not simply an appeal to individual consciences.

To describe the response more precisely, one could draw upon the distinction found in *The Declaration of Religious Freedom* of Vatican II. As John Courtney Murray observed, the text distinguished between the common good of society and that part of the common good which is public order. The latter, comprised by public peace, minimum standards of justice and public morality, is the responsibility of the state to protect through civil law. When an issue falls within the ambit of public order, it is a threat to the society as a whole.[24] The Church placed abortion in this category and set out to find an appropriate response to it. The clearest example of this public strategy was the early and consistent focus on a constitutional amendment as a means of redressing the damage of *Roe*. From the perspective of the 1990s it is clear that the constitutional amendment has failed as a *political strategy*, but it still illustrates the character of the Catholic response. By pursuing a constitutional amendment, the Church accepted the responsibility of demonstrating the public order threat posed by abortion, it accepted the requirement of addressing American society as a whole (not simply the community of believers) and it accepted the discipline of stating its case in moral language accessible to that wider community.

The conclusion that the amendment strategy failed should not obscure the public impact which the Church position has had over the last two decades. An adequate assessment of the public strategy must include a three-dimensional evaluation.

First, at the level of *cultural-moral perspective*, the public opposition to *Roe* has sustained a significant degree of resistance to the prevailing constitutional order of society. The opposition is not unified in its view of what the public policy on abortion ought to be, but the achievement in the cultural order, the world of ideas and attitudes, is that a prevailing, explicit constitutional endorsement of permissive abortion inaugurated by *Roe* has not silenced the moral critique of the jurisprudence which produced *Roe*, nor has it produced stable support for *Roe* as the basis of statutory law. Obviously *Roe* is in possession and has had dramatic consequences in the order of law and policy, but the significance of continued cultural-moral opposition to the logic and consequences of the *Roe* regime lies in the analogy that can be made to the history of race relations in the United States. In the 1940s, Gunnar Myrdal had argued that in spite of seemingly settled legal views on segregation, there was a fundamental split in the nation's conscience between what was affirmed as the ideals of American democracy and what was upheld in the law of the several states. From Myrdal to Martin Luther King, Jr., one can trace an appeal to a higher moral law which required review and redress of statutory law and policy. Myrdal's challenge stopped at the level of analysis; King, through a mix of religious argument and non-violent protest, pressed the moral challenge to the point of public resistance and political change.

The analogy with abortion is not exact, the sources of resistance to the prevailing constitutional order are not as unified as the coalition King led in the 1960s, but the recognition that it is possible to keep alive an appeal in the cultural-moral order which has the potential for revising or reversing existing law and policy should not be forgotten. Without the public institutional visibility of the Church's opposition to abortion, it would have been unlikely that the cultural-moral arguments against *Roe* could have been kept alive. The fact that the arguments continue as part of the public debate on abortion is one fruit of the public strategy of the Church.

Second, at the level of *law and policy*, the results of the public strategy have been mixed. Clearly the central premise of *Roe*, access to abortion as a constitutional right, has not been successfully challenged. The achievements in law and policy have been on two fronts. First, the Hyde Amendment in the U. S. Congress has been a restraint on the use of federal tax revenues for abortion. The restraint has held in spite of very well financed opposition to it and its effect has been to prevent abortion from being transformed into an entitlement supported by federal funds. Second, using the constitutional space gained from *Webster* and *Casey*, the Church has continued to work with others to restrict access to abortion at the state level. These two kinds of legislative achievements, at the federal and state level, do not threaten the core of the *Roe* regime, but they illustrate that a public strategy must be multi-dimensional. Rather than retreat to an enclave which resists *Roe* through ecclesial solidarity aimed at the members of the Church alone, the Catholic strategy has continued to struggle in the legislative arena, installing public restraints *within* a regime it fundamentally opposes, but so far cannot change.

Third, the arena of *public opinion* stands between the cultural-moral critique of *Roe* and the legislative-policy attempts to restrict its scope and consequences. If the cultural-moral arguments are ultimately ever going to triumph, it will be because of their ability to sway public opinion; the legislative strategy and tactics both depend upon the state of public opinion. After two decades of intense public debate the pattern of public opinion has reached a certain stability: twenty percent basically support *Roe*, twenty percent seek to reverse it in principle and sixty percent have not been convinced by either pole of the debate. While not disputing this linear assessment of American opinion, James Davison Hunter has argued that it is too simple. It fails to note how often a basic misunderstanding of *Roe* sustains public responses; and it also fails to illustrate how difficult it is to move someone on this spectrum of opinion. The reason is that an individual's conclusions on abortion are rooted in a more complex pattern of moral reasoning and "even deeper and more fundamental assumptions, about the sources of truth and goodness, about the ultimate meaning of life and so on."[25] Davison reinforces Kristin Luker's argument that the moral stance a person holds on abortion is part of a wider cultural perspective.[26] Changing the 20-60-20 configuration of public opinion involves a task of both classifying the factual meaning of *Roe* and addressing issues which are intellectually broader than abortion. The public strategy of the Church in the last twenty years has undoubtedly been a principal force in sustaining the twenty percent who seek the reversal of *Roe*. But a public Church style must be committed to addressing the sixty percent which Davison's statistics show includes Catholics as well as the broader public. To some degree the public strategy of engaging the whole society may have diminished the Church efforts to secure the views of its own community. Recognition of this fact has not eroded the consistency with which a public Church strategy has been followed.

Faced with a challenge to a core moral position, Catholicism in the last two decades has responded directly from ecclesial premises and a moral theory which are rooted in a conviction that moral wisdom can be shared across religious and cultural lines. This conviction in turn is supported by the view that failure to address the society as a whole on an issue which strikes at public order is both a tactical mistake and an abandonment of the public ministry of the Church. Institutional leadership on abortion has not been an unqualified success story for the Church, but it has illustrated how deeply the public Church premises are rooted in Catholic theology and polity.

THE OPPORTUNITIES AND OBSTACLES OF THE 1990s

The challenge for the Church in the 1990s is shaped by its post-*Casey* and post-Clinton character. At both the political and legal levels change at the opening of the 1990s promised to make the pro-life task more difficult than the 1980s. Charles Krauthammer, writing in the *Washington Post* in 1993 was stark in his assessment:

> The great abortion debate is over. With the courts overturning a Guam law criminalizing abortion and with the election of a down-the-line pro-choice president, November 1992 marks the end of the 20-year abortion wars. . . . One can reasonably declare

a great national debate over when all three independently (s)e-lected branches of government come to the same position.[27]

Krauthammer pointed to the *Casey* decision of the Supreme Court, President Clinton's campaign position on abortion and the victories of pro-choice candidates to the Congress to reinforce his internment of the abortion debate. This evaluation led him to recommend a shift of strategy for pro-life institutions: to change hearts not law, to focus on culture not politics. While the appeal is not cast in the language of Troeltsch's sectarian model, the logic of the proposal points to a sectarian role for the Church.

Krauthammer's perspective finds support both inside and outside the ecclesial community. The implications of the strategy would mean stepping back from the public engagement model of the last twenty years to focus on shaping a solid ecclesial consensus against abortion, providing a distinct witness through Church institutions and members in defense of life, and offering this pro-life way of life to others in society.

The proposal has intrinsic merit and its appeal is strengthened by the tactical situation confronting the Church. The primary effect of the *Casey* decision was its reaffirmation of the basic principle of *Roe*, even though it then opened the way to place further restrictions on the exercise of the right to abortion. Opposition to *Roe* will not find support in the leadership ranks of either the executive or legislative branches of government. Should the Church simply withdraw from a hostile public arena?

Such a move, in my view, would be a serious mistake. Neither the good of the Church nor that of civil society would be served by consciously adopting a Mennonite model. Theologically, the constriction of the Church's advocacy to a witness model amounts to a substantial change in its understanding of social ministry. To adopt a witness posture across the range of social issues would fundamentally alter the role of the Church plays in society. To adopt a strategy of witness *only* on abortion would isolate the issue in an unfortunate manner. In addition, a purely witness model will communicate to the wider society that the Church believes the public struggle is over. This would be forcing premature closure on the policy questions. Both law and policy are, to be sure, presently rooted in a pro-choice mode, but public opinion on the topic remains unsettled: it supports access to abortion, but it is clearly not comfortable with the consequences of *Roe*—1.5 million abortions a year.

Faced with the post-*Casey*/post-Clinton context the Church should maintain a public strategy in principle and in its witness; it should simultaneously seek to strengthen the existing ecclesial consensus (which is not perfect by any means) and it should carefully target the split in public opinion between its reluctance to rule out abortion in principle and its dissatisfaction with a radically permissive pattern of abortion.

Institutional leadership which is based on these premises and must be exercised in the political-legal context of the 1990s should distinguish long-term, mid-term and short-term goals. The long-range strategy should be focused on the *cultural level* of ideas and values. The work of Kristin Luker, James Davison Hunter, and Richard Neuhaus testifies to the significance of this level of the question as well as to its complexity. The strategy of a public Church at the cultural level must be long-term because it is an exercise of the teaching ministry of the Church—a continuing process—and because change at this level is a long, slow process. The cultural arguments which undergird the differences in perception about abortion go to the heart of the old argument between Catholicism and Liberalism. The social vision of Catholicism is rooted in premises which a liberal society entertains only with much hesitation. The public Church strategy of Catholicism is rooted in the conviction that abortion is a personal choice with immediate social consequences. These consequences are so significant for moral values, civil law, concepts of the family and societal responsibility that abortion should be treated as a public order issue. This conviction, virtually taken for granted in Catholicism, is precisely the dividing line in the cultural debate on abortion. The concept of the autonomous self, the description of abortion as a private choice, the way in which the state and civil law are conceived in the pro-choice position finds a public understanding of abortion threatening and alien. Beneath the specific differences on abortion lie Catholicism's understanding of the social nature of the person, its organic understanding of society, its positive conception of the role of the state and its conviction that civil law must be rooted in the moral law.

The cultural level of institutional leadership must be conceived as a long-term effort because each of these ideas is in tension with prevailing cultural ideas in American society. Thirty years ago John Courtney Murray catalogued the depth of the philosophical difference between the

Catholic and Liberal conceptions of society.[28] These divisions permeate the abortion debate today.

It will be very difficult to get a hearing on the Church's view of abortion as a social issue without some shared understanding of these deeper cultural-moral premises. The significant possibility in this regard is that several voices in American society today are willing to look at "the limits of liberalism" while stoutly maintaining its basic values. It is not clear how far the limits of liberalism debate will go, but it should be noted that Pope John XXIII in *Pacem in Terris* tried to present Catholic teaching on the person, society and human rights in a way which opened new possibilities for the Catholic-Liberal dialogue. Among the issues which could be in this discussion, abortion is one of the most difficult. But it should be part of Catholic strategy to engage the wider philosophical debate and to search for ways of relating it to the life issues in American society.[29]

The mid-term goals of a public strategy should focus on the *political-legal* issues. This is the engagement which voices from Krauthammer through Hauerwas (for different reasons) advocate forsaking. That idea should be resisted, but in the 1990s it will be necessary to revise the goals of the legislative strategy. In the 1970s, John Noonan argued that the fundamental flaw created in the constitutional order by *Roe* could only be addressed by an equally fundamental remedy: a constitutional amendment.[30]

The post-*Casey*/post-Clinton era makes this desirable goal virtually impossible. There is a need to shift the legislative strategy quite decisively to the space created by *Webster* and *Casey*: to place substantive restrictions on abortion at the state and possibly federal level. The goals here are more modest, but they are feasible. Moreover, they focus on the tension which seems to exist in the public mind between allowing abortions but seeking to reverse the prevailing pattern of permissive abortion. There are clear limits to this strategy; it falls far short of Noonan's fundamental remedy; it also allows the presumption of the law to favor abortion even as one tries to limit the consequences of such a law. The public strategy of the Church should keep Noonan's objective in mind, but recognize that this decade is not likely to produce an opportunity to realize it.

The short-term objective of the public strategy should be focused on internal reform and renewal *within the ecclesial community*. It is on this level that the truth of the Cuomo, Hauerwas, *et al.* proposals can be recognized. There is a critical role for a witness component in a public Church. The credibility of the life of the community is decisive for the public voice of the Church. The role of Catholic institutions (schools, universities, social service and health care facilities) can be shaped to provide a more effective witness in support of human life at each stage of its development. The argument of this paper is that this internal agenda of reform should be pursued in tandem with a larger public strategy; it should not replace the latter.

A particular question on the internal agenda is the role of Catholic political figures. For the past twenty years the many Catholics who today hold public office at the national and state levels have been very divided in their public positions. The 1990s do not offer incentives for political figures to take a vigorous pro-life position. Yet the different context for the abortion debate in the 1990s may provide an opportunity for a new conversation with Catholic political leadership. The constitutional amendment strategy never created a consensus among Catholic politicians. A more limited goal, restricting the number of abortions, may provide the starting point for a revised strategy to address the new setting of the 1990s.

Institutional leadership on the abortion question must be multidimensional. The basic religious and moral convictions which shape the Church's position are so central that silence or passivity is impossible. The ecclesial principles which shape Catholicism's understanding of the public order should be maintained; both the Church and the nation need a public strategy on abortion. The strategy needs to be revised and renewed; the 1990s have restricted the margin of choice and pose new obstacles for a pro-life position. But the very depth of the challenge which legalized abortion poses and the stringency of the options we face may create the opportunity for the Church to undertake the revision of public strategy which is needed today.

NOTES

1. Ernst Troeltsch, *The Social Teaching of the Christian Churches* (New York: Harper Torchbook, 1960), 201-382.
2. *Gaudium et Spes* (*The Pastoral Constitution on the Church in the Modern World*) [Rome: 1965], §2.
3. *Gaudium et Spes*, §3.

4. *Gaudium et Spes*, §39.
5. *Gaudium et Spes*, §76.
6. *Gaudium et Spes*, §40.
7. *Gaudium et Spes*, §42.
8. *Gaudium et Spes*, §42.
9. Samuel Huntington, "Religion and the Third Wave," *The National Interest* 24 (1991): 29-42, at 31.
10. Timothy A. Byrnes, *Catholic Bishops in American Politics* (Princeton, N.J.: Princeton University Press, 1991), 5.
11. Robert Bellah, "Religion and Power in America Today" *Commonweal* 59 (1982): 650-55.
12. Ralph B. Potter, Jr., "The Abortion Debate," in D. R. Cutler, ed., *Updating Life and Death* (Boston, MA: Beacon Press, 1968), 90.
13. Potter, "The Abortion Debate," 92.
14. *Gaudium et Spes*, §96.
15. Potter, "The Abortion Debate, 124.
16. Potter, "The Abortion Debate," 107.
17. John T. Noonan, Jr., "Raw Judicial Power," *National Review* (March 2, 1973): 260-64, at 261.
18. John T. Noonan Jr., "A Right Created Out of the Air," *Origins* 11 (1981-82): 296-99, at 297.
19. Mary Ann Glendon, "U.S. Abortion Law," *Wall Street Journal* (July 1, 1992): A15.
20. Noonan, "A Right Created Out of the Air," 297.
21. Stanley Hauerwas, *A Community of Character: Toward a Constructive Christian Social Ethic* (Notre Dame, IN: University of Notre Dame Press, 1981), 212-29.
22. Stanley Hauerwas, *A Community of Character*, 214.
23. Mario Cuomo, 1984, "Religious Belief and Public Morality," *Origins* 14 (1984): 166-205, at 239.
24. John Courtney Murray, "The Declaration on Religious Freedom," in John H. Miller, ed., *Vatican II: An Inter-faith Appraisal* (Notre Dame, IN: University of Notre Dame Press, 1966), 575-76.
25. James Davison Hunter, "What Americans Really Think About Abortion," *First Things* 24 (1992): 13-21, at 18.
26. Kristin Luker, "The Wars Between Women," *Washington Post* August 26 (1984): C-1, 4.
27. Charles Krauthammer, "Abortion: The Debate is Over," *Washington Post* December 4 (1993): A-31.
28. John Courtney Murray, *We Hold These Truths: Catholic Reflections on the American Proposition* (New York: Sheed and Ward, 1960), 303-20.

29. David Hollenbach, S.J., "Liberalism, Communitarianism and the Bishops' Pastoral Letter on the Economy," *The Annual of the Society of Christian Ethics* (1987): 20-53, at 20-25.

30. Noonan, "Raw Judicial Power," 264.

CONTRIBUTORS

Hadley Arkes is the Edward Ney Professor of Jurisprudence and American Institutions at Amherst College, Amherst, Massachusetts. He received his Ph.D. from the University of Chicago. He specializes in moral philosophy, law, and politics. His publications include *The Marshall Plan* (1973), *The Philosopher in the City* (1981), *First Things* (1986), *Beyond the Constitution* (1990), and *The Return of George Sutherland: Restoring a Jurisprudence of Natural Rights* (1994). He is a contributing editor to *National Review*, a monthly columnist for *Crisis* magazine, and he writes regularly for the journal *First Things*, for the *Wall Street Journal* and for the *Washington Post*.

Lisa Sowle Cahill is a Professor of Theology at Boston College, Chestnut Hill, Massachusetts. She received her Ph.D. from the Divinity School at the University of Chicago and was President of the Catholic Theological Society of America. She specializes in the study of sexual ethics, gender, bioethics, scripture and ethics, and the history of Christian ethics. Her publications include *Between the Sexes: Toward a Christian Ethics of Sexuality* (1985); *Religion and Artificial Reproduction* (1988) co-authored with T. A. Shannon; *"Love Your Enemies": Discipleship, Pacifism, and Just War Theory* (1994); and *Sex, Gender, and Christian Ethics* (forthcoming). She has been married for twenty-four years and has five children.

The Honorable Robert P. Casey was elected as the Governor of the Commonwealth of Pennsylvania in 1986 and reelected in 1990. As Governor he emphasized the importance of caring for children both before and after birth. He received his B.A. from Holy Cross College and his J.D. from George Washington University Law School, where he was a member of the Order of the Coif and research editor of the law review. In 1995 he founded the Campaign for the American Family, Inc., a lobbying group, and the Fund for the American Family, Inc., a foundation. Both organizations seek to make the well-being of America's families the top priority in formulating social and economic policy in America. His autobiography is titled *Fighting for Life* (1996).

J. Bryan Hehir is a Professor of the Practice in Religion and Society at the Harvard Center for International Affairs, Harvard University, Boston, Massachusetts. He received his Th.D. from the Harvard Divinity School. He specializes in social ethics and politics, religion and public policy (national and international), and institutional leadership in the public dimension of ecclesial life. He has contributed articles to many books and encyclopedias, and has published many scholarly essays in journals such as the *Annual of the Society of Christian Ethics, Chicago Studies, Christianity and Crisis, Ethics and International Affairs, Harvard Theological Review, Journal of Law and Religion, Journal of Medicine and Philosophy, Journal of Religious Ethics, Journal of Religious Studies, Origins, Social Thought, Theological Studies, Worldview*, and he contributes frequently to *America* and to *Commonweal*.

Russell Hittinger is the Warren Chair of Catholic Studies in the Department of Philosophy and Religion at the University of Tulsa, Tulsa, Oklahoma. He is also a Research Fellow at the American Enterprise Institute for Public Policy Research in Washington D.C. He received his Ph.D. from Saint Louis University. He specializes in the political, legal, and moral philosophy of medieval and contemporary periods and on issues of religion and culture. His publications include *Critique of the New Natural Law Theory* (1987).

Gerard Magill is Chair of the Department of Health Care Ethics and Director of the interdisciplinary Ph.D. program in Health Care Ethics at Saint Louis, University, Saint Louis, Missouri. He received his Ph.D. from Edinburgh University, Scotland, and he specializes in fundamental moral theology, health care ethics, business ethics, and the study of John Henry Newman. His publications include editing *Discourse and Context, An Interdisciplinary Study* (1993), *Personality and Belief, Interdisciplinary Essays* (1994) and co-editing, with M. Hoff, *Values and Public Life, An Interdisciplinary Study* (1995).

Kevin O'Rourke, O.P. is the Director of the Center for Health Care Ethics at Saint Louis University, Saint Louis, Missouri. He received his J.C.D. from the University of St. Thomas, Rome, Italy, and he specializes in health care ethics. His publications include *Medical Ethics: Sources of Catholic Teaching* (1993), co-authored with P. Boyle; *Ethics of Health Care: An Introductory Textbook* (1994, 2nd. ed.), co-authored with B. Ashley, O.P.; *A Primer for Health Care Ethics* (1994), co-authored with J. deBlois, C.S.J. and P. Norris, O.P.; and *Health Care Ethics: A Theological Analysis* (1996, 4th. ed.), co-authored with B. Ashley, O.P.

CONTRIBUTORS

R. Randall Rainey, S.J. is a Senior Fellow at the Woodstock Theological Center at Georgetown University, and Director of the Woodstock Center's Public Discourse and the Common Good program, which explores the theological and ethical dimensions of public controversies in civil society and democratic governance. He received his J.D. from Loyola University of New Orleans and his LL.M. from Yale Law School. Prior to joining the Woodstock Center, he was a member of the faculty at Saint Louis University School of Law, where he taught constitutional and administrative law. He specializes in First Amendment issues, mass communications law, and public discourse theory. His publications include "The Public's Interest in Public Affairs Discourse, Democratic Governance, and Fairness in Broadcasting: A Critical Review of the Public Interest Duties of the Electronic Media," 82 *Georgetown Law Journal* 269 (1993); "Law and Religion: Is Reconciliation Still Possible?" 27 *Loyola (Los Angeles) Law Review* 147 (1993); "Educating for Justice," 11 *Saint Louis University Public Law Review* 521 (1992); "After We're Healed: Imagining a Social Order Based upon a Justice that Reconciles," 34 *Saint Louis University Law Journal* 471 (1990).

William S. Sly is the Alice A. Doisy Professor and Chairman in the Edward A. Doisy Department of Biochemistry and Molecular Biology, as well as Professor of Pediatrics at Saint Louis University, Saint Louis, Missouri. He received his M.D. degree from the School of Medicine at Saint Louis University and was the Director of the Division of Medical Genetics at the School of Medicine at Washington University, Saint Louis, Missouri from 1964 until 1984. His academic honors include being elected as a member of the National Academy of Science, the Burlington Northern Faculty Research Award, the Passano Foundation Award, and Fellow of the Association for the Advancement of Science. He specializes in medical genetics, biochemistry, and molecular genetics. His publications include nearly two hundred articles and co-editing *Human Biochemical and Molecular Genetics* (1990) and *The Molecular and Metabolic Bases of Inherited Disease* (1995).

Basile J. Uddo is a Professor of Law at Loyola University School of Law, New Orleans. He received his J.D. from Tulane Law School and his LL.M. from Harvard Law School. He specializes in constitutional law, legal ethics, and compensation law. He has published numerous essays in books and articles in journals such as *America, The Human Life Review, Loyola Law Review, National Catholic Register, National Catholic Reporter, and the Tulane Law Review.* On prolife issues he has testified before Congress and several state legislatures, and he serves on the Prolife Advisory Committee of the United States Catholic Conference. He was appointed by Presidents Reagan and Bush to the National Board of the Legal Services Corporation.

James J. Walter is a Professor of Christian Ethics in the Department of Theology at Loyola University of Chicago. He received his Ph.D. from the Catholic University of Louvain, Belgium and has held teaching positions at the Catholic University of America and at St. Meinred School of Theology. He specializes in bioethics, Christian ethics, and professional ethics. His publications include *Conversion and Discipleship: A Christian Foundation for Ethics and Doctrine* (1986), co-authored with S. Happel; and *Quality of Life: The New Medical Dilemma* (1990), co-edited with T. A. Shannon.

INDICES

Name and Place Index

Subject Index